ARCHITECTURAL REFLECTIONS

Studies in the philosophy and practice of architecture

Second edition

Colin St John Wilson

Manchester University Press
Manchester and New York

distributed exclusively in the USA by St. Martin's Press

The right of Colin St John Wilson to be identified as the author of this work has been asserted by him in accordance with the Copyright, Designs and Patents Act 1988.

Every effort has been made to trace the holders of copyright material. However, if any omissions have been made, the author will be pleased to rectify them in future editions of the book.

First edition published 1992 by Butterworth-Heinemann Ltd
Reprinted 1994

This edition published 2000 by Manchester University Press
Oxford Road, Manchester M13 9NR, UK
and Room 400, 175 Fifth Avenue, New York, NY 10010, USA
http://www.man.ac.uk/mup

Distributed exclusively in the USA by
St. Martin's Press, Inc., 175 Fifth Avenue, New York,
NY 10010, USA

Distributed exclusively in Canada by
UBC Press, University of British Columbia, 6344 Memorial Road,
Vancouver, BC, Canada V6T 1Z2

British Library Cataloguing-in-Publication Data
A catalogue record for this book is available from the British Library

Library of Congress Cataloging-in-Publication Data applied for

ISBN 0 7190 5704 3 *paperback*

This edition first published 2000

07 06 05 04 03 02 01 00   10 9 8 7 6 5 4 3 2 1

Printed in Great Britain
by Redwood Books, Trowbridge

Contents

You must confine yourself to saying old things – and all the
same it must be something new.

Ludwig Wittgenstein

This book is dedicated to all my fellow-teachers
and students who have provoked it
but most of all to
M.J.

Acknowledgements

I am grateful to the publishers of the following, in which parts of
this book have previously appeared:

Perspecta (the Yale architectural journal):
Part of Chapter 8
Chapter 11

Architectural Review:
Chapters 1, 3, 4, 7, 10, 13, 14

Architects' Journal:
Chapters 15, 16

Architectural Association Publications:
Chapter 9 and part of Chapter 8

Alvar Aalto (1981) and *International Architect:*
Chapter 6

London Magazine:
Chapter 5

Program (Columbia University School of Architecture) and
Journal of Architectural Education:
Chapter 12

I would like to acknowledge my debt of gratitude to the following:

The Editors of the *Architectural Review*, the *Architects' Journal*
and *Perspecta* who have commissioned, cajoled and bullied me into
doing what I would never have done on my own.

The Organizers of the Alvar Aalto Symposium who have twice
invited me to present papers to their Symposia and in particular Juhani
Pallasmaa for a long-running exchange of views.

Anne Browning and Jane Powell who with inifinite patience
have typed and retyped endless drafts for each text.

And finally to my Publishers (and in particular Sally Chaffey) for
their patience and tolerance of my endless 'last minute' revisions.

C StJW

Introduction to the second edition

Pegging out the ground

To those in the know in schools of architecture around the world, this book has acquired a mythic reputation as a kind of 'bible'. But the limited number of the initial edition has made it frustratingly difficult to acquire. A new edition is both desirable and very timely, for the republication of *Architectural Reflections* celebrates a reciprocity.

The book collects together essays by Colin St John Wilson 'for the most part written as campaign dispatches to peg out and define [his] position during lulls in the fighting of the Thirty Years war to build the British Library at St Pancras'. The essays were the precursors of that building. It was a hard and painful 'war' and many vicious criticisms were made of the building during its design and construction, not least by Prince Charles.

Now the library has been completed to great acclaim. Views have been revised; even Prince Charles, it is said, has reversed his views. Most importantly, the library has been embraced by its users: the readers, the staff and the visitors to the building and its exhibition galleries and those for whom its public spaces, the courtyard, snack bars and restaurant, have become places of calm, inspiration, support and reflective thought, to meet or just to sit. Words such as 'dignified', 'friendly', 'invigorating', 'solid', 'inviting', 'uplifting' keep recurring in the letters and comments which stream back to the staff of the library and to Colin St John Wilson, the architect. There is a constant refrain from the users about how the building makes them feel good and about the qualities of space and light and material ('I've *had* to touch …'), in other words, about the way the building impinges upon their senses and, crucially, their sense of themselves. The way in which the building, although very large, appears to reinforce the sense of personal self-possession is explicitly summed up by the person who wrote that the building 'makes me feel somehow dignified'. This is a building which is successful in use not just at a practical level, difficult enough to achieve as that is with so many diverse and demanding activities, requirements and users, but in a deeper sense of use, that of dwelling. This, in the perspective of this book, is the true measure of success.

Yet, despite the acclaim and success, in many ways the British Library is an unfashionable building. This, which in itself is both a measure of the quality of the building and of the paucity of the status of 'fashionable', is not merely a consequence of the fact that the design which has been built is 25 years old. It is because it is rooted in what Colin St John Wilson has called the 'Other Tradition of Modern Architecture' in his book of that name.[1] Unfashionable as the building may be within the Babel of architectural language at the end of the millennium, it is a building which will clearly stand the test of time for it is already loved and embraced, even by those who shed tears on leaving the old British Museum Reading Room, steeped as that was in history and memories. It is a building which has that timeless quality which is instantly recognized and experienced but so difficult to define; a quality which is embedded in many of the ideas explored in these essays.

So in its use and presence the building triumphantly validates the ideas which are 'pegged out' and explored in these essays. But, like the building, the ideas themselves, which are in the humanist tradition of modernism, are out of fashion, an anathema to current architectural orthodoxies such as the fetishism of High Tech and the nihilistic relativism of postmodernism. Since the eighteenth century there has been an accelerating growth in architectural theories which have half lives seemingly inversely proportional to their rate of proliferation. As theories and styles fall away and transmute, the enduring qualities of buildings such as the British Library, though there are not many such buildings, will constantly raise questions of what are the ideas in which such a building is grounded. As we struggle in our current Babel to make sense the library prompts such questions with great immediacy for those who have the eyes of Alice to see through and beyond the 'Glass of Fashion'. So, just as the book originally pegged out the ground of ideas for the library, the building, in its reaffirmation of the enduring relevance and significance of these ideas, now reciprocates by tilling that ground to give life to the restatement of the ideas and prompting demand for the republication of the book.

The essays confront big and enduring questions and take stances which are deeply rooted in history. These are questions and answers which have stood the test of time but which repeatedly need restating. They are concerned with fundamental, inevitable but frequently ignored or misunderstood issues of the nature of architecture, in particular the nature of architecture as an art, an art grounded in use and of its ethical nature; the nature of architecture as an act of building; the relationship between the monumental and the utilitarian; and the sources of meaning in architecture in our bodily experience, in use and in tradition. These questions are repeatedly lost or neglected but as anyone who has practised or, in particular, who has taught architecture, knows, these questions do not go away. Each architect must confront them – knowingly or unknowingly – for they lie in that battleground where the inevitable assertion of the individual and the ego confronts a supposed freedom of expression, a freedom of expression which falsely and futilely struggles to free itself from the inevitable constraints of history, use, and human experience rather than maturely understanding these as the very ground from which new architectures, which may allow us to make sense of our changing world, must grow.

It is precisely because these questions lie at the heart of how we might make sense of our world and ourselves through architecture, and thereby may attempt to build a world of sense, that they require repeated excavation and re-examination. Colin St John Wilson takes a very clear and reasoned line setting out the arguments which bear reading and re-reading by each generation to help it find its way.

But these essays are also about values. As Micha Bandini says in her review of the book: '[it] establishes a strong argument on the ethical necessity for architects to take a stand with and through their architecture'.[2] In our world of the primacy of the image and the spin doctor – and of monuments to technology and consumerism and the great power of the State, the media and the multi-national corporations, how do we find an architecture which is a monument to other values, the values of literature, art and knowledge, and which values the individual? An architecture which may be monumental where monumentality is required but still in Asplund's words be of 'forms which do not threaten but invite'.

As Quatremère de Quincy and others have argued, aesthetics are inevitably a question of ethics. This is a central theme of the book. Today the ethical questions are so large and pervasive as to be often unrecognized. The realisations that we construct reality through our understanding and explanation of the world, that this reality changes, as through history we discover more and shift our cultural position, and that both as individuals and societies we have outer masks and inner selves (and even inner masks by which we screen the truth of our inner selves from ourselves) are no excuses for knowingly producing or promoting false realities, i.e. fictions, or for being preoccupied with only the mask, i.e. the superficial image. Wilson enables us to see through and beyond those seductions of pervasive imagery to an underlying world where meaning resides in experience and use and in the patterns of form and use.

In the essay entitled 'The historical sense' Wilson quotes T.S. Eliot in 1919: 'it is not only the pastness of the past but its presence … which makes a poet most acutely conscious of his place in time, of his own contemporaneity'. Because they search out the historical roots of the ideas they explore, these essays help those of us who design buildings and those who are interested in their design to an understanding of our contemporaneity, of our presence in our past, our past in our presence and the past that we are building.

Professor Roger Stonehouse

References

1   C. St John Wilson, *The Other Tradition of Modern Architecture: The Uncompleted Project* London: Academy Editions 1995.
2   *Building Design*, 4 December 1992 p. 14.

Apologia

'No one can be an architect who is not a metaphysician.' wrote John Ruskin.[1] In saying so he was pointing at the start contradiction that lies at the heart of architecture itself, torn as it is between those who would claim it to be 'Mother of the Arts'[2] and those who insist that it has nothing to do with art but is simply a question of 'function × economics'.[3] No other discipline claiming to be an art is so deeply divided within itself. Certainly it suffers from a condition of metaphysical distress and each of us is compelled to declare where we take our stand as if in some theatre of the Absurd. Would that we could simply abide by the advice of Matisse, who said to his students, 'If you want to paint you must first cut off your tongue because you have lost the right to express yourself with anything but your brush'. But architecture is a public and practical art based upon a spoken pact with its society. We are required to engage in a dialogue with those for whom we build in order to discover what to build.

But the realization of that pact, which seemed so easy in the springtime of Modern Architecture, and hailed by the poet Auden as 'a change of heart', has not been fulfilled. The reasons for that are many, and writing has been for me the best way to explore the issues at stake both in the broadest philosophical terms and also in response to the particular need that we each have to formulate a credo.

At the general philosophical level, the most urgent task, I believe, would be to repair the damage caused 200 years ago by the misguided application to architecture of the concept of 'aesthetics'. Even Kant himself finally saw that his definition of the aesthetic object as 'disinterested' and 'purposeful without purpose' was inapplicable to architecture.[4] But the damage was done and a wedge driven between the concept of Form and the concept of Use. This led to a class distinction between 'Architecture' (monumental and 'purposeless') and 'building' (day-to-day and 'utilitarian'). Inevitably such a distinction provoked counter-attack in the form of a rival concept called 'Functionalism'. Neither the Greek 'Ancients' nor the Mediaeval Schoolmen saw the need for such a distinction and I have tried to retrieve from these sources (Aristotle and Aquinas) the true and proper distinction between a Fine and a Practical Art. That distinction hinges upon the more fundamental Classical division between the 'speculative order' in which knowledge is pursued for its own ends and the 'practical order' in which knowledge is made to serve an end

other than itself. It is of the essence of architecture –
even, one might say, its unconditional imperative that
it belongs to the practical order, always serving an end
other than itself. It is fundamentally rooted in
purposefulness'; and in the later philosophy of Wittgenstein I find a mode of thinking that illuminates this
characteristic in a very rich way. One of the major
themes in his *Philosophical Investigations* was the
proposition that 'the meaning lies in the use'.[5] The
simple directness of this proposition makes possible a
unity of treatment on the subject of functional purpose
that is all of a piece across the entire spectrum of 'use'
from the simply utilitarian to the purely symbolic, from
the humblest shelter to the most exalted monument.

In order therefore to service an end other than itself,
an element of dialogue is intrinsic to the genesis of
a work of architecture. Only in that way can the uses
from which its 'meaning' will be derived attain
definition.

For architecture is inevitably drawn to reach
precariously out from its own discipline to make
contact with a world that is other – needs and resources
and disciplines that are other – and to make out of that
contact a common cause, an in-between order that is
neither the order of art nor the raw assimilation of
day-to-day experience, but the discovery of a common
theme through which conduct begins to find its true
rhythm, as stumbling feet are caught up in the measure
of a dance. A way of living becomes an order of spaces,
the need and the responding discipline inseparable,
truly a new found land. What is at stake is the
obligation to seek in things and in situations an inherent
but hidden order that needs to be identified, drawn out,
helped to find and enjoy its own identity – a search that is
very different from the urge to impose an order upon
things from outside (whether it be the old order or a
new invention). And it is only in this sence and this
proper sequence in the genesis of order that questions
of the balance between form and purpose can be
addressed without triviality. It would seem that no
other discipline claiming to be an art is so divided
against itself until it is understood that architecture can
never be 'pure' but will always share the double
allegiance of the Practical Arts. It is the essential, if
paradoxical, nature of architecture that only when it
serves a cause other than itself is it able to release the
benign powers that are uniquely its own. This paradox
embraces great responsibilities. Deciding where to take
up your position in the border territory that controls

the rival claims of 'Art' and 'Life' is to be thrown into the condition of ethical choice.

One aspect of this extension of meaning to the concept of function is the parallel extension to the repertoire of building form that grew out of the development in the nineteenth century of the English Free School of Butterfield (Figure A1), Street, Waterhouse and Burgess. Here the increased range of building types that emerged in response to new patterns of use in manufacture, cultural institutions and communications was matched by a protean inventiveness of form.

A1

We may note in passing that the birth of this School marked the first occasion on which English architecture introduced significant innovation in the language of architecture. It was quickly adopted in the United States by H. H. Richardson (Figure A2) and Frank Lloyd Wright before it returned to Europe where its possibilities have been enormously enlarged in our time by Haering, Scharoun, Aalto and others.

A2

Very pertinently, Wittgenstein himself, referring to Gothic architecture, threw out the phrase 'significant irregularity', the capacity to deal with 'differences': and as illustration of this we have the baffled attempt by Viollet-le-Duc to 'tidy-up' the irregularity of Butterfield's building language (Figures A3–4). This is not the picturesque. Samuel Taylor Coleridge put it well when he wrote, 'the form is mechanic when on any given material we impress a predetermined form . . . The organic form on the other hand is innate: it shapes as it develops itself from within and the fullness of its development is one and the same with the perfection of its outward form'.[4] This is a definition that gives to functionalism the rigour that we normally assume to be the prerogative of classical form, of which it is said that nothing can be added and nothing taken away without destruction of its integrity; and it is a definition that joyfully unites the invention of form to the unpredictable and inexhaustible appetite for novel experience that is born of use.

A3

When we look for the extension of this concept of functional form to our own time we find that, from the mid 'thirties, it has progressively diverged from the course set by the Modernist Orthodoxy established by the International Congress of Modern Architects and which both in its programme and its stylistic canon (the so-called 'International Style') already contained the seeds of its own destruction.

Certainly the grounds for criticism were in the wind

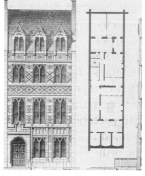

A4

from the start. There is evidence enough that in the
very springtime of the Modern Movement there were
voices proposing other aims, other measures. In the
earliest essay in this book (Chapter 11) I was
responding to the 'rediscovery' in 1959[3] of the work and
theory of an architect (Hugo Haering, Figure A5), who
had been silenced at the first meeting in 1928 of the
International Congress of Modern Architects. It is
understandable why the newly formed establishment of
the Congress leadership would silence him (and those
of his persuasion, such as Hans Scharoun). The politics
of launching a movement aimed to produce an
orthodoxy of method, technology and language on an
international scale could ill afford the sensitive and
responsive approach of someone who pleaded, 'we
want to examine things and allow them to discover their
own images. It goes against the grain with us to bestow
a form on them from the outside'.[7]

A5

My next-door neighbour at that time was Reyner
Banham, and in endless discussions with him and a
small group of friends[8] it was brought home to me that
a number of the 'lost causes' and 'zones of silence' in
the last 30 years of architectural exploration embraced
issues far more subtle and life-giving than the reigning
orthodoxies of CIAM. It was therefore in the full
awareness of this polemic that I began to formulate my
own position. In the first place it had become clear to
me that for my generation, the dice were loaded by the
momentous period in which we were born. The early
1920s were the pivotal years in the adventure of
Modernity. They witnessed achievements that were not
only gestures of iconoclasm but also achieved masterpieces of the New. Literature's greatest triumphs were
launched: *Ulysses, The Wasteland* and the *Duino
Elegies*: Wittgenstein published the *Tractatus* and Le
Corbusier *Vers Une Architecture*. Mies designed his
glass tower project, Rietveld the Schroeder House; and
neo-classicism delivered its last late lingering swansong
in Lewerentz' Chapel of the Resurrection and Asplund's project for the Stockholm Chancellery.

An so to those who were born at such a time it would
inevitably fall to inherit not only the masterpieces of
the avantgarde but also the intervening mediations of
the rearguard in their task of consolidation and
interpretation of the initial advance. And to us it
seemed that 'the victory' of Modern Architecture and
the orthodoxy of the Congress was a Pyrrhic victory. Its
positivism, its Cartesian Method for splitting that which
was complex into 'sub-problems' of mechanistic reduc-

tion became in the end narrowed down to a doctrinaire 'Modernismus'. Neither Joyce's Dublin nor Eliot's *Wasteland* stood to gain by sub-division into the Four Functions of the Athens Charter. And so it was doubly important to unearth the testimony of those earlier voices of protest that came from within the modern movement itself; and the authority of those who had protested was further confirmed by the survival in exceptionally good condition of much of their built work (which is to say that it has been taken to the heart of its inhabitants). I have accordingly tried in Part II of this book to bear witness to a handful of these 'Outsiders'.

That this group now takes on the aura of a Rogue's Gallery is no fault of theirs; the fact is that, when Siegfried Giedion published his grand testament of the CIAM in 1941 entitled 'Space, Time and Architecture', there was no mention of Haering, or Scharoun, Asplund or Lewerentz or Aalto. One could therefore even go so far as to infer the existence of an Other Tradition, a tradition furthermore whose origin lay in the English Free School. To its further credit it is a tradition that, since it never conformed to the shot-gun pact of CIAM and 'The International Style' has, in turn, as little to do with the shot-gun marriage-of-convenience that calls itself 'Post-Modernism'. And it is in my view the true inheritor of the rich and complex Modernism of the early 1920s.

Aalto himself, youngest of the Masters of the Heroic Period, came to stand for a critical resistance of a special kind: he was the first for whom the enemy was not so much the idols of the Old Order as the false gods among the New. He was particularly contemptuous of the increasing preoccupation with 'formalism' that he saw in America ('the smell of Hollywood') and on the other hand of what he called 'the slavery of human beings to technical futilities'. His own credo is summed up in the statement, 'We cannot create new form where there is no new content',[9] and for me his status as an exemplary resistance-fighter was epitomized in his Discourse at the RIBA in 1956 when, in speaking of 'the architectural revolution that had been taking place during these last decades', he said, 'It is like all revolutions: it starts with enthusiasm and it stops with some sort of dictatorship.'[10] He identified a deep link between a hard-fighting critical doubt and the highest form of creativity; and he spoke of the need to make up your mind where you must take your stand in the heat of battle.

Above all he (like Asplund before him) built buildings that significantly matched his own challenge that what matters is not how a building 'looks' on its opening day but how it 'performs' thirty years later. In this he has, alas, few rivals . . .

So much for the 'Metaphysics' and the 'Politics' of architecture: what of the 'Poetics'? Here I am confronted by the private need to understand why I can be so powerfully moved by the experience of certain buildings in ways that are not accounted for in the conventional terms of 'Firmness, Commodity and Delight'. One afternoon in Berlin in 1966 I was conducted around Scharoun's Philharmonie and then (crossing through 'Checkpoint Charlie') to Schinkel's Altes Museum. In formal grammar, use of materials and symbolic imagery no two buildings could be more different. What they did have in common was a set of spatial forms playing variations upon the theme of envelopment and release, of open and closed, of invitation and confrontation in various sequences and degrees of spatial 'pressure', and the cumulative effect of the whole sequence was of an indefinable exhilaration.[11] While the purely sensuous experience was an important factor, there is no ready explanation for the great urgency of the sensations experienced and their psychological resonance. What they both seemed to speak to was a form of body-language (Figures A6–7) whose code is based on feelings of being enveloped or exposed or on the 'threshold between', feelings that immediately became associated with the sense of being safe or in danger, reassured or threatened: feelings furthermore whose simultaneous conjunction of opposite modes are as inexplicable as they are exciting. Architecture is the organization of such experiences into spatial 'figures' which match the operational and ritual patterns of a building, so that we may say that the architectural order of a building will lie in the vital proportioning and sequential relationship of such figures.

A6

A7

The 'figures' can be understood in terms of degrees of enclosure from agoraphobia to claustrophobia and I present a number of instances from my own work as illustration. There is the totally enclosed room; the room without a ceiling (the courtyard Figure A8) or with a glazed ceiling (the Atrium Figure A9): the room with a wall or walls removed, (the portico or loggia Figure A17): and the threshold, a place of pause looking two ways between outer and inner. In proportion and geometry the variants upon this theme are endless: but most complex and subtle in address is the aedicule or 'little house' which takes the form of a space within a space (Figure A10).

In the Bishop Wilson School, Springfield there is a running play between experiences of 'insideness' and 'outsideness' at all scales with the particular intention of modulating the building down to the size of the younger children. An open courtyard – a 'room without a ceiling' – is enclosed within a ring of classrooms (Figure A11). Around the outside of that ring there stand a series of free-standing pavilions to house the Assembly Hall, the Library, the Sports pavilion and the Infants' School. This relation of open centre to closed ring is then reversed on entering the Library. There the centre is occupied by a canopied pavilion scaled down in size for the youngest children, and which acts as an 'aedicule' within the larger drum-shape of the Library as a whole (Figures A12–13). Here the aedicule offers the intriguing sensation of being an 'inside' juxtaposed to the 'outside' of the rest of the room – albeit that that too is 'inside' in relation to the 'real' outside.

In the Cornford House (Figure A14) there is a diagonal progression from the fire-place hearth which is the focus of the living-room – a tall top-lit 'Great Hall' space onto which, at ground and gallery level, enclosed rooms open inwards. This gives the large space the quality of 'outside' onto which the bed-room window looks down by analogy with houses looking into a square or courtyard (Figures A15–16). This sequence is then reversed since the enclosing ring is broken open on the diagonal to form a portico, (a room with two walls removed) to open onto a garden, forming thereby a sheltered threshold between inside and outside (Figure A17).

And so, while we will argue that the themes of purposefulness and use are the generating principles in the nature of architecture understood as a Practical Art it would seem that in the realm of means there lurk less rational impulses that are not addressed by the conventional categories of aesthetic, functional or technical assessment. No other art discipline deals with this experience, and we can now see that it is a form of experience that is overlaid with powerful psychological resonance. It is as if a kind of alchemy works upon private sensations of a shadowy kind and this too must be taken into account when we try to understand the force of our elation or exasperation in responding to our environment.

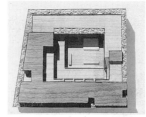

A8

A9

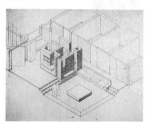

A10

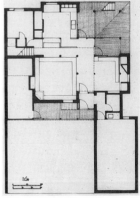

A14

A15

A16

A17

A13

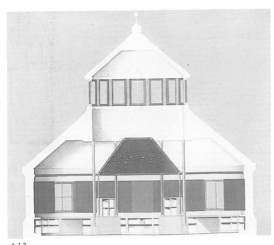

A12

A11

Finally it should be understood that these essays were
for the most part written as campaign despatches to peg
out and define my position during lulls in the fighting of
our Thirty Years War to build the British Library at St
Pancras. Perhaps all that needs to be said at this time is
that the black comedy that I describe in Chapter 15
'England builds', is open to interpretation as a *roman à
cléf* of sorts. . .

References

1. John Ruskin, 'The Poetry of Architecture'.
2. To the Greeks the 'Mother of the Arts' was memory not
   architecture.
3. Hannes Meyer, 'Building', 1928.
4. See Chapter 2 'The ethics of architecture' for a full
   development of this argument.
5. Ludwig Wittgenstein, *Philosophical Investigations*, Pt. I
   para. 67.
6. Samuel Taylor Coleridge, *Shakespearean Criticism*.
7. H. Haering: Wege zur Form, 1925.
8. The regular architectural members of the group were
   James Stirling, Alan Colquhoun, Robert Maxwell and
   Peter Carter. But this group was soon merged with the
   much larger Independent Group formed under the wing
   of the ICA – and that is another story.
9. Quoted in the third vol. of G. Schildt's biography of
   Aalto, *The Decisive Years* p. 226
10. RIBA Discourse (1957) 'The Architectural Struggle' in
    Sketches, MIT Press, 1978.
11. This theme is explored at some length in Chapter 1 'The
    Natural Imagination'.

Part I
FIVE THEMES

1

The natural imagination

'It is not the rationalization that was wrong in the first (and now past) period of modern Architecture: the wrongness lies in the fact that the rationalization has not gone deep enough. . .The newest phase of architecture tries to project rational methods from the technical field out to human and psychological fields'.
ALVAR AALTO, 1940

'But suddenly you touch my heart. . .'

In the prologue to his celebrated panegyric on the
Acropolis, Le Corbusier (Figure 1.1) draws attention to
a commonly felt distinction. 'You employ stone, wood
and concrete and with these materials you build houses
and palaces; that is Construction. Ingenuity is at work.
But suddenly you touch my heart. You do me good, I
am happy and I say: "This is beautiful. That is
Architecture".[1] He then makes a series of references
to 'a resonance, a sort of sounding-board which
vibrates in . . . an axis of organization'; and with
Ozenfant (in the first number of *L'Esprit Nouveau*) he
explores the 'physical-subjective facts which exist
because the human organism is as it is'. But, to use
Aalto's phrase, he did not go 'deep enough'.

1.1

Some kind of revelation has occurred, in pure
immediacy, unsought and unexplained: and that is a
mystery.

Most critics step down from the challenge because
they do not have an explanation that is neat. But the
mystery doesn't go away, we can still be moved deeply
by buildings yet have no adequate terms to deal with
the fact. We are normally very disinclined to talk about
this in the same way that we find a verbal account of
sexual attraction to be hopelessly inadequate. (There
are some common features in the psychic chemistry of
the two phenomena, a split-second immediacy of
sensation, a mingling of the visual and the visceral, an
uncanny awareness of some magnetic charge in the air,
of a jolting presence, of time suspended.) For my own
part I need to know why I can be so deeply moved in
the presence of certain buildings – on the turning of the
stair in the portico of the Altes Museum (Figure 1.2),
on the terraces of Garches, in the foyer of the
Philharmonie, in the nave of King's Chapel, the
impluvium of the House of the Tragic Poet, in the
Gallery of the Bradbury Building . . . It would seem
that to multiply examples would be merely of personal
interest – until one significant feature of the list is
noticed; these occasions have nothing in common at the
level of style, function or structure.

1.2

In traditional terms therefore we cannot look for an
answer to the Vitruvian categories of Firmitas or
Utilitas nor (if we take it to refer to stylistic rules)
Venustas.

Clearly therefore the secret of this elation lies in the
experience of some more primal conjunction of forms,
as if to say that our experience of architecture is

somehow divided in itself into frames of super- and infra-structure. It is as if we are being manipulated by some subliminal code, not to be translated into words, which acts directly on the nervous system and the imagination at the same time, stirring intimations of meaning with vivid spatial experience as though they were one thing – something like Wordsworth's great evocation of 'unknown modes of being' provoked by our wonder at Nature, only this time provoked by structures and images that are man-made. What is the chemistry of this transforming power, from what sources does its compelling force derive, and what is the code through which it works?

The natural imagination

The realm of architectural discourse today is much possessed by death and by the notion of architecture as the embodiment of memory. In so far as Memory, 'Mnemosyne' in Greek mythology, is the Mother of the Arts, it is the very source of that mode of the architectural imagination that feeds upon artifice and reflection – the whole culture of conventions, mythical and stylistic, that in turn transmutes the day-to-day transactions of utility and the prevailing lore of technology into symbolic statement. It is the world of ideal form, of abstraction and allusion and manner woven from a history that is unique in time and place; and what it draws upon is that body of knowledge and sensibility that we will call the Artificial Imagination. An eloquent example of it would be Borromini's San Carlino, which condensed the three geometric forms of octagon, cross and oval into a structural system that simultaneously offers and reiterates at different scales a formal triune reading that is explicitly symbolic in its reference to the Trinity: construction, abstraction and symbolization have rarely been pressed to such lengths.

But our experience of architecture is far from being encompassed by such learned response and reflection. Indeed in the very first instance quite other responses are at work, a whole array of instinctive reactions triggered by the nervous system and marked above all by the quality of immediacy.

One aspect of this instinctual reaction received its most celebrated formulation in *aesthetic* terms in the idea of *Einfühlung*, or empathy, first defined by Robert Vischer and Theodor Lipps as the reincorporation of an emotional state or physical sensation projected upon the object of attention. Its popularized expression in architectural literature appears in Geoffrey Scott's *Architecture of Humanism* where he writes: 'These masses are capable, like ourselves, of pressure and resistance . . . we have looked at the building and identified ourselves with its apparent state. We have transcribed ourselves into terms of architecture. . . It has stirred our physical memory . . .'[2]

Similarly Le Corbusier talks about the column as 'a witness of energy' and we are drawn into a world in which remote transpositions of the human figure participate in an exchange of forces, of pressure and release, of balance and counterbalance in which construct and spectator seem to become one.

But in its confinement to aesthetic sensation alone, the notion of empathy is patently too limited: yet it does bear witness to a level of experience that has far deeper repercussions and that is as deeply rooted as it is paradoxically unacknowledged – the sense, however abstracted, of a body-figure and the ensuing notion of Presence that flows from it (Figure 1.3(a)–(b)). Michelangelo (for whom the human body served as the supreme image for all that he had to say, both sacred and profane) in his one written statement about architecture testified to it when he wrote '. . . and surely architectural members derive from human members. Whoever has not been or is not a good master of the figure and likewise of anatomy cannot understand [anything] of it'.[3] With its stress upon anatomy this statement far outruns the conventional concern with the abstractions of Vitruvian symmetry. This mode of experience is real, active in us all, compelling in its impact. I hope to trace the source of this body metaphor and, in so doing, to show that it goes beyond instinctive sensation and is structured like a language, replete with its own lore and imagery no less so than the Artificial Imagination; furthermore it too has its memory, though of a more archaic order. And I will call it the Natural Imagination.

1.3(a)

1.3(b)

The concept of psychological 'position'

Two of the architects most notable for the subtlety and precision of their spatial compositions, Adolf Loos and Hans Scharoun, were given to quoting Kant's statement that 'all our consciousness is grounded in spatial experience'. From the moment of being born we spend our lives in a state of comfort or discomfort on a scale of sensibility that stretches between claustrophobia (Figure 1.4) and agoraphobia (Figure 1.5). We are inside or outside; or on the threshold between. There are no other places to be.

The writer who, more than any other, has offered us helpful clues by which to relate what I have called the Natural Imagination to this grounding in spatial experience is Adrian Stokes.

The background to his formulation lies in the unpromising discipline of psychoanalysis. However, he brings to bear upon it, first, the intentions and sensibility of a painter and, second, extraordinary powers of interpretation and evocation such that, in the phrase of David Sylvester, 'the texture of his writings is analogous to the texture of our actual experience of art'. Time and again his interpretations ring true.

From Melanie Klein's work on infant psychology Stokes takes the concept of two polar 'positions' or modes of experience through which (it is claimed) we all pass in infancy and against which all our subsequent experience in life is re-enacted. (That the word 'position' with all its connotations of physical space, presence and stance, was chosen to define a psychological state goes a very long way to meet the case that I shall be putting forward.)

The first 'position' is identified as an all-embracing envelopment with the mother, of oneness (Figure 1.6(a)). What Freud called 'the oceanic feeling', a kind of fusion which is most sheltering. This form of attachment is grounded in an intimate experience of the protective and sustaining qualities of the mother-figure, which at this stage is largely received as an unfocused, all-enveloping environment in a kind of emotional and aesthetic short-sight. By definition the nature of this mode of envelopment is spatial, physical, tactile. There is a close analogue to this 'position' in the architectural experience of interior space that is modelled in rhythmic forms of flowing and merging continuity (Figure 1.6(b)).

Secondly it is argued that this position of envelopment is succeeded by a fundamental and shocking change to the contrary position of exposure or detachment – of an otherness in which the infant becomes aware both of its own separate identity from the mother and from all other objects out there (Figure 1.7(a)). This experience is the beginning of objectivity and self-sufficiency. The architectural analogue for the 'position' of independence lies in the experience of open space and the external confrontation with a

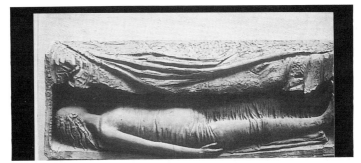

1.4

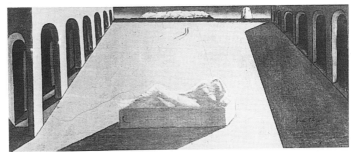

1.5

1.6(a)

1.6(b)

1.7(a)

1.7(b)

building's wholeness and self-sufficiency, the carved and massive frontality of its stance over-against you (Figure 1.7(b)).

Adrian Stokes points to the significance of 'the varying combinations by which these two extremes are conveyed to us':[4] normally, even in excellent buildings, one or other of these modes predominates. He then draws an extraordinary conclusion: that it is uniquely the role of the masterpiece to make possible the *simultaneous* experience of these two polar modes; enjoyment at the same time of intense sensations of being inside and outside, of envelopment and detachment, of oneness and of separateness (Figure 1.8(a)–(b)). A number of other writers have recognized the two poles of experience (Warburg's 'identification' and 'detachment', for instance); Stokes alone perceives the secret to lie in their *fusion*, and upon this rests the originality and the significance of his vision. 'In reflecting such combined yet antithetical drives a work of art symbolises the broader integrating processes. This is the unique role of art.'[5] (I liken this paradox to the well-known optical phenomenon of Gestalt psychology, which claims that it is not possible to register simultaneously both the vase and the kissing profiles (Figure 1.9). The counter-claim that great art can achieve this 'impossibility' is, of course, a criticism of Gestalt theory.)

Latent imagery of form

It is significant that, to Stokes, each of these two psychological 'positions' is charged, at the time of our first exposure to them, with emotional drama. The security enjoyed in the position of envelopment is destroyed by the exposure to otherness: and out of this conflict there is said to follow a whole scenario of frustration, aggression and remorse. Furthermore, it is claimed by this school of psychoanalysis that the process by which the infant repairs the psychological damage caused by aggression and rebuilds a figure of balance and self-confidence is both the beginning of objectivity and the source of all creativity.[6]

These ideas certainly help to suggest a possible source for the otherwise unexplained intensity of emotion underlying the experiences that we are seeking to explore. And in Stokes' *Greek Culture and the Ego* he further develops this interpretation to claim that

1.9

1.8(a)

1.8(b)

through this sublimation of aggression and through the ability of the artist to tolerate extreme experience of 'otherness' he is able to project in his work a concrete image of wholeness and balance to which Stokes assigns the title of 'Ego-figure'. He writes:

> I see it as an epitome of balance or stable corporeality, more concrete, more object-seeming, than any image of what is called the personality'. . . 'a witness of the ego's power to project a good image of its own balance that incorporates under this figure a symposium of meanings, many of which would else have suffered envelopment by one meaning.[7] In regard to human constructions, ugliness, badness as such, is not most feared, but emptiness, that is to say, lack of identity, lack of focus, promoting a feeling of unreality as may be transmitted, for instance, by an ill-proportioned flashy apartment yet designed, it seems, to banish space and time and so the sense of any function to be performed there. A crack in the plaster would be a relief. The squalid, the ugly, do not necessarily lend themselves to this numbing sense of unreality, deeply feared as proclaiming lack of relation, disintegration, the undoing of the ego-figure.[8]

Clearly there are profound implications in ascribing to art such a fundamental role in establishing for each culture its form of stability, the images of reconciled conflict and integration that strive to make us, in Hegel's phrase '*Einhausung*' – at home in the world. What is remarkable in this thesis is the claim that the concept of contradiction introduced here is grounded not just in aesthetics but in the resolution of certain subconscious dispositions of primary importance.

At this point, it is as well to recall that this essay set out to account for the emotion provoked by such ostensibly innocent experiences as the ascent of the staircase in the portico of the Altes Museum in Berlin, an emotion whose strength could not be accounted for at the level of the manifest evidence. It is presumably therefore not unreasonable to assume, in conventional psychoanalytical terms, that those manifest forms carry a significant charge of latent subject matter.

I think that it is to this tension below the aesthetic surface that Stokes alludes when he talks about the paintings of Piero and Cézanne in terms of 'the image in form' as distinct from 'the imagery of the subject-matter'(Figure 1.10). In other words, there is an

1.10

archetypal story latent in these conflicting forms themselves which has nothing to do with the story-telling of conventional anecdotes. And here once more we see Stokes' great originality; for Freud and all the other writers (except perhaps Kris and Ehrenzweig) who have brought psychoanalysis to bear upon art have exercised themselves mightily with interpretation of the anecdotal subject matter where Stokes, truer to the nature of the art, has read the inseparable message woven into the form itself. 'Formal relationships themselves entail a representation of imagery of their own though these likenesses are not as explicit as the image we obtain from what we call the subject matter.'[9] Form itself takes on the property of being a code and thereby becomes deep content: in architecture as in painting.

Artistic condensation

What this mechanism is doing precisely is to resolve a contradiction: and this it does not by logic but by the forms of condensation that are possible to art. 'A pervasive theme embodies more than one unity: each formal quality has further function in the pulsation of the whole. A doubling of roles characterizes the masterpiece by which we experience the sensation of having the cake and yet of eating it. *Form harmonizes the contradiction*: it is the setting for the evocative ambiguities, for the associative collusion, of imagery.'[10]

William Empson has exposed certain aspects of the workings of this resolution in terms of types of ambiguity, demonstrating that the moments of greatest poetic intensity gather around points of ambiguity, and thereby confirming once more the inseparability of form from latent content. The distinction between manifest and latent content is of course borrowed from Freud's interpretation of dreams; and it was Freud who pointed out that the treatment in dreams of the category of contradiction is simply 'to reduce two opposites to a unity or to represent them as one thing'.[11]

The analogy with dreams raises another question: for there the translation or coding of the latent content into the more innocent form of manifest content is an evasion carried out on material the mind has censored. So we must ask if it is in the nature of the work of architecture to deal in censored material.

I believe that this is so and that it is precisely the quality of those works about which Stokes writes most eloquently (of Romanesque architecture, of Piero, Alberti, Laurana, Palladio and Michelangelo) that the 'distance' between the patently ordered surface and the deep laid phantasy beneath is directly proportional to the haunting power that these works possess. 'Architecture, the more abstract of the visual arts, can afford to dignify those experiences with less disguise.'[12]

And what stirs most deeply in the latent imagery of architectural forms is the memory of the human body.

Embodiment

It is a marked property of the art most loved by Stokes that architecture and the human figure were linked as the supreme metaphors in a code through which all that is most urgent in human conflict and its resolution could be represented – the 'body-figure', Michelangelo's sole metaphor not only in sculpture and painting but also in architecture (Figure 1.11).

The code acts so directly and vividly upon us because it is strangely familiar. It is in fact the first language we ever learned, long before words; for it is that body of sensations and appetites and responses experienced by the infant in passing through the two polar 'positions'. Such body-images must have been the only metaphors available to the infant in its projection of phantasies, and from this conjunction must have gained a yet greater emotional charge. It is a language drawn from a wide range of sensual and spatial experience, of rough and smooth, warm and cold; of being above or under, inside, outside or in-between, exposed or enveloped. But then it is intrinsically these sensations that are the primary vehicle for architectural experience.

So the very language in which these early and dramatic conflicts are being experienced by the infant is precisely the language in which throughout the rest of our lives we experience and interpret architecture. It is of the essence of this body-language that it engages the whole sensorium; we hear space, we can smell it and in Louis Kahn's vivid phrase 'to see is only to touch more accurately'.

Literature bears witness here and there to this body language. Baudelaire pointed to a fusion of all the senses that speak to each other like the mingling of echoes from afar that blend into a profound unison:

1.11

Comme de longs échos qui de loin se confondent
Dans une tenebreuse et profonde unité,
Vaste comme la nuit et comme la clarté,
Les parfums, les couleurs et les sons se répondent.[13]

When Proust, to avoid an oncoming vehicle, steps back on to uneven flagstones, the memory of the uneven levels of the floor of St Mark's in Venice instantly floods into his mind. But it is in Wordsworth above all that we find intuitions of a pre-verbal language of the senses that yet taps the roots of the imagination. Furthermore this 'dim and undetermined sense of unknown modes of being' is also related back to the experience of infancy:

Those hallowed and pure notions of the sense
Which seem, in their simplicity, to own
An intellectual charm: that calm delight
Which, if I err not, must belong
To these first-born affinities that fit
Our new existence to existing things.[14]

In his pursuit of the body metaphor Stokes is careful to disclaim any attempt 'to anthropomorphize building in a literal sense. It would be indeed destructive to the architectural significance.'[15] Instead he is concerned to elicit 'the feel of a body surviving in a remote transposition'[16] in 'which architectural forms are a language confined to the joining of a few ideographs of immense ramification.[17]

It is of course the very essence of the humanist interpretation of classical antiquity that idealizations of the human body, like a mandala, contain the key to the fundamental order of the universe. In our own time, the Modulor of Le Corbusier is an attempt to win back some of this long-lost aura. And the most extraordinary demonstration of this 'remote transposition' is in the paintings of Picasso, where the iconic power of the body image defies the very violence of its abstraction: behind the most extreme distortion we still sense the human body in all its wholeness and self-sufficiency (Figure 1.12(a)–(b)).

1.12(a)

1.12(b)

Figures of architectural form

Architecture offers a whole typology of counterforms to the 'positions' experienced in this body language. Louis Kahn once said that 'certain forms imply certain functions and certain functions call for certain forms'. It is a reciprocity of just such a kind that binds a world of archetypal forms (aedicule, portico, column, roof) to the close world of appetite, fear and reparation that is enmeshed in the body language. Furthermore, the reciprocity embraces normative rules so that we could say, for example, that the aedicule is the very shape of a certain mode of spatial and psychological perception and that to each such level of spatial experience there is such a counterform. It is indicative of the primacy of these counterforms that they pre-empt all considerations of structure (the aedicule may be constructed of pisé, wood, steel or stone) and all discriminations of style (the aedicule is no more Gothic than it is Pompeian or Modern).

The simplest forms are ranged at each end of the spectrum that stretches between envelopment and exposure. The primary forms of *envelopment* are room and roof; both have a clear identity to which specific qualities of 'position' can be assigned. Here we should note that the Modernist concept of the free plan constituted a real challenge to these norms, and the determination with which Louis Kahn set out to reassert their autonomy lies at the heart of the most deeply contested shift in architectural experience of the last 20 years.

The opposite condition – *exposure* – is experienced not only in the extreme form of agoraphobia (in which the lack of protective boundary can lead to panic)[18] but also in the drama of confrontation that can take place between the façade of a monumental building and the visitor who, approaching across open space, is compelled to stand off a respectful distance and, in that intuitive act of deference, is made to feel vulnerable. Buildings vary in the degree of assertion with which they confront the visitor: this is in proportion not only to sheer size but also to the degree of frontality.

Frontality of façade is a prime condition of monumentality and, whether it be from Colin Rowe's analysis of Michelangelo's Modello for St Lorenzo or Le Corbusier's description in *Precisions* of the mechanisms of a frontal reading, we realize that frontality is also the prime consideration for the artifice of formal rhetoric. The Palazzo Farnese or the Villa at Garches alike assert what Le Corbusier called 'the primary plane of perfect form' whose tautness is stressed by the play of advanced or recessed forms parallel to the plane. Michelangelo's awareness of the formal significance of frontality is demonstrated by his carving procedure as described by Vasari: a wax sketch model was laid in a vessel of water progressively drained so that the elements of relief always emerge in relation to the level (frontal) plane of the water; the form was developed at all times in relation to that plane (Figure 1.13(a)).

This figural presentation of a building can take two main forms of 'Presence'. One is the form of assertion, of a confrontation whose challenge is instantaneous (Figure 1.13(b)). It is addressed to you; and what it demands of you is a certain submission by threatening to overwhelm your self-possession. The theatricalities of Speer and of Piacentini are clear cases in point. Conversely there are buildings that do not indulge such theatre, do not demand such submission and, in Asplund's phrase, 'do not threaten but invite'; whose frontal plane is deflected away from the line of approach, whose entrance is low-scaled and welcoming: buildings whose engagement with the visitor is more subtle, extended in time from the invitation to cross the threshold and thence to await the moment of reception within, the state of envelopment.

It is when these two polar positions enter into opposition that a greater tension surfaces. Thus the most vivid of these archetypal counterforms is the *aedicule*, (Figure 1.14(a)–(b)), the miniature shelter or canopy that creates a personal domain within a major or dominant space – a space within a space. Here the simultaneity of opposite 'positions' comes into play most vividly in the resulting juxtaposition between the inside and outside over which an unresolved ambiguity reigns. For instance, the aedicule will form an enclosure whose outside is still inside the major dominant space, thereby giving rise to a play between an inside–outside and the real outside. The classical convention of employing on the inside a cornice and other external building elements (for instance, in Alberti's St Andrea) invokes a similar play between real and fictive exposure; and in Lewerentz's Chapel of the Resurrection the free-standing portico is magically restated within the body of the Chapel itself by the free-standing 'baldacchino' over the altar.

1.13(a)

1.13(b)

1.14(a)

1.14(b)

Next the *threshold* – a defined place betwixt and between (Figure 1.15(a)–(b)), a moderating pause to acclimatize oneself to the difference between inside and outside. The staircase and the ramp bring to the condition of in-betweenness the dynamic of transition, expectation, disclosure. The outdoor room (courtyard, patio and impluvium) a portion of outdoor space that is captured (all but the sky) also has some of the in-between quality of the threshold, partaking equally of both outdoorness and enclosure (Figure 1.16(a)). Other variants on the in-between are the conservatory, the pergola and the arbour. Finally the terrace of the hanging garden and the balcony, both indoor and outdoor, shares the tension of betweenness with the further specific quality of overlooking other territory below (Figure 1.16(b)):

1.15(a)

1.15(b)

> A loggia of fine proportion may enchant us, particularly when built aloft, when light strikes up from the floor to reveal over every inch the recesses of coffered ceiling or of vault. The quality of sanctum, of privacy, joins the thunderous day. A loggia eases the bitterness of birth: it secures the interior to the exterior, affirms that in adopting a wider existence, we activate the pristine peace . . .[19]

One could multiply sub-categories of these counter-forms indefinitely but ultimately they are few, 'confined' (in Stokes' phrase) 'to the joining of a few ideographs of immense ramification'.[20]

Conclusion

In setting out to explore why I can be deeply moved in the presence of certain buildings I have been encouraged by Aalto's talk of 'psychological fields' to go beyond the story of my feelings to seek the common features of that experience.

All our awareness is grounded in forms of spatial experience and that spatial experience is not pure but charged with emotional stress from our initiation to 'first-born affinities'. There is a domain of experience, born before the use of words, yet structured like a language replete with its own expectations, memory and powers of communication: a domain that is indeed the primary source of the one language that is truly universal and to which we have given the name of 'body

1.16(a)

1.16(b)

language'. The structure of this primordial language is ordered in terms of two complementary psychological 'positions' in which spatial, sensual and psychological components are linked in a code that is, in turn, reflected in mirror symmetry with our experience of the primary forms of architecture.

From this all-important insight a number of conclusions readily flow. To the traditional understanding of the tie between day-to-day utility and architecture we have to add the yet closer tie of a running narrative, charged with emotion, that has impressed upon all forms the character of danger and desire.

The great painters further confirm this emotive content of architecture; for they quite explicitly use architectural forms to provoke in us those strong and identifiable mental states of 'danger and desire'. Just as Freud found a suitable point of entry to arrive at his picture of the workings of the normal mind by an analysis of the hysteric, so de Chirico's use of architectural forms to induce states of anxiety, disorientation, menace and oppression is a remarkably potent proof of the emotive powers of architecture (Figure 1.17). The façades of the buildings confront me with blind windows and arcades whose repetition and indifference to my presence undermine my self-possession. What elements there are of protection or envelopment have all the quality of being a trap. The tipping floor plane challenges my instinctive sense of posture and balance. I am in the classic 'position' of exposure but this time in such a way that the exposure is aggressive and demeaning rather than a stimulant and reinforcement of my 'Ego-figure'.

1.17

Conversely Piero's images reinforce in us all that is benign, secure, harmonious by the use of architectural forms that represent attributes of measured calm, a marriage not only of contours, but of emblematic metaphors (Figure 1.18). Here there is a neighbourliness between the forms of the figures and the architecture. The proportion in the column between capital and shaft echoes the proportion between head and body in the Madonna figure. There is a belongingness between form and form and yet each form has its own identity and self-possession.

Both artists are concerned with the emotive empathy and sensual charge of architecture: and both put these powers to the task of creating a frame of attention or theatre for an event. They do not simply employ the imagery of architectural elements but use these elements to convey very directly the 'positions' that are

1.18

archetypal in the language of the natural imagination.
What then is the relationship of the artifical imagination to the natural imagination? The natural imagination is the infrastructure of architectural experience. It
acts as both initial provocation and sustaining scaffold
upon which the intellectual constructs and cultural
symbols of the artificial imagination are erected.
Clearly the further the abstraction or conceit is pressed
the less will be the role of such a scaffold; and in the
case of purely conventional symbols there will be
virtually none.

However, in the field of structure it offers that first
instinctive reaction to the 'witness of energy' claimed in
the theory of empathy: and while it touches little upon
the field of functional or operational performance,
much archetypal imagery (the dome, the column, the
arch) derives its origin from the language of the body.

There is a stream of awareness just below the level of
day-to-day self-consciousness that monitors the field of
spatial relationships around us. What is surprising is
that it is a realm of perception without common
recognition – and this lack of acknowledgement is the
more remarkable in view of the extent to which in
actuality it pervades our day-to-day experience. It is a
condition that we do not see but see through – a
baffling and perhaps dangerous transparency.

For it is not only for an insight into our mysterious
moments of elation that we look to it but also as the
catalyst for those responses of alienation and exasperation provoked by the buildings that, as we vaguely say,
'do not work'. Architecture, it would seem, is the
inescapable condition of our life: we had better know
how deep are the roots of that condition.

References

1 Le Corbusier-Saugnier, *Vers une Architecture*, 1923;
   trans. *Towards a New Architecture*, Architectural Press,
   1946, pp. 187 and 192.
2 G. Scott, *The Architecture of Humanism*, 1914, p. 213,
   London: Constable & Co, 2nd edition, rep. 1947.
3 Michelangelo, *The Letters of Michelangelo*, No. 358,
   Peter Owen, 1963.
4 A. Stokes, *Three Essays, The Luxury and Necessity of
   Painting*, p. 11, Tavistock Press, 1961.
5 *Ibid.*, p. 14.

6 There is reinforcement for this thesis in D. W. Winnicott's identification of the infant's 'transitional object' (Teddy bear or Linus' blanket or whatever) that is both a *physical* object existing in outer reality (that can get lost – and every parent knows the irreparable disaster that is then acted out) and a *magical* object (that is the focus of play and phantasy in the inner reality of the child). This 'object' belongs in that vulnerable 'in-between' realm that becomes the place of all cultural experience in later life.

7 A. Stokes, *Greek Culture and the Ego*. p. 27, Tavistock Press, 1958.

8 *Ibid.*, p. 9.

9 *Ibid.*, p. 52.

10 A. Stokes, 'The Image in Form' in *British Journal of Aesthetics*, Vol. 6, No. 3. p. 246.

11 S. Freud, *The Interpretation of Dreams*, section VI.

12 A. Stokes, *Michelangelo*, p. 75.

13 C. Baudelaire, 'Correspondances' in *Fleurs du Mal*.

14 W. Wordsworth, *The Prelude*, 1805 version. Bk. I: lines 419–20 and 576–83.

15 A. Stokes, 'The Impact of Architecture', *British Journal of Aesthetics*, Vol. 1 No 4.

16 *Ibid.*

17 A. Stokes, *Smooth and Rough*, p. 59, Faber & Faber, 1941.

18 One of the major factors in the collapse of morale among the German forces invading Russia in the Second World War was the unrelenting exposure in traversing the apparently limitless plains.

19 A. Stokes, *Smooth and Rough, op. cit.* p. 55.

20 *Ibid.*

2

The ethics of architecture

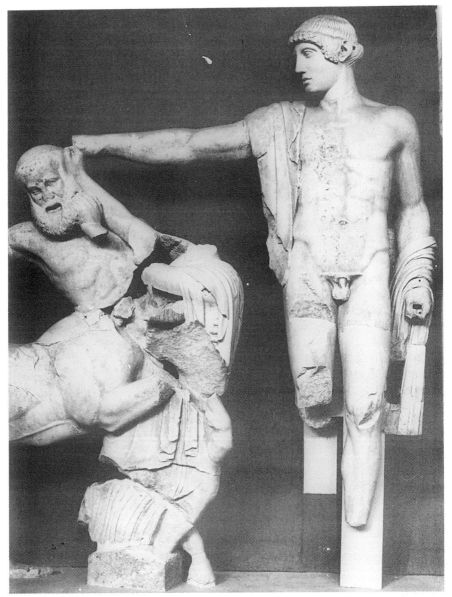

A torn condition

'Today the difference between a good and a poor architect is that the poor architect succumbs to every temptation and the good one resists it.'[1] This remark by Wittgenstein reminds us that architecture invites judgement in ethical terms in a way that the other arts do not. That this is so points to a paradox at the heart of architecture.

In the first place it is open to dispute whether or not architecture has the status of an art at all. Division of opinion on this point is radical. Hannes Meyer, who was Director of the Bauhaus after Gropius, argued that 'building is a biological process . . . not an aesthetic process. Composition or function? The idea of the "composition of a dock" is enough to make a cat laugh!'[2] For him architecture was the servant of the day-to-day needs of society. His check-list for the factors to be addressed in the construction of a house ran to forty-seven items among which we find 'the behaviour of the postman and the burglar' and 'the life of domestic insects',[3] but no mention of visual form at all.

Conversely it is claimed that architecture is 'frozen music' (Schiller), the epitome of the timeless, or the archetype of forms so perfect that, in the words of Alberti 'nothing could be added, diminished or altered but for the worse'.[4] By some it has even been assigned the role of 'Mother of the Arts',[5] and by yet others elevated to a plane on its own, serving itself only – '*l'architettura autonoma*'.

Thus we are presented with two contradictory claims – that architecture is pure art or pure pragmatism. We need to look more closely at the phenomena in order to discover if either of these propositions meets the case to our satisfaction.

In the absence of a common acceptance of the role of 'art' in the discipline of architecture there is a conflict of view about the role of ethics within the discipline. Opposition to the ethical comes from the advocates of art for art's sake on whose behalf Nietzsche declared 'Art is with us in order that we may not perish through truth.' This is reason enough to start with an examination of the 'pure art' thesis and its origins in the birth of 'aesthetics'.

The role of 'aesthetics'

There is no true work of architecture that does not
enjoy some systematic play of forms. But the status of
such enjoyment in the life of architectural forms is no
simple matter. Alberti states his priorities as follows:
'All building owes its birth to necessity, was nurtured
by convenience and embellished by use, pleasure was
the last thing consulted in it . . .'[6] This order of
priorities is not to be discounted as the puritanical
whim of a zealot. It is a clear-eyed view of the uneasy
balance of forces that come into play in the field of
architecture; for however compelling the demands of
use and of necessity, there can be no doubt about the
nature of the rival demands of the pure work of art nor
about the inner drive that informs it.

It is out of the attempt to define this aspect of the
work of art that the language of 'aesthetics' was
developed. It was a late arrival in the history of culture,
offspring of the eighteenth-century Enlightenment. Its
clearest philosophical definition is in Kant's *Critique of
Judgement*, which sets out to study the mode of
consciousness encompassed by 'feeling' over against
the earlier Critiques of Knowledge and Desire. The
work considers two kinds of judgement – of taste and of
purpose: and immediately a firm distinction is laid
down. The beautiful is deemed to be 'entirely
disinterested'[7] rather than concerned with the purpose
of the object in question; and out of this distinction we
are led to the extraordinary conception of 'purposiveness without purpose',[8] exemplified by objects which
are serenely detached from engagement with the real
world, yet reassuringly look 'as if' they had a purpose.
These are said to be the conditions for aesthetic
enjoyment.

Kant then argues that aesthetic judgement determines not only the beautiful but also 'the Sublime',
which induces an emotion of awe before forms that 'do
violence to the imagination' and whose nature is not
just 'without purpose' but is positively opposed to any
sense of purpose. In the context of these abstract and
almost Surrealist ideas Kant introduces the concept of
'the Genius'[9] who has the gift to invent that which is
utterly unpredictable by any set of rules and whose
essential property is originality. And it is these values
of 'taste', visual form, freedom from purpose and even
an anti-rational extravagance that are then taken up to
inform the critical base of the schools of architecture
that were being formed at this time.

Above all these values were enshrined in the Ecole des Beaux Arts, which was to become the dominant school of architecture in the Western World. The course-work of the school hinged upon two disciplines – 'composition' (exercises in visual order) and the invention of symbolic forms evoking the 'character' of the project in question (*l'architecture parlante* – for example, Boullée's National Library (Figure 2.1). Within that regime the pursuit of the sublime was encouraged and the ensuing effusions were permitted to pass unchallenged by any test of reality. [Almost from the start we find in the 'functionalism' of Ledoux (who called himself 'Architect to the World') a sort of lunatic disregard for the realities of function in the form of a house for the Guardians of the River (Figure 2.2(a)) or the Farm (Figure 2.2(b)).] On the one hand, rules of visual composition (such as symmetry) were allowed to overrule the rights of operational disposition: for example elements born of use (such as a balcony) could now be so disposed as not to serve that use but to offer 'visual interest'. On the other hand the borrowing of sacred and symbolic forms became easy currency in a game of rhetoric that had little relation to the cultural purpose that begat them. Phantasy was substituted for reality and applauded.

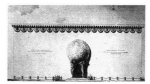

2.1

2.2(a)

2.2(b)

'Aesthetics' thus came to preside as sole criterion for the annual Prix de Rome competition in which all that was put to the test was the power to make exquisite and erudite patterns on paper: a royal staircase could exist in a vacuum (Figure 2.3). Before the invention of aesthetics there was no such thing as 'paper architecture'. The schools have been at risk ever since against bewitchment by it.

More subtly the concepts of aesthetic 'distance' and 'purposelessness' have, in our day, eroded the essential grounding in reality of the relation between things to the point at which, on the one hand, the Surrealists could introduce the concept of a total 'dissociation of objects' (Figure 2.4) and on the other the advocates of 'autonomous art' could retreat into the studio and lock the door. Adorno, champion of autonomous art, declared that 'art, with its definitive protest against the dominance of purpose over human life' suffers once 'it is reduced to that practical level to which it objects in Hölderlin:

For never from now on
Shall the Sacred serve mere use.

2.3

2.4

We note the disdain with which 'use' is relegated to the status of 'mere use'. But we also note the unacknowledged presumption that art is now to be equated with 'the sacred'.

The reality of architecture

Real architecture cannot breath an air so rarefied. Far from being a form of release from the blind enslavement of day-to-day living it is itself the very framework of the world of everyday experience, of *vita activa* rather than the purity of *vita contemplativa*: and its medium is actuality – real structure in real space. Elsewhere in his writings, Kant makes a significant contribution to this counter-argument, for it is a fundamental tenet of his *Critique of Pure Reason* that 'all our awareness is grounded in spatial experience'[10] and if we spell out that experience in terms of envelopment and exposure (of being inside or outside or on the threshold between) then it is not a far cry to call all such experience, even if it is in the forest or at the cliff edge, at one with the essential medium of architecture – the purposeful inhabitation of space. I have explored in Chapter 1 the sense in which that spatial experience when first learnt in infancy became imbued with traumatic emotions of insecurity or assurance, submission or aggression.[11] What I wish to register here is the persistent presence (in our consciousness) of architectural experience whose very medium of sensation is at the same time the filter of our common experience 24 hours of the day. And it is a form of experience that is remarkable for the discrepancy between our unawareness of it and the extent to which it has a dominating effect on our psychological responses. From the very nature of its medium therefore architecture is rooted in our everyday experience and can never enjoy the 'detachment' that is so dear to the aesthetes.

The eminent Greek scholar Gilbert Murray emphasized the reality of architecture when he wrote: 'We can see why Aristotle, though living in a great architectural age, never classes architecture among the "imitative" arts . . . The architect makes real houses and temples: he does not make imitations'.[12] From this it follows that the social (Aristotle would say 'political') role of architecture also differs radically from that of any of the other arts. Here again the absence of that 'detachment' is most marked. Architecture is of its nature assertive – it proposes a certain way of doing things, of bringing together or separating activities – and this will either create an order that affronts or one that enhances the quality of life. Rilke's poem 'Archaic Greek Torso' concludes with the famous injunction 'You must change your life', and Auden echoed this in his reference to the new architecture as 'a change of heart'. 'Pure' art makes no such demand upon us.

The form of our buildings is the form of our life. We could turn that proposition around by asking 'Why do we demolish buildings?' Here again comparison with the fine arts is illuminating: for instances of the destruction of works of art are few (the passion for ideological orthodoxy is perhaps the only significant motive) but buildings are demolished every day and for many reasons. In fact a substantial treatise could be developed on the range of motives – ideological tyranny, functional obsolescence, economic gain, stylistic dogma, sociological misfit, technical faults, physical obsolescence, area redevelopment. The swinging ball never ceases to perform its unholy office. There can be no doubt about the brutal accountability of architecture to its society.

No other discipline that claims to be an art is so deeply torn with competing claims and contradictions such as these: and in so far as these conflicts are played out in the marketplace, the workplace and the home it is clear that they are not going to be settled in the rarefied world of 'pure aesthetic values'. Decisions have to be made over values that range far outside the neat disciplines of visual order. They are answerable to claims about the quality of life, and about the equivocal relationship of architecture to power and to productivity. As the frame of reference within which to understand the world the category of aesthetics is patently inadequate. It is therefore to the opposite school, the pragmatists of functionalism, that we must now turn.

2.5(a)

'Naive' functionalism

Certainly Hannes Meyer (Figures 2.5(a)–(b)) and the early champions of 'functionalism' had no qualms about addressing the questions of 'reality', politics and 'the quality of life' – a task that they considered to have no relation to the world of art. It could even be argued

2.5(b)

that the extreme claim that the aesthetic object should be 'purposeless' was itself the inevitable provocation of the counter-claim of 'functionalism'.

We have already referred to Meyer's checklist of forty-seven items for the design of a house, and we now need to address the grounds for his claim that architecture has nothing to do with aesthetics. 'All things in this world are a product of the formula: (function × economics): so none of these things are works of art.'[13] The tone is accusatory and makes for a curious parallel with the *odium theologicum* of Ruskin, only this time it is *odium profanum* – a deeply reformist opposition to the movements based upon art-for-art's sake and a whole-hearted commitment to accountability in social, economic and technical terms.

A quite new emphasis upon the social commitment of architecture was identified by Bruno Zevi in his book *Towards an Organic Architecture* (1941) as a prime influence. In seeking for the definition of an architecture that would be responsive to 'the needs of the actual users of a building' he concluded that it would be 'based therefore on a social idea and not on a figurative idea'.[14] This point was seized upon by John Summerson as central to his own discussion of *The Case for a theory of Modern Architecture*.[15]

He proposed that 'the source of unity in modern architecture is in the social sphere, in other words in the architect's programme'. And he referred to this as 'the one new principle involved in modern architecture', defining the 'programme' as 'a description of the spatial dimensions, spatial relationships and other physical conditions required for the convenient performance of specific functions'. He went on to assert that 'the character of these relationships may well be something different from the relationships in a predetermined stylistic discipline . . . The resultant unity can . . . be described as a biological or organic unity because it is the unity of a process'.

Clearly this is a line of thought that will not for long remain confined within the terms of 'convenient spatial relationships'. Where now do you draw the boundary between the world of 'architecture' and 'a social idea'? In Nolli's map of Rome (1748) the buildings conceived to be 'architecture' are represented by the interior delineation of their floor plans, while all the rest of the city fabric is represented as an undifferentiated mass (Figure 2.6). In this way it is clearly shown that to Nolli only a tiny proportion of the built world, the monuments, were deemed to be 'architecture': all the

2.6

rest was 'mere building'. But from now on, it is suggested, no such distinction exists. Architecture as 'a social idea' has burst the bounds of architecture as an aesthetic discipline.

This is not surprising. 'What is the use of art if it is not art for all?' asked William Morris and so too did Tolstoy. Thus architecture, a discipline proud to address the Gods, was also proud to attend upon the needs of Everyman; and those needs had now spread into a vast new range of building types and functional operations. Certainly under that banner a great new emancipatory power seemed to be imminently matched by an equally great advance in the field of technical development. The new materials and new methods of production and construction were of the greatest interest to the protagonists of 'New Building'.

But whether or not an 'organic unity' could be achieved through the values and processes proposed by Hannes Meyer is open to serious question. In pursuit of what he called 'the Scientization of architecture' he wrote as follows: 'I taught my students at the Bauhaus to be critical of the diffuseness of "ideal reality" and together we tried to come to grips with the only reality that can be mastered – that of the measurable, the visible, the weighable.'[16] 'Architecture is no longer the art of building: building has become a science. . . social, technical, economic and psychic organization.'[17] He went on to insist that the architect must be 'conversant with the biological sciences. For without hygiene or climatology or the science of management he will have no functional diagrams i.e. no data on which he can elaborate his architectural forms'.[18]

This is the language of a functionalism that Aldo Rossi acerbically stigmatized as 'naive' functionalism; and he was right to do so. Its philosophical basis is two-fold. In method it is indebted to Descartes, who set out in his *Discourse on Method* the classic procedure for problem-solving. This method, modelled on mathematics, proposed that any problem should be tackled by breaking down its complexities into the simplest possible sub-problems each of which could then be factorized in isolation. The most celebrated application of this Cartesian Method was Le Corbusier's brutal reduction of city structure by division into Four Functions (work, dwelling, recreation and transport). See Figure 2.7(a)–(b).

In doctrine it is indebted to the extension of Cartesian analysis into the logical positivism of the Viennese School. Here the dependence upon calcula-

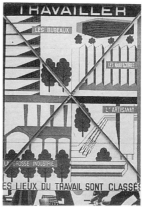

2.7(a)

2.7(b)

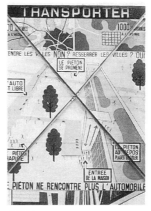

2.7(c)

tion and demonstration lead to the rejection of all
evidence but 'the measurable, the visible, the weighable'. Any aspect that does not submit to calculation
and verification is dismissed as 'nonsense'. This
resulted in a world picture in which human relationships and activities were broken down into 'functional
diagrams' of observable patterns of activity. When
Meyer celebrates one of these diagrams with the claim
that 'The Plan determines itself from the following
factors. . .', we are confronted by the extraordinary
claim that the method itself is grounded upon some
irrefutable logic of design (Figure 2.8). This is
determinist nonsense. There is no such thing as a 'logic
of design'. Design and invention are dependent upon
the formation of a hypothesis – a 'quantum leap' –
which is not reducible to the sequential steps of logical
deduction but which does offer a proposition to be
submitted to methodical test. Quite simply the claim to
'Scientization' is either a piece of rhetoric (to be set
against the presumed fuddy-duddy of aesthetic discourse) or a sorry mechanism for dragging the whole
argument down to the level of those few instances that
are open to calculation. And they are few indeed. For
example we have the oft-repeated diagrams demonstrating the relation between the angle of incidence of
the sun and the interspace between residential building
blocks (Figure 2.9–10); but since this can never be
anything more than one among many rival factors in
the layout for a city, it will frequently be eliminated as a
determinant.

Meyer pursued his theoretical position into design
proposals of remarkable force and integrity and in
doing so went some way to support his claim that there
is a vivid authenticity (if not infallibility) in the
self-evident forms that emerge from the functional
approach. 'Its forms are as rich in content as life itself:
"ripeness is all".'[19] Nevertheless he not only declared
that his League of Nations project (Figure 2.11) was
'neither beautiful nor ugly' (since 'the result of a
process of organization does not stand or fall by any
aesthetic assessment'),[20] but added further, that 'it
does not symbolize anything'.[21] This deliberate absence
of reflection is in large part a polemical conceit; but it is
impoverishing, none the less.

Clearly the theory underlying 'naive' functionalism
fails to account for the part to be played in response to
functions other than those that deal in the measurable.
We need to find the definition of an 'art' that does not
stop short either at the brink of the purposeful as

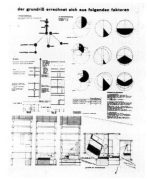

2.8

2.9

2.10

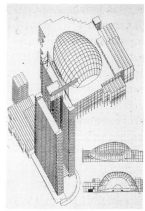

2.11

defined by aesthetics or the demonstrably instrumental as defined by the positivists.

Such a definition does exist in the thought and practice of both Ancient Greece and the medieval masters of High Gothic.

Fine art and practical art

Neither aesthetics nor 'naive' functionalism have satisfied our search for a credible definition of architecture. It is therefore significant to notice that neither classical antiquity nor medieval scholasticism had any use for those concepts either. When sacrificial blood ran down the steps of the Parthenon, when the first visitor to Haghia Sophia (Figure 2.12) cried that he did not know whether he was in heaven or still on earth and when the priests of St Denis crushed by the multitude on feast days and 'having no place to turn, escaped with the holy relics through the windows'[22] there was no talk of 'taste' and 'disinterested contemplation'. Instead we meet concepts of 'orderly arrangement' and 'practical skill', of 'truth' and 'the well-made thing', which relate the work back to its origin in both patterns of use and the cosmological symbols of the way of life that called it into being. Even ornament in so far as it was deployed to assert relative values in a hierarchy of forms was pressed into the service of explanation rather than diversion.[23] Order, proportionality and clarity (desired equally by the Schoolmen as by the ancients) were metaphysical ideas before they were translated into optical facts. They were held to be properties of the work, not subjective sensations in the eye of the beholder; all that was communicable to the eye was answerable first to the mind.

2.12

For Aristotle 'the virtue of a thing is related to its proper function'.[24] S. H. Butcher, in his classic book on *The Poetics*, wrote that 'Aristotle's omission of architecture from the list of Fine Arts is quite in line with the usage of his countrymen who simply reckoned architecture among the Useful Arts.'[25] 'Building is essentially a form of production that is truly reasoned.'[26] It is important to distinguish between our present limited use of the word 'function' to denote efficient performance only and Aristotle's teleological concept of function as the fundamental fulfilment of a specific goal or vocation. 'Every art or applied science. . . seems to aim at some good.'[27] In the same way his concept of the good life (*Eudaimonia*) is the fulfilment of the gifts particular to each individual.

He makes a clear division between the practical order, in which knowledge is made to serve an end, and the speculative order, in which knowledge is pursued for its own ends. The practical order is in turn divided into the two spheres of action (*Praxis*) and making (*Poiesis*) and it is in the relation between these two spheres that the nature of architecture is realized. The sphere of making deals with the proper use to which a building is to be put.

Aristotle's ethics focus upon the man who is 'good' in so far as he tackles life with a truly reasoned approach to the essential nature of each thing or situation, gathering together the meaning of things – almost, one might say, the essence of what makes life worth living. The word *Kalon* embraces the notions of 'the beautiful' and of 'that which is worthwhile of its own nature', as if they were one and the same. We have no such conjunction of meanings in our vocabulary, which is to say in our culture, but it was the epitome of Greek as of scholastic culture and it is a conjunction of the kind that 'functionalism' failed to evoke.

In this context it is the task of *tekne* to produce by reason and skill those things 'whose form is not predetermined by natural law', and which therefore require an act of invention to bring them into being.[28] Such freedom begets responsibilities; and it is not to be construed as the freedom to escape from necessity but rather to serve an end other than itself in a way that is 'truly reasoned'.

This terminology of practical order is adopted virtually lock stock and barrel by the medieval schoolmen – for whom Aristotle was 'The Philosopher'. Aquinas restates the theme of art conceived of as the right way of going about making things (*recta ratio factibilium*)[29] at the same time serving the purpose of drawing out the intrinsic qualities and virtue of something and re-presenting them with the 'beauty of intelligibility'. This definition is developed to encompass the notion of 'the principle determining the peculiar perfection of everything which is, constituting and completing things in their essence and their qualities, the ontological secret, so to speak, of their inmost being. . . the peculiar principle of intelligibility of everything'.[30]

St Augustine distinguished between 'that which is beautiful in itself' and 'that which has a perfect relation to something else',[31] so that once again we have the emphasis upon the interaction between things, 'mutual fitness', rather than the isolated object of pure contemplation.

In the light of this overwhelming consensus of traditional opinion about the nature of architecture as practical art it is only fair to recall that, after all, even Kant himself found that architecture did not fit comfortably into his scheme of 'purposiveness without purpose'; after a number of evasions he conceded that for an 'architectural work' it is 'the suitability of a product for a certain use (that) is the essential thing. . .'[32] Loss of purity is compensated for by a gain in richness; and he finally concedes that at its highest point this 'adherent' beauty 'includes a moral significance'.

Origin of the work of architecture

The call to being

The essential characteristics of a work of practical art are significantly shaped by the way in which it is called into being in the first instance. For a work of architecture this differs radically from that process in the other Arts – indeed the clearest indication of architecture's status as a practical rather than a fine art is demonstrated by this process.

A work of architecture is called into being to serve the cause of innumerable and unpredictable patterns of operation in day-to-day life. Its conception can therefore never be immaculate. It has a concrete historical provenance growing from a whole complex of conflicting aims that are themselves grounded in initiatives and agencies far removed from the discipline itself: and when completed it has to stand in real space and time in defiance of all that nature and the whim of man may bring to it. Summoned out of such unpredictable and uncontrollable circumstances the work is required to open itself to the demands of the day-to-day or the timeless; to whatever task, region or timetable it may be summoned.

In a number of contexts Aquinas adopts from classical precedent the concept of an 'appetite and its satisfaction', and it is a phrase that, in its celebration of life, comes closest to the definition of what should generate the 'brief' for a building. It is in the initial analytical stage of the design process that it will be essential to arrive at a proper definition of the 'appetite' in question: Aquinas would say that it lies in 'the rectitude of choice' – appetite qualified by true need. But for the architect during that first stage it will be necessary above all to observe and to listen. It is the opportunity to discover something that enlarges the range of the 'forms of life' by a challenge extending the scope of the discipline from outside it.

There is then a second stage in which the design process paradoxically becomes a critical tool, challenging some of the assumptions made in the brief; for the early stages of the design process, which are necessarily exploratory, are in themselves a test of the hypothesis of the brief in the sense that they for the first time bring those verbal suppositions into three-dimensional realization. Contradictions or undesirable relationships inherent in the written brief can often only be discovered in this way.

The design process then is not simply the clapping of solution on to problem, like a snuffer on a candle, but is the interaction of two agents in a reiterative process of discovery. This exchange of energies has no parallel in any other art; and it is the reason why there can be no such thing as 'autonomous architecture'. Unless it be born out of this dialogue, no work can ever achieve the status of architecture: it can only be a folly.

The unveiling of truth

Here again the Greeks help us to understand the mysterious thing that happens at such moments of realization. To Aristotle both *Tekne* and 'prudence' are ways of arriving at truth; and the Greek perception of truth is of something concealed that has to be brought into the light. The philosopher Heidegger has very convincingly related this perception to the origin of the work of art.[33] What is at issue is an act of revelation drawn out of day-to-day experience by the alchemy of art. James Joyce appropriated the term 'epiphany' for this phenomenon, in which the perception of some specific detail or gesture suddenly opens up in depth a whole new perspective of meaning that is made articulate and recognizable for the first time.

This points to the acute tension between the roles of architecture as invention or midwifery. For here it is a question of the realization of a need or appetite that lies coiled within a given situation, the potentiality of its 'virtue'. It is significant to note at this point the similarity in language between Heidegger the philospher who speaks of 'letting-be', of allowing things to come into the open of their own accord, and Hugo Haering, the architect who says 'We must discover things and let them unfold their own forms. It goes against the grain to impose a form from outside.'[34] What happens at this delicate stage of interpretation is an exchange of energies between a creative discipline and the tentative realization of a way of life: and the mood is closer to that of attending upon a birth rather than the exercise of artistic *prepotenza*.

This process of discovery, dialogue and exchange is not a condition required for the creation of a 'pure' work of art, but it is the categorical imperative for the creation of a work of architecture.

The element of play

So much then for the way of arriving at an authentic statement of what is required. How then do we proceed to invention? We have already seen that there is no 'logic of invention'. Here we have an extraordinary insight into the very process itself from Alvar Aalto. In an essay entitled 'The Trout and the Mountain Stream' of 1947 he writes as follows:

When I personally have to solve an architectural problem I am confronted, almost always, with an obstacle that is difficult to surmount, a kind of 'courage de trois heures du matin'. The cause, I believe, is the complicated and intense pressure of the fact that architectural design operates with innumerable elements that internally stand in opposition to each other. They are social, human, economic, and technical demands that unite to become psychological problems with an effect on both the individual and the group, on group and individual movement and internal frictions. All this becomes a maze that cannot be sorted out in a rational or mechanical manner. The large number of different demands and subproblems form an obstacle that is difficult for the architectural concept to break through. In such cases I work – sometimes totally on instinct – in the following manner. For a moment I forget all the maze of problems. After I have developed a feel for the programme and its inumerable demands have been engraved on my subconscious, I begin to draw in a manner rather like that of abstract art. Led only by my instincts I draw, not architectural syntheses, but sometimes even childish compositions and via this route I eventually arrive at an abstract basis to the main concept, a kind of universal substance with whose help the numerous quarrelling subproblems can be brought into harmony.

When I designed the city library at Viipuri (I had plenty of time at my disposal, five whole years) for long periods of time I pursued the solution with the help of primitive sketches (Figures 2.13–14(a)–(e)). From some kind of fantastic mountain landscapes with cliffs lit up by suns in different positions I gradually arrived at the concept for the library building. The library's architectural core consists of reading and lending areas at different levels and plateaus, while the centre and control area forms the high point above the different levels. The childish sketches have only an indirect connection with the architectural conception, but they tied together the section and the plan with each other and created a kind of unity of horizontal and vertical structures.

2.13(a)

Aalto refers to the significance of this element of 'play' in the act of creation as an important theme in the philosophy of his friend Yrjo Hirn. In terms of philosophical treatment it is a theme which which has been significantly developed by Hans Georg Gadamer today.

Here we touch upon the high paradox of all art – that the responsible approach to freedom is a certain kind of play of two kinds. Firstly, there is the need for an imaginative 'leap' that puts forward a hypothesis open to test against the stipulated requirements. This is the moment of pure creativity. That first moment of hypothesis takes the form of an adumbration only. At this point a different mode of 'play' takes over, one in which modalities and variations are explored until the 'rules' have been established – and the points at which they are to be broken if vitality is to be sustained. It is fascinating to see (as in these studies by Le Corbusier, Kahn and Stirling, Figures 2.15–17) an architect 'thinking out loud'.

This is the moment at which the analogy to musical structure is appropriate. Nevertheless what is unique to the kind of 'play' here is that it must be the translation of a set of needs in society, which is perhaps the nearest that the art of architecture will ever come to the classical condition of 'mimesis'. What is then remarkable is that Art chooses no longer to be free from

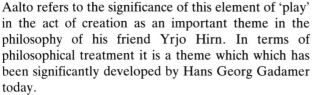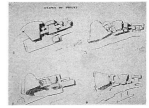

2.15

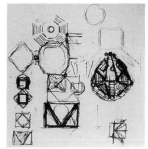

2.16

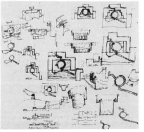

2.17

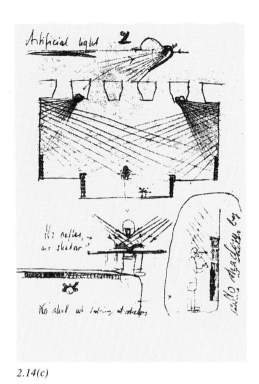

2.14(c)

2.13(b)

2.14(a)

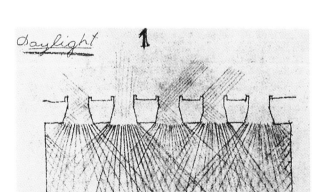

2.14(b)

2.14(d)

2.14(e)

necessity but instead to lay down a set of rules for play, imposing limits upon itself. In Gadamer's words 'Art begins precisely where we are able to do otherwise.'[35] To play is to submit willingly to a certain set of rules. This is the code that underlies the nature not only of every game but also of ritual; and from this strange alchemy of play a number of positive issues flow.

In the first place, it enables the functions to draw attention to themselves and thereby to register their identity. All activities have the capacity to be enjoyed in their own right if only they can achieve 'visibility' and therefore identity. This is the working basis upon which any culture will establish its hierarchy of signs and it is the very essence of all ritual which could not exist without the form-giving powers of play. Secondly, the formality of play makes possible a common participation in the enjoyment of a shared freedom. This introduces a mode of being that transcends the individual. It is a conscious submission to a common form of participation in which behaviour is structured – becomes indeed transformed into a structure. This is the moment in architecture at which form emerges as identity – as meaning that is shaped and shared.

Finally, it is only by virtue of the monetary 'distancing' from necessity that formal or ritual language-games come into play; and by doing so invite the observer to respond in like measure with a reciprocal spirit of play, releasing thereby the powers of recollection, reflection and even phantasy.

The meaning lies in the use

If the unique mode of its origin is the first characteristic of a work of Practical Art then the second most significant characteristic lies in its relation to use.

At the beginning of this essay we identified two interpretations of the nature of architecture. On the one hand the claim (grounded in the theory of Aesthetics) for an art 'without purpose', Art-for-Art's sake: on the other hand the claim of the 'Naïve' Functionalists that 'architecture = function × economics' (art has no part in it). Adolf Loos, writing in 1910, argues that both of these views were true because architecture itself is divided into two parts which correspond to these definitions – the monumental and the utilitarian: and that this discontinuity confirmed the

Classical distinction between 'that which serves only itself' (the aesthetic) and 'that which serves an end other than itself' (the practical). He said that, 'only a very small part of architecture belongs to art: the tomb and the monument. Everything else that serves a purpose is to be excluded from the domain of art . . . the house has nothing in common with art . . .'[36]

But this distinction is too much in thrall to Kantian aesthetics and we have seen that architecture eludes this category thanks to the Classical and Mediaeval distinction between the Fine Arts and the Practical Arts: for within the terms of those two categories there is no doubt that architecture lies exclusively within the realm of Practical Art. We need then to explore more concretely the content of that realm – what activities, building types, technical disciplines, commitments are embraced within it.

Clearly Loos' house and the category that he refers to as 'the rest – everything that serves a purpose', belong there, together with the objects and values acclaimed by Hannes Meyer and the 'Naïve' functionalists. The question then is what, within the realm of building, we should exclude? Are there not really stronger reasons for including 'the Tomb and the Monument' than excluding them? Is there not after all a class of structures embracing the entire field of building and thereby bringing together a whole gamut of values from the shed to the monument?

In order to bridge the gap insisted upon by Loos we can usefully employ an argument proposed by Wittgenstein to describe the nature of language, (I substitute the word 'architecture' for his 'language'). "Instead of producing something common to all that we call 'architecture' I am saying that these phenomena have no one thing in common which makes us use the same world for all – but that they are *related* to one another in many differrent ways. And it is because of these relationships that we call them all 'architecture'."[37]

To illustrate what he meant by this he took the example of, "the proceedings that we call 'games' . . . I mean board-games, card-games, ball-games, Olympic games and so on; what is common to them all? . . . If you look at them you will not see anything that is common to *all* . . . (but you will see) a complicated network of similarities overlapping and criss-crossing . . . that crop up and disappear."[38] And in another analogy he points to the ties of family-resemblance.[39]

To describe this characteristic of discrete elements that yet link up to make some kind of 'family' group he uses the metaphor of a thread that is made by the twisting of fibre on fibre. 'The strength of the thread does not reside in the fact that some one fibre runs through its whole length but in the overlapping of those fibres.'[40]

This line of thought offers us certain advantages. Firstly we do not have to accept a discontinuity between 'building' and 'monument' when it is quite clear that they do share, albeit in varying degree, many 'overlapping' terms in common. Some relation to the Vitruvian qualities of *Firmitas* (Technology) *Utilitas* (Function) and *Venustas* (Form).

Without being too fanciful we could even imagine the grid as a three-dimensional lattice in which the x, y and z axes correspond respectively to Technology, Function and Form. Such a lattice will therefore contain the logical location for every possible type of building, as broad and rich as the appetites and demands of life itself and quite free of any artificial discontinuities or class distinctions. It will then be the task of Ethics to assign in terms of propriety at what point within the lattice any one building task should be located. The monument and the shed will occupy very different positions there but at least they will not have been denied unnecessarily what they have, however remotely, in common. (Let us not forget that the temple started out as a shed of sorts!)

Underlying Wittgenstein's concept of family resemblance is the theory of language that dominated his later work and which hinged upon taking as the point of departure for any philosophical problem the following injunction: 'don't ask for the meaning; ask for the use'.[41] In a sense his later philosophy was an exemplary functionalism: but it was certainly not naïve. Indeed, insofar as it was addressed to dealing with problems that fell outside the limits of positivist language, it demands that we should look for the definition of a functionalism that embraces the whole range of usage from the most primitive to the most sophisticated.

Why should we limit the use of the word 'functional' solely to those activities that are measurable in performance?

In the language of architectural representation there are two forms of philosophical 'discourse'. Firstly there are the 'literal' forms that follow very closely the configuration required by Summerson's 'convenient performance of a specific function'. Their strength and their weakness lie in the directness of their attack upon specific objectives. In order to extract the maximum explicitness of form from that 'performance' they automatically limit themselves both physically and semantically to that one activity alone.

On the other hand, when Wittgenstein claims that 'Architecture immortalises and glorifies something: hence there can be no architecture where there is nothing to glorify'[42] he is clearly pointing to an area of 'use' which is specifically symbolic. There is indeed a sense in which a building form can convey an idea by simply 'showing' what cannot be 'said' in any other way. The case has been very convincingly argued that the infinite pains taken by the Ancient Greeks to compensate for optical distortion in the presentation of the forms of the Temple is the supreme demonstration of the Greek concept of a Timeless Idea.

> Let proportion be carried to a point of perfection before our eyes and the same act of consciousness which reveals the apparent and visual significance of the principle reveals also and carries deep into our minds its intellectual and ethical significance . . . Visual perception passes into ethical conception . . . We think with the eye and see with the mind . . .[43]

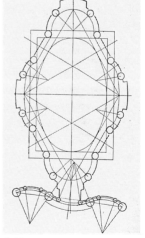

In a very different way the church of St Carlo alle Quattro Fontane weaves variants upon the mystery of the Trinity by the interlocking of three geometric figures (Figure 2.18). Here the theme is not one of timeless serenity but of restless time-bound tragedy and complexity: but the architecture of Borromini embraces the themes triumphantly.

However (as we shall shortly explain) these symbolic and figurative powers are strictly answerable to the challenge of propriety. Playing fast and loose with the authority and values that they discharge is the essence of Kitsch. One of the charges held against Ceasar was that he appropriated the form of the Temple for his own house. Symbolic form should be reserved for sacred purposes only – for 'the tomb and the monument' to which Adolf Loos referred. The only absolute discontinuity is that which opens up between the temporal and the eternal.

2.18

But few buildings have so singular a purpose that their reality is to be encompassed by any one sign-system only: more meanings than one are to be conveyed at the level of operational use alone.

The architect who first and most sensitively perceived the need to extend the territory of functionalism into wider and deeper areas of appreciation was

Alvar Aalto. As early as 1935 he was writing of rationalism as follows:

> We can say that one of the ways to arrive at a more and more humanely built environment is to expand the concept of the 'rational'. We should rationally analyse more the requirements connected with the object than we have to date. All the different requirements imaginable that can be made of an object's quality form a sort of scale, perhaps a series similar to a spectrum. In the red field of the spectrum lie social viewpoints, in the orange field questions connected with production etc., all the way to the invisible ultraviolet field, where perhaps the rationally undefinable requirements still invisible to us, which exist in the individual human being, are hidden. Whatever the case, it is at this end of the spectrum, where the purely human questions reside, where we will make most new discoveries.[44]

This is a functionalism that has nothing to do with 'the house as a machine for living in'. On the contrary we are for instance asked to consider whether or not, "the candle's yellow flame and the interior decorators' inclination to glorify their light compositions with yellow silk rags came closer to the mark vis-a-vis human instincts than the electrical technician with his luxmeter and this schematic concept of 'white light'."[45]

The classical theory of 'mimesis' as a mode of the fine arts is focussed upon the representation of the necessary actions of men in exemplary situations and guided by the rules of propriety. And although Aristotle did not relate the term to architecture it is illuminating to make an analogy here with the proper embodiment of some exemplary functions in architecture. There is a dynamic in such an interpretation which carries with it the notion of archetypal forms that have evolved at moments of exceptional coherence in history and have then over time assumed the status of representational symbol.

A cardinal tenet of this interpretation would lie in an obligation to seek out the truth-functions of that situation.

And if, for a moment, we return to Aristotle, we would do well to link this exploration to that quality of the arts that, in his view makes it one of the instruments and skills by which we discover truth, 'gather together the meaning of things' and realise their own particular good: or James Joyce's conception of the artistic discipline as a rigorous submission to the 'epiphany' or reveleation of the nature of what is 'out there' not what is pre-empted by a pre-conceived form of order.

In this search for the truth of each situation a building has work to do. In serving public institutions and occasions or the private realm it makes possible the happening of whatever is most significant and appropriate to that occasion: the realization of 'a frame for the actions of men that suddenly focuses into a place where those actions are not merely made possible but are made manifest: are made perhaps for the first time vivid and recognizable to themselves'.[46] Each element, while being entirely true to itself, yet enters into a relationship of unique reciprocity with other elements. Each form comes to its realization in the presence of another is completed only by coming together with another and finds its meaning in that conjunction. It is from such revelations alone that real meaning will come. It cannot be invented, it can only be discovered and drawn out – 'shown'.

In the realm of building suffice it to point to a pair of exemplary situations that have evolved over time. Rarely have audience and music been brought into such direct presence as in the Philharmonie by Scharoun (Figure 2.19(a)–(c)). Here the 'appetite' resulted in the invention of a new form – 'music-in-the-round'. The desire that enjoyment of the performance should be shared equally by all members of the audience, the additional enjoyment derived from an awareness of that shared participation, the respect paid to each member of the audience (by breaking up the mass of seats into terraces with separate access), and, above all, the unprecedently vivid sense of occasion – all of these virtues are achieved by a novel interpretation of the 'arena' form. It is the revelation of a hitherto unknown truth in the Greek sense of unveiling a latent potentiality. This enjoyment of the musical performance is compounded by a foyer space composed of an array of staircases and promenade galleries that do not merely serve the circular distribution of access points but also encourage the audience to participate, during the interval, in a kind of *ballet des flaneurs* of its own. In all this we have an exemplary case of an appetite being translated into its essential good ('what it wants to be') by the invention of spatial forms.

One of my reasons for choosing this building is that, although the absence of conventional rhetoric in the façades has distressed the formalist critics, it is notable that the sheer energy of the forms designed from the inside outwards has given the building a vitality of

2.19(a)

2.19(b)

2.19(c)

image that led to its popular nickname of the 'Karajani Circus'.

However, let us take a case in which the stylistic criteria would be received by the aesthetes as exemplary but which yet puts those means at the disposal of a functional operation of the greatest elaboration and precision. I have referred above[47] to the very powerful spatial sensation that I experienced on entering the portico of Schinkel's Altes Museum (Figures 2.20(a)–(d)). The magic of that experience lies in the changes of pace introduced into what becomes a measured 'rite of passage'. The great breadth of the outer run of columns is dramatically narrowed down within the portico to the five-bay opening in the centre, and this in turn reduces to the single entrance bay from which to the right and left the two 'dog-leg' staircases spring. This dramatic compression laterally is mirrored by a similar reduction in height (and in the level of light) as you pass beneath the upper landing to climb the first half-flight of the staircase that lies beneath its shadow. Enveloped in that shadow you believe that you have passed into the building. But then, turning on the half-landing, you re-emerge into daylight beneath the full ceiling height of the portico. The sudden sense of spatial release coincides with the surprise realization that your are still 'outside' after all. Ascending the second flight you arrive back on the central axis of the building to take the view into the Lustgarten between the capitals of the giant order whose profiles cut the air sharp and clear as a trumpet call.

The purpose behind this elaborate 'passage' is not, as one might at first suppose, merely to avoid a too peremptory penetration of the wide but shallow portico, although that is certainly achieved by diverting progression forward into a sawing motion at right angle to the line of advance. In actuality those movements, changes in direction, hesitations, pauses and re-orientation are no less than the marvellous offering to every visitor of eight possible ways to enter the building. This is an architecture of invitation, and, in so far as it offers options and invites choice, it responds fully to a function which, because it belongs to that territory that Aalto described as 'the invisible ultra violet field . . . where the rationally indefinable requirements are hidden', is rarely acknowledged within the terms of a building brief but is in actuality essential to the real life enjoyed there. The choices and hesitations breed a certain lingering, which in turn promotes the possibility of the chance encounter of

2.20(d)

2.20(e)

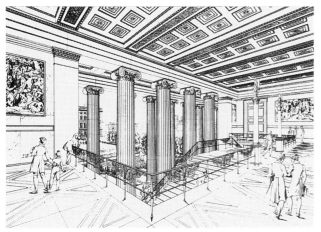

2.20(c)

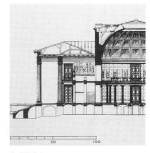

2.20(b)

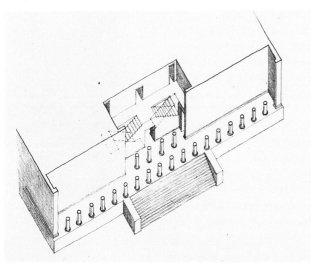

2.20(a)

friends or the first-time meeting of strangers. This is, after all, one proper function of such a building, so that we might say that Schinkel's multi-level portico is as great an invention in the world of the museum as we found 'music-in-the-centre' to be in Scharoun's Philharmonie. What is important is that in both cases a new life form has been offered and that the issue of 'good taste' or style has not weighed in the matter, either by its assertion in the former or its suppression in the latter.

2.21(a)

There is an interesting contrast between the way in which just such an occasion as this (exemplified by Garnier's Opèra House (Figure 2.21(a)–(b)), where the façade acts as a billboard and the crowd scene at arrival or intermission was raised to the level of grand ballet itself) stands in relation to the near-contemporary National Library of Labrouste (Figure 2.22(a)–(b)) which adopts the opposite strategy. Labrouste deliberately avoids a declamatory façade, providing instead just a hole in the wall that in turn leads into a secluded courtyard. Here the building is addressed not to a crowd but to an individual, the scholar, and the tempo is duly modulated.

In each case what is present is a living organism of great sophistication and this has nothing in common with Rossi's 'naive functionalism'. For each type of building there is an appropriate imagery, and this will in turn carry its appropriate rhetoric, pitch of address, ratio of envelopment to exposure, range of dimensional scale and resonance of acoustics – even perhaps a smell. These properties are not academic. Their resolution impinges directly upon the experience of those enjoying the building, and in summary will constitute the grounds upon which the public will interpret the character of the building, will enter it into the public repertoire, will name it in that unacknowledged register of public acclaim or affection that either takes a building to its heart or suffers it grudgingly, welcomes it to the family of that community, giving it perhaps an affectionate nickname (such as the Philharmonie's 'Karajani Circus'), or sees it as a kind of obstacle to be overcome. The building may even in these terms be a little awkward and still be successful, for awkwardness is not what is most feared so much as lack of identity, lack of character, lack of presence. The meaning grows out of the use. The reciprocity of use and form is absolute – and vulnerable. Omit either element and the meaning drains away, leaving only a museum piece or 'tourist attraction'.

2.21(b)

2.22(a)

2.22(b)

The ethical

In exploring the origins of the work of architecture and its place in society we have found that architecture comes into being at the very point at which life and art are at the moment of greatest tension, the anarchic spontaneity of one confronted by the will to order of the other. It is historically the task of architecture to draw them together and to make of that very occasion an act of discovery, a revelation about a way of framing the daily activities and celebrations and rituals of society in ways that offer them both place and identity.

This polarity calls for the need to choose between rival interpretations, tactics, trade-offs. In this conflict it will necessarily be the role of the ethical to pursue that which is most fruitful in the weaving together of innumerable patterns of operation in day-to-day life.

In times of cultural stability, when traditional interpretation and values hold their own, the call for radical decisions does not exist. Prevailing conventions carry or are gently adapted. But at times of innovation the need to make such decisions introduces an ethical challenge of a special nature. The very constraints that were once accepted as ground rules have become dissolved. Not only the conventions of style but also constraints upon the ways of building have been undermined by the possibilities of new materials, techniques and structural forms. Above all, however, new needs, appetites and new scales of undertaking go in search of new patterns of operation, new identity.

Little wonder then that in the attempt to find new bearings there have been those who, like Christopher Alexander, have craved for a 'design method' that will generate for each building firstly an exhaustive list of requirements and then a Cartesian formula that will break the list down into manageable 'sub-problems'[48] (Figure 2.23). Once again we confront the attempt to turn the incalculable into the calculable. But there can be no 'solution' to a state of affairs that never had the structure of a 'problem' in the first place. Sooner or later the riddle of 'values' blocks the way and judgements must be weighed: 'art begins where it is possible to do otherwise'.[49] And this is where the test begins and the temptations hover. The answer will probably require what Aalto called 'the courage of three o'clock in the morning'. The questions will be ethical.

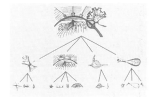

2.23

The concept of the ethical proposed here is not that of the censor but of a creative force directing the agencies at work to their proper end, and drawing upon whatever is essentially their intrinsic good to make possible a form of life that is wanted. In the field of architecture its task is to foster the transformation by which the appetite, once identified, is translated into building forms. Propriety is its cutting edge. In his lecture 'On Ethics' (1929) Ludwig Wittgenstein goes a long way to cover the ground opened up by such questions. In that lecture he was not content to pursue the conventional view of ethics (represented by G. E. Moore) as 'the enquiry into the nature of the Good'. Instead he saw it as 'the enquiry into what is valuable or into what is really important ... into the meaning of life, into what makes life worth living, the right way of living.'[50] These definitions lie very close to what we have seen Aristotle to mean when he uses the word *Kalon*.

On the other hand, as we have seen in our discussion of positivism it is a subject for which it is very difficult to find an appropriate language since the subject matter is focused upon problems of value rather than of fact or logic. In the *Tractatus* Wittgenstein had written: 'When all possible scientific questions have been answered the problems of life remain completely untouched.'[51] And in this lecture he illustrated the limitations of what can and cannot be said in the language of science by the image of a teacup 'that will hold only a teacupful of water even if I were to pour out a gallon over it'.[52] In relation to this limitation in language he asked: 'Won't it be a hopeless task to draw a sharp picture corresponding to a blurred one? ... This is the position you are in if you look for definitions corresponding to our concepts in aesthetics or ethics.'[53] The inadequacy, however, lay in language not in ethics, which he continued to explore as a vital 'thrust against the limits of language'.[54]

It was of course Kant's original goal to find a language that was not dominated by the factual discourse of science, a language which yet allowed questions of art, ethics and religion (Wittgenstein's 'problems of life') to be explored in their own terms. But whereas his strategy was to divide the subject into 'pure' categories, Wittgenstein works in the opposite direction to apprehend whole 'forms of living'. 'To imagine a language means to imagine a form of (*Lebensform*).'[55] If at this point we bring together those two concepts of a 'language game' and a 'form of living' it is only a short step to see that every discipline has its own ethos according to the ends that it is to serve.

The teleogical integrity and interdependence of all created things was, for the Ancients and for the schoolmen, absolute. In the words of Aristotle, 'Since there are many activities, arts and sciences the number of ends is equally large.'[56] In our description of the origins of the work of architecture we saw how wide was the number of agencies engaged, how diverse the fusion (and conflict) of interest that they entertain. Confronted by much bafflement in the search for the core of an issue, it is difficult to respect the claim of facts that do not at first seem to fit together. The temptation to evasion is great, and self-justification in the act comes easily. For instance, Paul Rudolph once wrote: 'All problems can never be solved. . . it is a characteristic of the 20th Century that architects are highly selective in determining which problems they want to solve. . . Mies, for instance, makes wonderful buildings only because he ignores many aspects of a building.'[57] Here the implication is that the 'potency' of design needs to flee from the real state of affairs into the immunity of some higher zone made safe for aesthetics.

There are many other forms of evasion, ranging from the strict imposition of a preordained set of rules (whether they fit or not) to the rejection of all rules in favour of 'total flexibility' of use (which fits nothing in particular). All these evasions – often shared, often promoted by a client who is not the actual inhabitant of the building – fall within the interpretation of the functional remit of a building. Inauthenticity at this stage is poison at the root and no ingenuity of design can bring to life that which is still-born. But can one speak of the ethics of design – of play? Here temptation lies in the very special kind of indulgence that is of the essence of play – self-indulgence. This bias is hard to correct because the force of the temptation is in direct proportion to the inventive strength of the talent at play. However, we have already seen that it is of the essence of architectural play that it is the translation of a need. Even then the excitement of play (the making and the breaking of the rule) can lead to a bewitchment of the player by the play for itself. This is the bewitchment that we call 'formalism', which is play claiming to be an end in itself.

Finally, it is in the nature of play that it can also lend itself to treachery. The corruption of play is kitsch (Figure 2.24). It is the attempt to capture the effect without entertaining the substance. It copies but its point of departure does not lie in the life that generated what it copies but the appearance of the forms only. It is not the translation of a necessity but the imitation of 'an effect'.

Comparison between the authentic and the kitsch will show that the kitsch building, instead of deriving its origin from use, will have derived it from a previous work; instead of revealing relationships hitherto concealed, it will seek to crib a received idea: instead of resisting compromise, it will be open to every concession that enables it to 'please'; instead of daring to attack from a new angle, it will seek the respectability of prestigious precedent; instead of inviting people to sustain its form of life, it will never have come to life in the first place; instead of achieving transformation of the necessary, it will toy with caprice; instead of inventing a vocabulary that is unalterably apt, it will offer the arbitrary forms that are open to any 'convenient' modification. Nor are we fooled by the attempt to redeem as irony (cf Warhol's Thirty are better than one', Figure 2.24(b)) that which is irredeemably kitsch at bottom (see Philip Johnson's tower of false 'Palladian' windows, Figure 2.24(a)).

Every one of these evasions is born of the aesthetic fallacy, and the 'poor architect' of Wittgenstein's accusation who will have succumbed to this temptation will have his head stuffed with the cribs and rules of thumb offered up in the curriculum of the Ecole des Beaux Arts (Figure 2.24(c)).

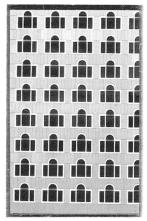

2.24(a)

2.24(b)

2.24(c)

Conclusion

We have seen that architecture, more than any other form of art, has suffered from a radical contradiction within itself for the last 200 years. Ever since the Enlightenment the battle has raged between the claims of 'art' and of 'utility'; and during this century even that issue has been made worse by the champions of 'art', who have channelled the whole argument into terms of one form of art competing against another (classical v gothic, traditional v modern, purism v constructivism) – utility being reduced by all parties to 'mere utility'. This claim has, not surprisingly, provoked the counter-claim that is equally unbalanced – the 'naive functionalism' of the kind that we have seen epitomized by Hannes Meyer.

The authentic terms upon which architecture is grounded are quite other, and we have had to go back to classical antiquity and the medieval scholastics for testimony to those terms. They are founded upon the classical distinction between the 'Practical' and the 'Fine' arts. Architecture is incontestably one of the practical arts, whose obligation is to serve ends other than itself. We have therefore had to look again at the complex nature of an art that can place itself at the service of causes that lie far outside its own discipline.

The one principle that could bridge the gap is a reinterpreted perception of use. Where the strictly utilitarian interpretation of that principle stopped short at the boundary of 'the measurable, the visible and the weighable', we have found in the late philosophy of Wittgenstein a very different interpretation. He attributed to use the authority of being the bearer of meaning and carried the principle of functionalism to a breadth and depth of application that have yet to be fully identified, articulated and addressed. 'Meaning, function, purpose, usefulness – interconnected concepts'.[58] This is the Uncompleted Project hinted at in the springtime of the Modernist adventure and which is still unfulfilled. In the work of Alvar Aalto we can find some examples of such a reconciliation both in his practice and in his writings that seek to explore 'the end of the spectrum where the purely human questions reside and where we will make most new discoveries'.

It is no easy claim to make, as we have seen in rehearsing the origins of a work of architecture. Between the patient drawing out of the concealed agenda (what the Greeks called 'the hidden truth') and the discipline that will ensure relevance to the power of invention a certain alchemy is required to fuse the rigour of the one with the gift of 'play' of the other.

All in all the operation is a delicate one beset with temptations – to turn a blind eye to awkward issues, to pre-empt the outcome by importing a ready-made 'solution', to accept only those parameters that are measurable, to indulge in the play of forms for their own sake. So we ask what is the necessary power that will control these rebellious forces?

Inevitably there comes to mind that image out of Greek philosophy of the charioteer and his pair of untamed horses: and here, as in antiquity, the discipline that is embodied in the figure of the

charioteer is the ethical. The metaphor of a command
that can harness divided energies into one is apt for the
role of ethics that Wittgenstein defined as the pursuit of
'what is valuable ... what makes life worth living'.

But there is another aspect of the morphology of
architecture that relates to the proper sequence of
operations, an order that insists that the point of origin
lies in the demand of some functional need or appetite
to be matched by its counterform in building. In the
fine arts, form is born out of previous form. This is not
so with architecture, for which form is born out of use,
shaped by use, energized by use and (Alberti's phrase)
'embellished by use'. It cannot draw its sustenance
from any other source.

Once again an image out of Greek mythology comes
to mind. The giant Antaeus, whose mother was
Goddess of the Earth, drew all his strength from
physical contact with the earth. Of all his contestants
only the wily Hercules observed this phenomenon and
contriving to hold Antaeus up so that his feet no longer
touched the ground rendered him weak as a babe in
arms and vanquished him. And for architecture it is a
contact no less mysterious and no less vulnerable to
separation that ties it to the World of day-to-day usage,
necessity, custom, use, function – call it what you will;
and it is no less true that divorce from such a contact in
the origin and grounding of a work of architecture
results in something that is not architecture at all, but
merely a decorator's 'folly'.

Alvar Aalto summed up this perception which he
wrote as follows: 'The New Architecture strives to
assess the content of the work (on which its form
depends) correctly and to make it the only point of
departure in creating form ... We cannot create new
form where there is not new content.'[59]

This condition of dependence is as true of the most
humble building as it is of the most sublime and in
that fact we come full circle back to the claim that in
recognizing use as the primary criterion for meaning we
acknowledge the status of architecture as a practical
rather than a fine art. In saying this, we are saved from
the misbegotten distinction that has for so long sought
to separate 'architecture' from 'mere building'. The
authenticity celebrated in Aalto's sketch of a Spanish
farm (Figure 2.25) takes its rightful place beside his
Civic Centre for Seinajoki (Figure 2.26), humble
certainly but no less a member of the common family of
structures in which property determines the rightful
station between factors of use and play.

2.25

2.26

In defiance of the claim of aesthetics for an art that is 'purposeless', purpose is the very driving force of architecture, its reason for being and its enjoyment. Every need for a building carries its own ontological code within it, and it is the task of architecture to draw out the intrinsic qualities and virtues of that appetite, and by so doing give form to a form-of-life, 'a local habitation and a name'.

References

1 Ludwig Wittgenstein, *Culture and Value*, p.3 (1930), Basil Blackwell, 1989.
2 Hannes Meyer, 'Building: 1928', in *Hannes Meyer: Buildings, Projects and Writings*, Claude Schnaidt, Tiranti, 1965.
3 *Ibid*.
4 L. B. Alberti, *Ten Books on Architecture*, Book VI, Chap. II.
5 To the Greeks the Mother of the Arts was Memory (Mnemosyne).
6 L.B. Alberti, *op. cit.*, Book I, Chap. IX.
7 Immanuel Kant, *Critique of Judgement*, Pt. 1: First Moment, # 5.
8 *Ibid*. Second Moment, # 10.
9 Theodor Adorno, 'Functionalism Today', *Oppositions*, No. 17.
10 Immanuel Kant, *Critique of Pure Reason: Transcendental Aesthetic*, First Section.
11 See Chapter 1, 'The Natural Imagination'.
12 Gilbert Murray, 'Poeisis and Mimesis', in *Tradition and Progress*, Houghton Mifflin, 1922.
13 Hannes Meyer, 'Building 1928', *op. cit.*
14 Bruno Zevi, *Towards an Organic Architecture*, p. 76, Faber, 1941.
15 John Summerson, 'The Case for a Theory of Modern Architecture', *RIBA Journal*, June 1957.
16 Hannes Meyer, 'My dismissal from the Bauhaus', 1930, in C. Schnaidt, *Hannes Meyer, op. cit.*
17 Hannes Meyer, 'Marxist Architecture', 1931, in C. Schnaidt, *Hannes Meyer, op. cit.*
18 Hannes Meyer, Education of the Architect, Lecture, Mexico City, 1938, in C. Schnaidt *Hannes Meyer, op.cit.*
19 Hannes Meyer, 'Bauhaus and Society', 1929, in C. Schnaidt, *Hannes Meyer, op. cit.*
20 Hannes Meyer, 'Marxist Architecture', *op. cit.*.
21 *Ibid*.
22 Abbot Suger, quoted in Jean Gimpel, *The Cathedral Builders*, (trans. C. Barnes) Evergreen Books: London 1961.

23 See Hans Sedlmayr's 'Art in Crisis' (trans. Battershaw, Hollis & Carter 1957) and Karsten Harries' 'The Rococo Church'.

24 Aristotle, *Nichomachean Ethics*, Book VI: 1139a, 16b2.

25 S.H. Butcher, *Aristotle's Theory of Poetry and Fine Art*, p. 147, Macmillan, 1898.

26 Aristotle: *op. cit.*, Book VI: 1140a, 1–23.

27 *Ibid.*, Book I: 1094a, 1–2.

28 *Ibid.*, Book VI: 1140a, 1–23.

29 St Thomas Aquinas, quoted in J. Maritain, *Art & Scholasticism*, Sheed & Ward, 1947.

30 J. Maritain, *Art & Scholasticism*, p. 20, Sheed & Ward, 1947.

31 St Augustine, *Confessions*, Bk. IV, Chap. XX.

32 I. Kant, *Critique of Judgement*, Pt. 1: Fourth Moment.

33 M. Heidegger, 'On the Origin of the Work of Art', in *Poetry, Language, Thought*, Harper, 1971.

34 Hugo Haering, 'Wege zur Form', 1925.

35 Hans Georg Gadamer, *Truth & Method*, First Part: 2; and *The Relevance of the Beautiful*, p. 125.

36 Adolf Loos, *Architecture*, 1909.

37 L. Wittgenstein, *Philosophical Investigations*, Pt. 1, # 65, Blackwell, 1953.

38 *Ibid.*, # 66.

39 *Ibid.*, # 67.

40 *Ibid.*

41 *Ibid.*

42 L. Wittgenstein, *Culture and Value, op. cit.*.

43 Lisle March Phillips, *The Works of Man*, Chap. IV, p. 110, Duchworth, 1911.

44 Alvar Aalto, *Rationalism in Man, 1935 Sketches*.

45 *Ibid.*

46 Colin St John Wilson, see Chapter 12.

47 See Apologia.

48 See Christopher Alexander, 'Notes on the Synthesis of Form', Harvard, 1964 and 'A Pattern Language', Alexander, Ishikawa and Silverstein; Berkley 1968.

49 Gadamer, *op. cit.*

50 L. Wittgenstein, 'Lecture on Ethics' (1929), *The Philosophical Review*, 74, 1965.

51 L. Wittgenstein, *Tractatus Logico-Philosophicus*, # 6.52.

52 L. Wittgenstein, *On Ethics*, 1929.

53 L. Wittgenstein, *Philosophical Investigations*, Pt. I, # 77, *op. cit.* (Blackwell: 1953)

54 L. Wittgenstein, *On Ethics, op. cit.*

55 L. Wittgenstein, *Philosophical Investigations*, Pt. I, # 19.

56 Aristotle, Book 1:1094a, 1–2, *op. cit.*

57 Paul Rudolph, in *Perspecta*, The Yale Architectural Journal, No. 7, P. 41.

58 L. Wittgenstein: *Tractatus Logico Philosophicus*, # 6.21.

59 Alvar Aalto, article in *Uusi Aura* 1928 quoted in E. Schildt, *Alvar Aalto*, The Decisive Years, p. 226, Rizzoli 1986.

3

The play of use and the use of play

An interpretation of Wittgenstein's comments on architecture

'Architecture immortalises and glorifies something. Hence there can be no architecture where there is nothing to glorify.'[1] This statement was written in the private notebook of the philosopher Ludwig Wittgenstein (Figure 3.1) in 1947 at a time when the Modern Movement was about to enter into its inheritance as the universal mode of construction after the destruction of World War II. It is a dark saying, and it could not have been written by any of the leaders of that movement. But it has a history, and 40 years later it is central to the architectural dilemma of our time. It was the fruit of a debate that took place 40 years earlier in Vienna, and the nature of that debate is only just beginning to receive its due in the wake of a movement that has not delivered all that it promised. Inevitably attention is focused upon the origins of that movement and upon the acceptance or rejection of those influences that presided at its birth. Of these figures the one who casts the longest shadow is Adolf Loos (Figure 3.2); and with the increasing exposure and exposition of his ideas we are at last beginning to understand the extent to which his influence was rejected.

3.1

3.2

Paul Engelmann, one of his students, suggested that the full significance of Loos' position was illuminated by its close relationship to the work of Wittgenstein and Karl Kraus. Not many architects can be said to share an affinity of ideas with a great philosopher and a great cultural satirist. Certainly they both saw Loos, who wrote much and wrote well, as a philosopher–architect above all.

For instance, in accounting for the furious controversy over Loos' building in the Michaelerplatz (1909–11) Kraus made the wry statement that 'he has built them an idea over there',[2] and this comment is later echoed by Wittgenstein's note 'Remember the impression one gets from good architecture, that it expresses a thought',[3] and the nature of that thought is illuminated at a number of points, particularly by Wittgenstein himself, of whom Loos is reported to have said 'You *are* me'.

This relationship was reciprocal, and there are many fascinating points of contact between Loos and Wittgenstein. When in 1931 Wittgenstein named ten people who had influenced him, Loos was one of them – in the company of Frege, Schopenhauer and Spengler; a quite extraordinary compliment. Furthermore when Wittgenstein, whose family was very rich, gave away all his inheritance in anonymous gifts, Loos was one of the beneficiaries. Wittgenstein perceived common ground between the modes of thinking in philosophy and in architecture, a common need for probity in ambiguous situations, saying that 'working in philosophy – like work in architecture – is really more a working on oneself. . . The poor architect succumbs to every temptation and the good one resists it'.[4] This remark perhaps carries a special sting, since one of Wittgenstein's sisters had persuaded their father to pay for the construction of the Secession Building by Olbrich – who was one of Loos' pet hates. Again, from 1926 to 1928, Wittgenstein took over the architectural design and execution of a large house in Vienna whose initial design had been prepared by Paul Engelmann. Although Wittgenstein decried it himself as no more that an exercise in taste, it is an austere, powerful and haunting building, and Engelmann conceded final primacy of authorship to Wittgenstein.

3.3

What is most significant for us today in the bond between Loos, Kraus (Figure 3.3) and Wittgenstein is that they shared in a view of Modernism (one might say the Modernism of Vienna) that is radically different from the manifestos which gained pre-eminence in the activist establishment of the 'international' Modern Movement and which have since become the scapegoat of current abuse. It was a view of Modernism that was common in the world of literature – indeed pre-eminent in the sense that it was the view of the dominant writers, Eliot and Joyce. Where the charter of the CIAM Group was optimistic, Utopian, indeed wonder-fully generous in its dream of a Brave New World, the Modernism of Vienna, while equally avid for the new, was yet, in a fiercely critical and tough-minded way, committed to continuity rather than revolution. 'You must confine yourself to saying old things – and all the same it must be something new,' wrote Wittgenstein.[5]

Overall there hung an Augustinian pessimism in the judgement of human nature. It even retained a place in its hierarchy of values for the sacred – or at least marked the spot of its desertion 'where there is nothing to glorify'. And it is in this unique compounding of an old sense of propriety with a new sense of values in use that the novelty of its contribution lies.

To divide correctly

Engelmann attributed to Wittgenstein, Kraus and Loos the gift 'to separate and divide correctly'.[6] Karl Kraus said that 'Loos' first concern was to separate the work of art from the article of use'. 'All that Adolf Loos and I have ever meant to say is that there is a difference between an urn and a chamberpot. But the people of today can be divided into those who use the chamberpot as an urn and those who use the urn as a chamberpot.'[7] Here the accusation of an impropriety in use ('a whole culture') draws upon a dichotomy that is persistent in Loos' writing – the distinction between the utilitarian and the monumental. Loos himself said: 'The work of art is brought into the world without there being any need for it. The house on the other hand satifies a need. . . Only a very small part of architecture belongs to art: the Tomb and the Monument. The rest, everything that serves an end, should be excluded from the realm of art.'[8] And the fact that Wittgenstein himself held to some such view of architecture is shown by his own statement that 'Architecture is a *gesture*. Not every purposive movement of the human body is a gesture. And no more is every building designed for a purpose architecture.'[9] 'The work of art is the object seen *sub specie aeternitatis*.'[10]

The dichotomy (architecture and building) is very persistent in German architectural discourse. What lay behind Loos' division between work of art and article of use was his particular abhorrence of the fashionable aestheticism of his time (exemplified by Hoffmann), which allowed the architect to dictate even the colour of his clients' slippers to be worn in the bedroom and nowhere else. It was part of a Krausian polemic. For Wittgenstein the issues were much broader. His later philosophy introduces us to such a rich interpretation of the modes of use that we begin to see that the disjunction between 'that which serves an end' and 'that which is an end in itself' is false to the nature of architecture. Indeed I hope to show that by transposing to architecture certain arguments used by him in an exploration of the use of language we begin to understand that architecture embraces a paradox precisely by overcoming the terms of this disjunction (see also Chapter 2). For in architecture 'article of use' and 'work of art' undergo a sea-change, freed, once and for all, from both the dreary obligations of the utilitarian and from the airless camp of the aesthete.

Wittgenstein did not write any extended work about architecture but there are many remarks scattered in his notebooks and a number of statements reported by students and friends that bear upon architecture. By appropriating arguments used in his philosophy proper, I have tried to build bridges between these points to see if they offer a pattern of explanation that will carry us further in our understanding of architecture.

The meaning lies in the use

Firstly, there is the use made in Wittgenstein's later work of the analysis of language. Starting from the injunction 'Don't ask for the meaning ask for the use,'[11] he evolved a powerful analogy in his concept of a 'language game' as the means of exploring through case-studies the meaning in use of particular words or concepts. The meaning of a word is not fixed; it is something dependent upon operational performance and demands interpretation in terms of the particular context in which it is working. Words cannot be understood outside the (non-linguistic) activities into which the use of language is woven. In terms of a language-game we uncover in usage a particular area of meaning. Words are like tools in a toolbox – 'a hammer, pliers, a saw, a screwdriver, a rule, a gluepot, glue, nails and screws. The functions of words are as diverse as the functions of these objects'.[12] Elsewhere he says 'our language can be seen as an ancient city: a maze of little streets and squares, of old and new houses, and of houses with additions from various periods; and this surrounded by a multitude of new boroughs with straight regular streets and uniform houses'.[13]

'And to imagine a language means to imagine a form of life (*Lebensform*).'[14] In a very literal sense this consideration of forms of use relates directly to the classic functionalism of Meyer, Stam and the ethos of *die Neue Sachlichkeit*. Loos himself wrote: 'I maintain that use determines the forms of civilised life, the shape of objects. . . We do not sit in such-and-such a way because a craftsman has built a chair in such-and-such a way: rather the craftsman makes the chair as he does because someone wants to sit that way.'[15] Use determines the meaning, not the other way round.

At this point we recognize some convergence of meaning with the term used by Hugo Haering in

describing 'the form arising out of operational performance: *Leistungsform*. . . We want to examine things
and allow them to discover their own forms'.[16] And
Wittgenstein's exploration of language as use is always
vivid with its examples of 'activities', 'customs',
'institutions', 'norms' and 'occasions'. Language is
society's means of communication and exchange. In a
lecture on aesthetics he said: 'In order to get clear
about aesthetic words you have to describe ways of
living. . . connected with all sorts of other gestures and
actions and a whole situation and a culture.'[17] He
continued:

> A philosophical question is like an inquiry into the
> construction of a society. It is as if a society met
> without clear written rules but in a situation where
> rules are necessary; the members have an instinct
> that enables them to observe certain rules in their
> dealings with one another, but everything is made
> more difficult because there is no clear pronounce-
> ment on the subject, no arrangement for clarifying
> the rules. Thus they regard one of their number as
> president, but he does not sit at the head of the table
> nor is he in any way recognisable and this makes the
> transaction of business more difficult. So we come
> along and bring order and clarity. We seat the
> president at an easily identifiable place with a
> secretary near him at a special table, and we seat the
> other, ordinary members in two rows on either side
> of the table and so on. . .[18]

Language-game and gesture-language

But there are many different language-games, and in
his explorations Wittgenstein makes a number of
tantalizing references to aspects of language in which
the notion of 'use' harbours suggestions of a very
different order from the pragmatic: 'What belongs to a
language-game is a whole culture.' For instance, in his
notes on Frazer's *Golden Bough* he writes: 'Our
language is an embodiment of ancient myths'[19] and 'A
whole mythology is deposited in our language'[20] or
again 'The ritual of the ancient myths was a language'[21]
and 'We have in the ancient rites the use of an
elaborate gesture-language'.[22]

One is here reminded of the way in which W.R.
Lethaby, in trying to go beyond the conventional

histories of architecture of his time (which were committed to explanation in terms of the phenomena of structure and the appearances of styles) wrote that 'at the inner heart of ancient building were wonder, worship, magic and symbolism',[23] and he went on to trace the motif of many a latter-day decorative feature back to its origins in magical representation (of, for instance, real lions or bulls as guardians of the gate).

If we remember Wittgenstein's statement to the effect that architecture (as opposed to building) is a gesture, and then relate that in turn to these statements about 'the use of an elaborate gesture-language', we are led to ask what it is within the language-game of architecture that performs this role.

First, we have the notion of an inherited language that is loaded with meanings of a special kind. (Remember his metaphor of the ancient city.) Second, he defines the nature of ritual language as *formal* by virtue of its commitment to repetition and strict rules. If we now compare this usage with the language-game of Haering's *Leistungsform* (operational form), we can begin to conceive of a scale of 'use' that runs between two extreme poles; the 'gesture' of 'ritual' and the 'purposive movement' of day-to-day 'functions'.

Let it be said at once that calibrations along this scale have nothing to do with questions of more or less ornament. For Loos that would be infantilism or 'crime'; for Wittgenstein 'just gassing'.

The meaning of play

The sense in which Wittgenstein uses the word game is limited to notions of rule, assent and structure. All of these have direct relevance to architecture, but in the arts there is a further sense in which the notion of play itself is relevant – the will to play, entertainment of the arbitrary, ascent beyond necessity, the drawing-out into pattern of that which in necessity alone is raw appetite. It is not a question of detached pleasure, of ornament to fill the void: it is the achievement of such mastery over necessity that a position of freedom is won that will allow the transforming powers of art to act upon the exigencies and importunities of use so that, in the phrase of Aldo van Eyck 'Space and Time become Place and Occasion', and the institutions of man become intelligibly embodied. Hans-Georg Gadamer has given an extended philosophical treatment of the structuring role of aesthetic play resulting in a form of *knowledge*.[24] Play is archetypally the form of self-sufficiency, of an end in itself, and in so being it paradoxically gives back to the performance of utility something of the aura enjoyed by the end in itself. Coomeraswamy in *Lila* draws our attention to the interpretation in Greek oriental and medieval thought of the divine nature of play, not only as a disinterested enjoyment but also as a form of wisdom.[25] And just as for Aquinas and the Schoolmen, art was that which draws out the particular clarity of something, 'the beauty of intelligibility,' so we find that in Heidegger's description of the Greek temple[26] stone, rather than being used (and therefore used up) as an instrument (for example, an axe), comes into its own at last as a 'presence, sharp-arrised, veined, massively gleaming-. . .truly itself for the first time. . . Something has been uncovered, something *understood*'.

Now it is the unique nature of architecture that it is a special form of art – the transformation of utility into icon. Its meaning is born of an exchange, of a process of question and answer in which 'use' is the source of questions and architecture the affirmation of a 'way of life': the ensuing *Lebensform* would not have come into existence but for that interaction. In the reciprocity lies the vitality of architecture.

It is, however, a condition of this transformation that its origins lie in use, and are humble, since there is always some need to shelter or enframe some action or object special to its culture; and that if it loses its roots in that necessity, it loses its status as a transforming agent.

It follows that the notion of pure architecture is meaningless. At the same time, paradoxically, the notion of *game* is of its essence; for architecture play is not so much a metaphor, certainly not an aesthetic indulgence, as a fundamental property of its being.

So we find that when we apply Wittgenstein's own method of analysis to the definition of architecture, the formula of 'meaning in use' unfolds a spectrum of astonishingly wide applications – yet all belonging to the same family of 'games'.

In attempting to define the way in which many games are very different in kind yet share a relatedness that makes them one language, Wittgenstein uses the image of a thread: '. . .in spinning a thread we twist fibre on fibre. And the strength of the thread does not reside in the fact that some one fibre runs through its whole length but in the overlapping of many fibres'.[27] And so

I would claim that it is one 'thread' that runs from the shed to the cathedral.

'There can be no good use without art,' said Aquinas,[28] and that is true of any occasion for building, however humble. So by using Wittgenstein's method I am brought to challenge that extreme of disjunction between the 'work of art' and the 'article of use' upon which Loos placed such emphasis. At both ends an eloquence is apt, but equally at all points along that spectrum architecture is serving an end. (It is the only art that is *not* an end in itself.) Architecture is not the prime mover; it does not *bring together* things that but for it would not have come together. Rather it makes possible the coming together of that which wants to come together but had no way else to do so. 'It is born of necessity,' wrote Alberti.[29] It follows that the limits of an architecture are the limits of the culture that it serves. It is the embodiment of values that have been worked out before by a culture in all its levels of awareness (religious, political, economic). The cathedral after all did not invent religion!

Concluding reflections

We have now come a long way down the route of Wittgenstein's concepts of meaning in use and language-game, of *Lebensform* and ritual, of thought and gesture to arrive at a certain plane of understanding about the nature and genesis of architecture. My own formulation of that understanding would be as follows. Architecture only comes into being by answering to a call from outside its own discipline to serve a set of needs in society.

3.4(a)

By this we mean two things. First, to set up a spatial order that makes possible the fulfilment of manifold operations in an *effective way*. This is the base of common use.

Second, to bring to life an order of representation that embodies those occasions so that they can be recognized in an *intelligible* way. This is the part of gesture, the use of play.

3.4(b)

The only way in which the representation can be arrived at is by a form of play that transforms utility to a level above that of necessity and thereby invents forms that truly celebrate a 'way of life'. For this to happen the play must complement the way of life, and propriety ensure that the urn and the chamberpot each

3.5

have their rightful use in the language-game of an undivided universe.

Where there is no necessity, there can be nothing to celebrate (a folly is not architecture). And where there is no play, there can be no celebration.

The only book that Wittgenstein published in his lifetime was the *Tractatus Logico-Philosophicus* – in the same year as Eliot's *The Wasteland* and Joyce's *Ulysses*.

3.6(a)

It was largely devoted to a technical argument about the nature of the language of logic that limits its capacity to make meaningful statements about the world. On such technical grounds the 'riddle' of ethics and aesthetics and religion was also denied its place – but not without regret ('even if *every possible* scientific question were answered the problems of our living would still not have been touched at all').[30] The book concluded with austere resignation – 'Whereof we cannot speak thereof we should be silent.'[31] And this elected silence was shared by Adolf Loos, who declared that 'the building should be dumb on the outside and reveal its wealth only on the inside',[32] (Figure 3.4(a)–(b)) and likened the rhetoric of Vienna's Ringstrasse to the villages of cloth and cardboard built by Potemkin in the Ukraine as *trompe l'oeil* to minister to Catherine the Great's appetite for culture.

3.6(b)

Now it seems that when in 1927 Wittgenstein took over the design of his sister's house from Engelmann (Figure 3.5), he really believed that there was nothing to glorify and that the interior also should be made dumb. Certainly he produced an architecture of unparalleled minimalism (Figure 3.6); austerity and the paring away of detail arrive at an almost metaphysical intensity. Nothing could be further from the world of Hoffmann and Klimt hitherto enjoyed by his sister.

3.6(c)

One of his students wrote of an occasion on which 'as we passed Swansea's immense new Guildhall, Wittgenstein expressed horror and disgust. The magnificent stairway in particular annoyed him; he said it was the architecture of a religion which nobody now professed'.[33] And to another student he said, of Canada House (Figure 3.7) in Trafalgar Square (which he considered to have taken over certain rhetorical forms without saying anything with them), 'That's bombast. That's Hitler and Mussolini' – and then added, 'how truly it showed that they were one in spirit with us!'[34] Conversely, another student reported that in speaking about the Georgian architecture of the Dublin streets Wittgenstein said, 'The people who built these houses

3.7

had the good taste to know that they had nothing very important to say; and therefore they didn't attempt to express anything.'[35]

We have seen that the limits of architecture are the limits of the culture that it serves. Wittgenstein's own interpretation of the limits of the culture of his day was deeply pessimistic. Fundamentally he was out of key with his time, 'an age without culture', and with its gestures – 'What nowadays passes for architecture'.[36] He held that we have lost the habit of doing the simplest things in a normal way. One here recalls Loos' story of the saddle-maker and the professor of design: 'Sir, if I knew as little about leather and horses and riding as you do, I would be able to appreciate the imagination in your saddle designs . . .' Wittgenstein died in 1951 and was therefore spared the Surrealist irony of the current attempt to reconstruct that 'tradition' by grasping the baton of Speer and the other henchmen of Hitler's neo-classical *Volkswille*. Mercifully, too, he was spared the appropriation of the notion of 'ritual' to the 'Post-Modernist' idea of 'fun'. For his own part he concurred with that most withering charge in which Kraus spoke of 'This Great Age . . . bereft of imagination, where man is dying of spiritual starvation while having no feeling of spiritual hunger.'[37]

At best he arrived at a certain resignation – 'what's ragged should be left ragged',[38] even at times a certain affection – 'the earlier culture will become a heap of rubble and finally a heap of ashes but spirits will hover over the ashes'.[39] But his final word remains the accusation implicit in that most resounding statement. . . 'Where there is nothing to glorify, there can be no architecture.'

For us perhaps the lesson is summed up in Auden's dedication:

Since the external disorder and extravagant lies,
The Baroque frontiers, the Surrealist police,
What can truth treasure, or heart bless,
But a narrow strictness.[40]

References

1 L. W., *Culture and Value*, p. 69.
2 Karl Kraus, *Die Fackel*. December 1910.
3 L. W., *Culture and Value*. p. 22.
4 *Ibid.*, p. 16.
5 *Ibid.*, p. 10.
6 P. Engelmann *Letters from Ludwig Wittgenstein*. p. 131.
7 Karl Kraus, *Nachts* 1918 in Bei.
8 Adolf Loos, *Architektur*, 1909.
9 L. W., *Culture and Value*, p. 22.
10 L. W., *Notebooks*, p. 3.
11 *Ibid.*, para 11.
13 *Ibid.*, para 18.
14 *Ibid.*, para 19.
15 Adolf Loos, *Kulturenartung*, 1908.
16 Hugo Haering, *Approaches to Architectural Form in Die Form*, 1925/1.
17 L. W. *Lectures on Aesthetics*, p. 11.
18 Quoted from L. W.'s ms 213, 415 by A. Kenny in *Wittgenstein on the Nature of Philosophy*.
19 L. W., *Remarks on Frazer's Golden Bough*, p. 10.
20 L. W., *Remarks on Frazer's Golden Bough*, draft.
21 *Ibid.*, draft.
22 *Ibid.*, p. 10.
23 W. R. Lethaby, *Architecture, Nature & Magic*, p. 16.
24 Hans-Georg Gadamer, *Truth and Method* (trans. 1965) and *Philosophical Hermeneutics* (trans. 1976).
25 Coomeraswamy, *Selected Papers*, Vol. 2 148 (Bollingen Series LXXXIX).
26 M. Heidegger, *The Origin of the Work of Art*.
27 L. W., *Philosophical Investigations*: 1; 67.
28 St. Thomas Aquinas, *Summa Theologiae*: 11–1.57.3 ad 1.
29 L. B. Alberti, *Ten Books on Architecture*; bk 1 ch. IX.
30 L. W., *Tractalus Logico-Philosophicus*, 1922, para 6.52.
31 *Ibid.*, para 7.00.
32 Adolf Loos, *Heimatkunst*, 1914.
33 Karl Britton, *Portrait of a Philosopher*.
34 Rush Rhees, *Ludwig Wittgenstein: Personal Recollections*.
35 M. O'C. Drury, *Conversations with Wittgenstein*.
36 L. W., *Culture and Value*, p. 6.
37 Karl Kraus, *In diese Grossen Zeit*, 1914,
38 L. W., *Culture and Value*, p. 45.
39 *Ibid.*, p. 3.
40 W. H. Auden, *Look Stranger*, 1936.

4

The historical sense

T. S. Eliot's concept of tradition, and its relevance to architecture

T. S. Eliot's theory of the relationship between tradition and novelty is exceptional for its power and originality. It grew from a remarkable interaction between critical intelligence and poetic vision. In fact Eliot's final triumph lay precisely in the uncovering of a structure of relationships between the old and the new, the temporal and the timeless, innovation and quotation; each had its place in a precise order of a kind that no other artist in our time has achieved. And that order hinges upon a paradoxical interpretation of tradition as the springboard for innovation.

The first statement of this theory appeared in the celebrated essay of 1919, 'Tradition and the Individual Talent', and I take the liberty of transposing the familiar passages in it into terms of architecture[1] rather than poetry, as follows:

Tradition . . . cannot be inherited, and if you want it you must obtain it by great labour. It involves in the first place, the historical sense, which . . . involves a perception, not only of the pastness of the past, but of its presence; [and] compels an [architect] to work not merely with his own generation in his bones, but with a feeling that the whole of the [architecture] of Europe from [Ictinus] and within it the whole of the [architecture] of his own country has a simultaneous existence and composes a simultaneous order. This historical sense, which is a sense of the timeless as well as the temporal and of the temporal together, is what makes an [architect] traditional. And it is at the same time what makes an [architect] most acutely conscious of his place in time, of his own contemporaneity.

No [architect], no artist of any art, has his complete meaning alone . . . you must set him, for contrast and comparison, among the dead. I mean this as a principle of aesthetic, not merely historical, criticism. The necessity that he shall conform, that he shall cohere, is not one-sided; what happens when a new work of art is created is something that happens simultaneously to all the works of art which preceded it. The existing monuments form an ideal order among themselves, which is modified by the introduction of the new (the really new) work of art among them. The existing order is complete before the new work arrives; for order to persist after the supervention of novelty, the whole existing order must be, if ever so slightly, altered; and so the relations, proportions, values of each work of art toward the whole are readjusted; and this is conformity between the old and the new. Whoever has approved this idea of order . . . will not find it preposterous that the past is altered by the present as much as the present is directed by the past. And the [architect] who is aware of this will be aware of great difficulties and responsibilities.

In a two-way process Eliot, changed by Dante, has in his own work changed Dante for us. This depth of reference and interchange operates in a number of benign ways. Memory (in Greek mythology the Mother of the Arts) becomes the key, and it carries with it an incomparable depth in terms of allusion or direct quotation.

The power of condensation it gives to communication can be most clearly demonstrated by an analogy in literature. Virgil, in writing the greatest Roman epic, plants his hero, Aeneas, in the midst of the greatest Greek epic, Homer's *Iliad*; and 1300 years later Dante picks Virgil as his guide in the *Divine Comedy* (during which they meet both Ulysses and Aeneas). So that it only requires James Joyce 600 years later to entitle his novel *Ulysses* for a vast apparatus of allusion and analogy to come into play and to be available to anyone informed of classical Christian culture.

By contrast we may take the following statement by Walter Gropius: 'Modern Architecture is not built from some branch of an old tree but is a new plant growing directly from roots.' In the light of this assertion it is not surprising to learn that there was no teaching of history at the Bauhaus. And out of such an attitude the notion was fostered that a brave new world could be built only by breaking free from custom and association: that the past was the enemy of the future. This is a clear case of what Eliot (in a later essay entitled 'What is a Classic?') referred to as 'a provincialism, not of space, but of time: one for which history is merely the chronicle of human devices which have served their turn and been scrapped, one for which the world is the property solely of the living, a property in which the dead hold no shares'.

The first thing to be said about the juxtaposition of these two viewpoints is that we are not confronted by a simple conflict between the futurist and the conservationist. Both Gropius and Eliot were equally resolved to discover 'the really new'. Furthermore both started from the same point – a moment of deep critical unrest at the beginning of this century. In architecture a typical reaction to the self-indulgence of Art Nouveau was Karl Scheffler's flat statement: 'We have had enough of "originality"; what we need is the self-evident.' Shortly after that Eliot wrote of the need for verse 'to recover the accents of direct speech' in a context vitiated by 'the pathology of rhetoric' and that the best way to go about it would be to concentrate attention upon 'commonplace objects'.

In fact what we are confronted with is something much more complicated – a deep division within Modernism itself. In the field of architecture that division came into focus at the attempt to establish a new orthodoxy by the founding members of CIAM at La Sarraz in 1928. The assertion of new norms, the establishment of a common language, was all the cry. Impatient of contradiction the new orthodoxy was proclaimed.[2] But how can orthodoxy exist without reference to precedents, to a body of doctrine that is to be reinterpreted and developed?

That is the rub: and it now seems clear to us that this rejection of historical continuity (something that could have been easily embraced within the vision of their elders such as Loos, Perret, Wright, Berlage and Mackintosh) was bound to make the new law seem alien. At the very least it amounted to throwing away not only a wealth of allusion but also a whole groundwork of the familiar upon which alone confidence in the new can be constructed. At the Bauhaus itself Paul Klee lamented, 'The people are not with us.'

But before we condemn the founders of CIAM too readily we should try to understand that they were guided not only by their sense of the urgency of the new issues that had to be confronted and for which there was no precedent – '*Les problémes du grand nombre*' (mechanized transport, mass production, population explosion) – they were stupefied at the ludicrous abuse of image and precedent that was flaunted by their elders.

Architects like Sir Gilbert Scott had brought the Battle of the Styles to such a level of cynical manipulation that the battlefield was strewn with broken images. The story of his Foreign Office design is

4.1

a case in point. The first design in 'French Gothic' (Figure 4.1) was rejected by the Prime Minister. The second in 'Byzantine Renaissance' (!) eventually finished up as 'Ordinary Italian' (Figure 4.2). The farce was then consummated by the re-birth of the first design as a basis for St Pancras Chambers. As to the written justification of such manipulation, you merely

4.2

have to read the sort of inflated platitudes written by a
typical protagonist such as John Belcher (in his
Essentials of Architecture) to know what Eliot himself
meant by the Hollow Men ('Shape without form . . .
paralysed force . . . this broken jaw of our lost
kingdoms'). In fact it would be fair to say that those
who claimed above all to be the inheritors of Tradition
did more than anyone else to devalue the only terms
under which it could be sustained: they had made it into
a language that could only tell a lie.

Furthermore there were those who, shortly after,
were prepared to use history and associations for more
sinister reasons under the banner of the 'Recall to
Order'. This was (and still is) the euphemism under
which the so-called 'right thinking' intellectuals provided the soft talk for Fascism. Eliot, who had come
near enough to Charles Maurras to scent the danger,
had himself pointed out that to carry into practice his
interpretation of the working of tradition would lead to
'great difficulties and responsibilities'. For certain
appeals to memory will all too readily conjure up
images of malign power. 'In the back of every Dictator
there is a bloody Doric Column' (Herbert Read). It is
an uncomfortable fact that the forms of neo-classicism
only too readily embodied the mythology not only of
Nazism,[3] but also of Communism ('The People too
have a right to Columns,' said Stalin; see Figure 4.3).
And Giuseppe Pagano, editor of *Casabella*, summed up
the danger when he wrote of Mussolini's Third Rome
that it was 'the exaltation of a lie perpetrated out of a
love for tradition . . .'(Figure 4.4).

We need then to establish criteria by which that
insight can be pursued; by what means we can judge the
value of any appeal to the authority of the past, and
also by what means we can reveal the intentions that
underlie it. Such an appeal takes the form of an allusion
or quotation in which a new form is associated with an
existing precedent for any one of a number of reasons.
The analogy may be formal, technical or semantic;
rewarding, trivial or false; and the intention behind it
may be in good or bad faith. It can be simply analysed
as a relationship between two terms; and the originality
and power of Eliot's formulation is to suggest that it is a
two-way relationship, that the precedent is changed by
the new term as much as the new is informed by
analogy with the old. Thus when Alberti transposes the
Roman triumphal arch onto the façade of the Christian
church at St Andrea in Mantua (Figure 4.5), the

4.3

4.4

4.5

analogy is very rich. It brings together the New Learning, Christian theology and the Roman celebration of victory at the same time that it announces a rediscovery and reassessment of the Classical language of architecture. Both of the terms are changed by the relationship and gain in their range of significance.

The use by Aalto in the Villa Mairea of regional Karelian forms on the back of the building (the 'primitive' sauna) and on the front a very sophisticated commentary on Purist themes, together with their progressive overlapping and fusion throughout the house, is another case in which both new and old terms are transformed and gain by the encounter. On the other hand, when Mussolini set out to celebrate victory (the bombing of defenceless Abyssinian villages) by building the Third Rome, we are only too aware that the relationship is one-way – an attempt to appropriate to the new the aura and authority of the old (Figure 4.6) by an act of symbolic inflation. The original source of reference gains nothing by the analogy – is in fact diminished by any degree to which the claim of association could be made to stick. This is almost a definition of kitsch. The Stalinist proposal to dress up Aalto's Viipuri Library in 'Classical' garb is a case in point (Figure 4.7).

4.6

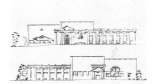

4.7

In fact the Fascist experience is prefigured by historical claims of a more complex nature which are open to analysis in the same way. For in the work of Muzio (Figure 4.8) and the early Terragni the claim to recall the ancient spirit of 'Romanità' carries some conviction; akin to the metaphysical forms of de Chirico a haunting juxtaposition is set up between the solemnity of Roman forms and the stripped geometry of Loos. It constituted a Surrealist gloss upon late Rome and in this way the exchange between new and old is not merely one-way, however equivocal it may seem to be.

Where the analogy is directed more to building language, the relationship of new to old is very vulnerable to pastiche, since development in technology will probably have undermined any direct grounds for quotation. For instance Kahn in Dacca (Figure 4.9) has invented a new form of masonary construction laced with reinforced concrete tie beams, and this new form stirs memories of Roman monuments in a way that is sufficiently sympathetic for us to feel that the Romans themselves might have welcomed it. By contrast Michael Graves uses the keystone motif in the

4.8

form of curtain walling for his Portland building (Figure 4.10). Such use can only be understood as an ironic gesture: for here the language of building construction is more travestied then transformed; and the relationship of the new to the old comes close to a further definition of kitsch (by Demetri Porphyrios) as 'the evocation *in toto* of a style simply by means of one of its attributes used out of context'. One is reminded of Eliot's description of Romanticism as 'a short cut to the strangeness without the reality'. In these terms all forms of revivalism are open to challenge, whether Victorian, Edwardian or Post-Modern. Certainly kitsch can never, in Eliot's terms, enlarge upon the meaning of the exemplar to which it alludes, for the new relationship proposed is itself a perversion not an extension of the original.

4.9

It is of course dangerous to transpose a thesis formed in the study of literature to the context of architecture. On the other hand, in so far as the use and abuse of history takes the form of allusion or quotation, the essential relationships of novelty to tradition invoked by Eliot can be seen to obtain. What you do about that fact will be very different in each discipline. What of the old is to be referred to and what to be rejected, what of the new has substance and will prove irreversible – all such questions relate to an interpretation of what is the 'ideal order' within any one discipline and not in another. But even what Eliot finally came to see about his own art of verse is not without relevance to the future of architecture.

4.10

> What we call the beginning is often the end
> And to make an end is to make a beginning.
> The end is where we start from. And every phrase
> And sentence that is right (where every word is at
>   home
> Taking its place to support the others,
> The word neither diffident nor ostentatious,
> An easy commerce of the old and the new,
> The common word exact without vulgarity,
> The formal word precise but not pedantic,
> The complete consort dancing together)
> Every phrase and every sentence is an end and a
>   beginning. . .[4]

References

1 I have put the transposed words into brackets.
2 And resisted. Hugo Haering denounced the formulations that were put forward and which shortly became the established doctrine of CIAM. He was one of a number of architects (among whom Frank Lloyd Wright, Aalto and Asplund were pre-eminent) whose work constituted a sort of running resistance to CIAM 'Orthodoxy'; but that is too large an extension of the present argument to be explored here. See Apologia and Chapter 6 'Alvar Aalto and the state of modernism'.
3 See Chapter 13 'Speer and the fear of freedom'.
4 'Little Gidding' from *Four Quartets* by T. S. Eliot, Faber and Faber, 1944.

5

Architecture and the figurative arts

This country is unique in Europe in its official attitude to art: there is no legislation requiring expenditure of any consequence upon works of art to be included in the construction of public buildings.

But suppose we did have the money, would we know what to do? In 1956 a number of artists and architects got together to 'work in collaboration' and put on the exhibition at the Whitechapel entitled 'This is Tomorrow', in which each one of twelve groups made its own stand. The exhibition came into being after a walk-out against an earlier set of terms proposed by the Groupe Espace: English go-it-alone v European 'Synthese'; but in practice the word 'competition' would more correctly describe the goings-on than 'collaboration' (not merely between, but within, the groups).

In the catalogue the architect James Stirling wrote: 'Why clutter up your building with "pieces" of sculpture when the architect can make his medium so exciting that the need for sculpture will be done away with . . . the painting is as obsolete as the picture rail. Architecture, one of the practical arts, has along with the popular arts deflated the position of painters and sculptors – the fine arts.'

Not so long after that I had a visit in Cambridge from Mark Rothko. We went punting on the river and he told me of his commission to paint murals for Philip Johnson's Four Seasons' Restaurant on the back of the Seagram Building. The language that he used to describe what he hoped his painting would do to that space sent the ducks packing to Grantchester in blue streaks: he wanted, in a word, to destroy it utterly.

Two tough cases perhaps, but not so very exceptional. There could be little accommodation between an architecture whose proudest claim was a fierce extension of its means to become the sole mediator between a 'user' and a prescribed set of 'uses', and a mode of painting that sought to purify itself through a reduction of means.

Twenty years later we reached the end of the road. Karl Scheffler once wrote, 'You can kill a person with a building as easily as with an axe,' and it is still easier to kill a work of art. Mies Van de Rohe's Berlin National Gallery did for Rothko once and for all: you could not see a single painting there, hung as they were against the blinding curtain of huge glass walls.

The two most prestigious galleries constructed in recent years have been, to put no finer point on it, no less intolerant. Indeed it is precisely the quality of our despair that those buildings which have achieved exceptional excellence in the field of technology have somehow conspired to kill the very things they were made to serve. I know of no more patent instance of the contradictions in our culture. 'The distinction between theories and values is not sufficiently recognized but it is fundamental. On a group of theories one can found a School; but on a group of values one can found a culture, a civilization, a new way of living together among men.' Thus Ignazio Silone reproves all forms of narrow polemic. Today we have had enough of 'schools' of painting and of architecture, of the trivialization and narcissism to which their 'purity' has brought them.

5.1

Can we yet specify the conditions under which painting and architecture could come together and mean something – mean one thing, so that put to the test, the removal of some part of either would destroy the significance of both? Think of St Mark's in Venice (Figure 5.1) without the mosaics: it might still have a kind of poetry, white-domed, luminous (St Front, Perigueux, Figure 5.2) but Byzantium would never have been. Or think of the Raphael Stanze in the Vatican: did you ever stand in a space that was more precisely gauged to the space in the paintings both physically (your size, its size) and intellectually (iconography and structure), envelopment in the phantasy of the painting going step by step in measure with your tread in the 'real' space? And in neither case are we talking about a merely aesthetic experience: we are talking about a whole culture made manifest and, on those occasions, for those moments, being manifested uniquely through those means (Figure 5.3).

5.2

Labrouste, in the Bibliothèque Nationale, had recourse to a form of illusionism by depicting sky and foliage in the spandrels of his vaults, recalling the pleasure of reading in the Luxembourg Gardens, transforming his thin vaults into a velarium in the Garden of Academe, a gentle and unpretentious transformation.

But the illusionism of 100 years ago does not work for us; and certainly there is one form of the pictorial imagination that has come a long way to meet architecture – is itself a kind of painted architecture. For our first project for the British Museum restaurants Richard Smith evolved an enormous relief painting as direct extension of the architecture, taking account of the fall of light from above, the coffered module of the ceiling structure, the triple height of the space (viewed

5.3

at the top level by one restaurant and at ground and
mezzanine level by another). It was as if his painting
had in turn found a natural extension to its own
preoccupations. And Paolozzi's sculpture and graphics
have generated a language of forms both symbolic and
decorative that has always had a mysterious but quite
natural affinity to architecture (Figures 5.4 and 5.5). In
a more conventional way Le Corbusier,
painter–architect, made a number of wall paintings and
designs for huge enamelled doors and tapestries at
Ronchamp and Chandigarh, and these introduced
subject matter in the form of symbols and figuration in
his own post-cubist idiom: there was, however, no real
equivalence between a form of painting that seemed
always a little too willed and too blatant and an
architecture that was effortless in its power but subtle in
its handling of contradictions (Figure 5.6).

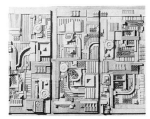

5.4

5.5

5.6

But I have in mind a kind of painting that is more
ambitious in its claims to deal with subject matter –
matter which in this case would rely upon a certain level
of scale, a certain pitch in confrontation, a context of
before and after, to create the frame of attention within
which alone its meaning could be developed and
experienced. A kind of painting that desperately needs
to be public if only it can find the right way to be so.
(Consider, for instance, how absurd it would be for
'Guernica' to be in a private study; but ask also if a
museum suits it very much better.) At the technical
level its rendering of space will avoid the illusionism to
which we can no longer respond as much as it will avoid
those hermetic abstract signs that are legible only to a
small sect. Thus its space disposes and exchanges
relations with our space easily, alternately distancing
and enveloping us: contributing at one level to the long
lost art of decoration but focusing here and there into
incidents of intensely concrete reference, far from
decorative self-effacement, able to suggest, to evoke
and dissolve yet able also to strike hard and shock. In
its stance to the viewer this painting will owe much to
Matisse but much also, in dealing with occasion, to
Brecht; and in its range of presentational techniques it
will have learnt much from the cinema. Perhaps in its
capacity for alternative readings it will not need to go as
far as the Shakespeare sonnet of which Empson wrote
that it yields 4,096 possible movements of thought
('with other possibilities'), yet it will take longer to
'read' than it takes to peel a banana. It will be clear by
now that my model is based upon an imagined

extension of the art of Kitaj (Frontispiece and Figure 5.7) not because it is unique but because it is that with which I am most familiar; but the case still holds for the work of many other artists whose scale and themes aim to make public rather than private statements.

The essential point is that any of these painters have the power to match the demands of such a mode of painting. But this is not something that can be willed: it must be a response to a need. It is as if the artists were trapped in a world of private reference not out of choice but because it is all that they can trust – and trust, authenticity, good faith are the heart of the matter. Such caution is easy to understand. Public art has in this century been so vilely appropriated to the rhetoric of the dictators that even artists of great natural talent, Arturo Martini (Figure 5.8) and Mario Sirone (Figure 5.9), have allowed themselves to be false-footed. As for Architecture, it too could easily serve that cause if only the occasion could occur, the intentions be clarified and the limits of its discipline specified.

What is above all the missing factor for both painting and architecture is that proper place and occasion and the need so stated that the response in good faith can be given; and society alone must specify that if it is to evolve the culture of which Silone spoke.

5.7

5.8

5.9

Part II
FIVE CASE STUDIES

6

ALVAR AALTO
and the state of Modernism

The year in which Aalto launched his career (at the age of 24) with the group of structures at Tampere was a remarkable year: 1922. It was, for instance, the year in which Joyce's *Ulysses*, Eliot's 'The Wasteland' and Wittgenstein's *Tractatus* were published, and Le Corbusier's *Vers Une Architecture* was completed; Mies Van der Rohe had just produced his most astonishing vision of the glass tower, and Le Corbusier his project for a contemporary city for 3,000,000 people. It was indeed the year in which Corbu himself set up his practice in Paris, and it was the year adopted by Barr, Hitchcock and Johnson as the birth of the International Style.

By the time that Aalto joined the CIAM Group, at their second meeting in Frankfort in 1929, he was engaged in the design of what appeared to be one of the most sophisticated, and certainly one of the largest, monuments of that International Style, the Sanatorium at Paimio. The sudden flowering of this architecture on a broad international front had been celebrated at the Weissenhofseidlung Exhibition in Stuttgart of 1927, and one year later the CIAM Group had been formed at La Sarraz.

Such apparent conformity was, however, deceptive. Hugo Haering (Figure 6.1) protested at the very meeting against what he saw to be the impatience of the revolutionary who must seek to substitute overnight a new order. His plea for the gentler mode of dialogue and discovery was silenced by the champions of unity, whose fighting manifesto required a new and instantly recognizable canon. The suppression at that time of some inherent contradictions certainly stifled the sort of diversity that the movement needed in order to be sustained beyond the initial attack.

6.1

The theme around which the Frankfort Meeting was organized was the nature and standards of the *Existenzminimum*. Almost immediately Aalto was expressing critical reservations about such an approach.[1] We find that the first thing to be said about his relation to the new architecture is that, like Haering and Scharoun, he began almost immediately to set a divergent course from that of the CIAM Group as a whole. The extent to which this represents an 'other' tradition is the main substance of this chapter. For the moment let us simply note the extent to which Aalto's work from this time on took the form not only of a substantial corpus of building but indirectly acted as a critique of what was being done concurrently by the 'established' avant-garde. Perhaps it is for this reason that he has always seemed to be closer to our generation than the other principal figures of the so-called Heroic Period. He was the only one for whom the enemy was not the dead hand of the past but false Modernism, a sort of bad faith.

We note also the quite extraordinary compactness with which Aalto's career fitted into a crucial period in the history of his country, at a time when most of the great creative talents that forged the modernist sensibility were expatriates (Joyce, Pound, Eliot, Wittgenstein, Le Corbusier, Mies, Picasso, Brancusi and Stravinsky). This is, however, no coincidence, for the quality of rootedness in the work itself is inherent in the intention and the methodology that Aalto evolved: a form of pact.

'Dictatorship' and the other tradition

In his discourse at the Royal Institute of British Architects in 1957, Aalto started by saying, of the revolution of modern architecture, 'like all revolutions it starts with enthusiasm and stops with some sort of Dictatorship', and he went on to talk about architecture as a kind of battleground for the quality of life of the man-in-the-street, a fight for certain freedoms against the twin enemy of technocratic stupidity, on the one hand, and the bad faith of formalism, on the other. Now the probity with which Aalto senses the dangers, and stakes out the positions on which to make a stand and fight, lies at the heart of all that he had to offer. It brought to his gifts as an artist a very special passion and precision.

In his review of Asplund's Stockholm Exhibition of 1930 he declares himself unequivocally in favour of 'the gains architecture has made by setting itself the goal of being a social factor instead of . . . dedicating too much attention to decorative and representational view-points'; and he sees it as 'a very positive manifestation that the artist is . . . democratizing his production and bringing it . . . to a wider public'.[2] Now democracy is arguably the most precious and vulnerable secular value of our time, and the architecture that is proper to it, sustains and reinforces it, is the most elusive of all, since architecture's own relationship to power is necessarily equivocal. Aalto knew the risks, and the way in which certain Scandinavian architecture became thereby emasculated is recalled in his anecdote in later life about the man who awakened from a nightmare crying 'Who can save me from Vallingby?' Nevertheless he set up the interests of 'the little man' as his criteria for judging architecture – though here we add straightaway that he was also writing in 1930 about the emancipation of women: indeed he took 'the modern working woman' transformed from a subordinate position to become an equal working companion (Figure 6.2) as the symbol of the cultural changes of that time. (And we should note in parenthesis that by his insistent acknowledgement of the roles played by Aino and Elissa Aalto in his own working life he was a man who practised what he preached.) We have already noted his reservations about the *Existenzminimum* and to those we can add (also in 1930) arguments in favour of mixed-use planning rather than the single-function zoning of the CIAM theorists.[3] When, just after World War II highrise housing was about to be adopted on a large scale, he declared himself to be 'one of those who only against his will accepts highrise dwellings in a location where lowrise is at all possible'.[4]

6.2

In contrast to the emphasis at the Bauhaus upon production method as the chief parameter in the design of light fittings he gave priority to the form of the object itself and to the quality and variety of light to be created (Figure 6.3). In general it was under the sign of the biological rather than the mechanical that his formal sensibility was modelled (Figure 6.4). This reflected not only his passion for natural forms and his exploration of nature's resources (such as his experiment in the early fifties with solar heating at Muuratsalo), it also fostered a willing acceptance of the agencies of growth and change in planning in built form and in the selection of materials that welcomed the action of time. In an age when taste dictated a predilection for the bare and the minimal he developed out of functional detail a whole language of rich decoration. Above all a healthy scepticism, controlled indulgence in dogma and the schematic, and he was alert from the start to the emergence of formalism, arguing already in 1935 that Modernism and traditionalism 'have grown closer and together form a large formalist front in opposition to a rational view of life and art'.[5]

6.3

Clearly one of the things that he had meant by 'Dictatorship' was that periodically a form of architectural language tends to be imposed upon the requirements of a building brief. Indeed the history of style is the succession of tyrannies imposed by the great

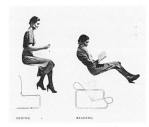

6.4(a)

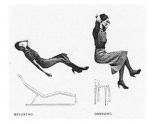

6.4(b)

innovators, whose poetry blinds their followers to all but itself, and it may even be argued that the authority of that poetry is directly proportional to its hypnotic power to paralyse rational judgement.

In the same year that he gave his discourse we can see this form of dictatorship clearly exemplified in the entries for the competition scheme for the City Hall of Marl. We get one proposition after another in terms of the grid-frame structure in the manner of Mies, which was then universal.

6.5

Then suddenly the box is burst open. First we have the project by Aalto that opens like a hand in a beautiful controlled gesture (Figure 6.5) and then the project by Hans Scharoun whom I have already mentioned as sharing Aalto's opposition to the CIAM canon. Here we see in varying degrees, in these two projects, an extraordinary independence of parts brought together in a collage of powerful juxtapositions that defy not only the Miesian discretion about selectivity but almost all conventional rules of formal continuity. And here I am reminded of a passage from an author to whom I shall make a number of references, namely Adrian Stokes:

> In regard to human constructions, ugliness, 'badness' as such, is not most feared, but emptiness, that is to say, lack of identity, lack of focus, promoting a feeling of unreality as may be transmitted, for instance, by an ill-proportioned flashy apartment yet designed it seems to banish space and time and so the sense of any function to be performed there . . . The squalid, the ugly, do not necessarily lend themselves to this numbing sense of unreality, deeply feared as proclaiming lack of relation, disintegration, the undoing of the ego-figure. Shape, pattern, growth, rhythm, interlocking parts of whatever kind, restore ourselves to ourselves.

6.6(a)

6.6(b)

We should note that the first characteristic of this responsive architecture is the vitality that flows from permitting the individual elements to have their own space and representation, and therefore identity. Now it is part of a thesis about which I argue further in Chapter 7, that for Aalto (as for Haering, Scharoun, Duiker and the early Melnikov) expressionism was the bridge to an extraordinary enlargement of the language of architecture (Figure 6.6), at a time when most of the early protagonists had rejected it in favour of the new reductive canon of purism. Avoiding that overemphatic

6.6(c)

rhythm (in which all impulses run parallel), but
accepting the means (stepping, polyrhythms, justaposi-
tion, changes in scale and material), he elaborated a
syntax whose capacity to accommodate the circumstan-
tial and the contradictory precisely matched, as we will
see, his insatiable desire to embrace and depict the
variety of human occasions. Louis Kahn once said that
'some functions suggest forms and some forms suggest
functions', and in this sense Aalto transvalued the
lexicon of expressionist forms. That the apologists of
the time, and the historians since, have failed to
appreciate this transformation has done much to
obscure the lines of continuity in what I would call 'the
other tradition' of responsive architecture.[7] And, in
doing so, it has compounded some journalistic confusions of our time about 'the death of modern
architecture'.

The lion and the programme

Two months after Aalto's Discourse at the RIBA, John
Summerson read an important paper there entitled
'The Case for a Theory of Modern Architecture'.[8] That
paper came to a halt with a dilemma, as both
Summerson and his critics saw it. He started by making
a bold claim and one that I have examined at some
length in Chapter 2. He said that the social sphere or
'the programme as the source of unity is . . . the one
new principle involved in modern architecture'. He
then went on to 'the crux of the whole matter' by
realizing that 'the conceptions which arise from a
preoccupation with the programme have got, at some
point, to crystallize into a final form . . . but there is no
common theoretical agreement as to what happens at
that point . . . One may even be speaking of a missing
achitectural language'.

Now Summerson is alluding not just to the vast
increase in the range of building types which require
research into their operational parameters, but also to
the sense in which architecture became engaged in a
form of social contract of the type to which Aalto
referred. Now the programme, as the vehicle through
which information and intentions of this order are to be
transmitted, is indeed far removed in terms of
complexity from the *utilitas* of Vitruvius.

To come to grips with it, we must start by acknowledging quite frankly the fundamental ambiguity in

its nature, which gave rise to Summerson's dilemma. I
have likened this below to Freud's classic distinction
between the manifest and the latent content of a
dream, in order to evoke the uneasy sense that we all
too often have that the so-called architectural 'problem'
stands in a false relation to the real world of people's
desire.

But a more appropriate analogy to the nature of
Summerson's 'programme' would be the formula for
dealing with the structure of genetic coding known as
DNA, in which a helix of double and single strands of
code link in a simple way to form the most complex
message of all – life itself. If we then liken the first of
the two coding strands in our DNA formula to those
conventional aspects of the programme that deal with
the operational and environmental parameters, we find
in Aalto's work from the late 1920s onwards an 'attack'
whose freshness, professional rigour, and technical
imagination, amounted to a form of significant
innovation in themselves. If we take, for instance, his
analysis and solutions to the needs of the tuberculosis
patients at Paimio, we find a case-study of a different
order from the idealized and abstract models of
functionalism proposed by his contemporaries. A
whole range of novel 'detail' is invented to respond to
the nervous condition and particular needs of a patient
in terms of heat, light, ventilation and quietness. All
these considerations conferred upon the 'programme'
an unprecedented density of relevant detail, the
draught-free filtering of natural air through double
windows; the varied use of colour to relax or stimulate;
special wash basins; specially designed doorfurniture
cupboards and beds – even the notion of putting out a
flag on the sun-terrace to celebrate each recovery of a
patient (Figure 6.7).

6.7

Aalto was, however, very aware of the dangers
inherent in the design methods that grew from seeking
a total solution by solving the secondary or subordinate
operational factors in isolation, one by one. He
illustrated this with the following anecdote:

As a teacher I once heard a student present his thesis
project. It concerned a children's hospital. He had
attempted to find the overall solution not only
through one secondary method but through many.
The analysis of movement patterns took half an hour
of the speaker's time. There were the space needs for
children of different ages, different light angles in the
window systems, easy maintenance of surfaces, etc.

All of them good things in themselves if one understands them as subordinate elements, but they were in this case not sufficient to create a humane environment or a functioning whole. When the student had finished counting up all these methods and presented his technical solutions for all the cases, I could not help but say: 'You have apparently still left out at least one possibility. How would the building and the sick children in it function if a wild lion jumped in through one of the windows? Would the dimensions be suitable in such a case?' The answer was a deep silence in the whole auditorium. Only the laugh of the paediatrics professor from Harvard could be heard.[9]

To the student the manifest programme was a checklist of predictable behavioural parameters and nothing else: to Aalto the programme had to embrace another story as well, and his surrealist image of the lion has the dream quality that encourages me to re-invoke for a moment Freud's concept of latent content in dream-work. Aalto's lion, like an apocalyptic beast, sloped towards our student in search of a quarry that did not exist in that student's imagination.

To return therefore to our DNA model, we find a second set of questions operating enigmatically at another level, and answered by a second strand of code, one just as important as that dealing with operational requirements, but here dealing not only with Summerson's 'missing language' but also with ambiguous psychological and cultural demands and those symbols for what Aalto called 'life's ungraspable difficult unity'.[10] In 1940 he said 'rationalization has not gone deep enough . . . the newest phase of architecture tries to project rational methods from the technical field out to human and psychological fields'.[11] And it is this second strand in the genetic code of our model that I wish to examine by exploring that new range of 'psychological fields', wherever it may lead.

In the same way that certain forms (in Kahn's phrase) suggest the accommodation of certain functions, so do certain clusters of form congregate under the sign of one or the other of two major spatial experiences of overriding psychological potency that we have examined at length in Chapter 1 – envelopment and isolation. And there we found that what seems to be at work here is the instantaneous fusion of nervous sensation and half-buried memories, a Proustian chemistry of the nervous system which takes the form of a body-language operating just below the level of self-conscious awareness yet colouring all our spatial experience (see Figure 6.8(a)–(b)).

6.8(a)

So we must add to the specification of our code a component of body language; but note that it is not just the innocent version (so beloved by aesthetes) of 'empathy' (of translating, in imagination, the statical thrust of the columns into a load upon your own shoulders – what Corbu called 'the witness of energy'). It is a language in which the human body, your body,

6.8(b)

once had to be the sole metaphor you had for dealing with every emotion, frustration or fantasy, fear or joy and which owes its emotional charge to its reconciliation of contradictory material. And it is one of the most marked characteristics of Aalto's work that it so dangerously engages with contradictory elements which it yet manages to control.[12]

But there is also yet a third reading to be built into our code. This is the realm of traditional associations, the ancestral hall of conventional symbols and collective beliefs, the local colour of every cultural reign.

And so we have come a long way in our attempt to spell out what Summerson's 'programme' has to cover if it is to match adequately, not only the criteria of function and environment, but also the other interlocking codes that together spell out both the private and the subliminal reactions, and the public realm of conventional narrative; and then, above all, so to weave the strands together that one can begin to conceive their counter-form in the architectural language that was 'missing' in Summerson's view of the programme as he conceived it. A language whose words are dense and multi-evocative; portico and hall, aedicule and roof, hanging garden and atrium, column and wall, mixing memory with need, sensation with reflection, doubling meanings with profusion.

The missing language

At least we now know that in looking for Summerson's missing language we are not looking for something simple. We are looking for an architecture that can encompass in its narrative all the strands of codes that we have explored – and which are indeed the essential structure of any of the cultures that are the glory of our history books. Now a culture cannot be conceived in the brain of one man alone, nor does it, like a

mushroom, grow overnight. A theory or a school of
thought can, but not a culture which is collective,
cumulative and necessarily imbued with much reflection and resonance: composed, furthermore, of many
individual strands that, as in the fibres of a cord, may
be discontinuous yet bond together under tension into
one thing. Aalto said 'it requires time for all that
develops and crystallizes in our world of thoughts.
Architecture needs this time to an even greater extent
than any other creative work.[13] He used to say that
what matters is how a building looks thirty years after it
was built – a test that his own work survives
exceptionally well (Figure 6.9).

6.9

6.10

That is precisely the question that was posed back in
1922 when *Vers Une Architecture* was completed by Le
Corbusier. Have we had enough time yet? Looking
back now our judgement would be that timing is as
crucial as time itself. Reflecting upon the achievement
of Le Corbusier, for instance, it is the impatience of the
man that seems most touching – even tragic. He did try
to do it overnight, and he did try to do it almost alone.
In view of this, it is extraordinary that his architecture
did at least address itself to all the levels of our
programme except perhaps one – the level of
conventional symbols. And for that reason his work,
which was a paragon to the rest of the world, lacked the
necessary rootedness in the French prejudices of the
time to avoid disfigurement (Figure 6.10).

On the other hand, for Alvar Aalto time and country
meshed perfectly with his talents, largely because he
made them do so. The language of his architecture
followed very closely the contours of the building
programme that he was studying at any one time, and it
did this because of one very striking characteristic in
the 'structure' (abstractly speaking) of his creative
attack. This can be epitomized by drawing two forms –
an ideograph of two lines, one straight, the other
serpentine. We can transform the lines into planes, and
whether we view it as plan or section, it will recall to us
the archetypal Aalto space, in which the juxtaposition
of a strictly flat plane with a rhythmically wavelike
surface seems to charge the air of the space like the
beating of a giant wing (Figure 6.11). But these two
forms can also be imagined as the lines of an
encephalogram – an imprint of the brain's processes –
in the sense that there seems always to be in the
'argument' of an Aalto building a complementarity
between the rigorous plane of analysis and the
turbulent wavelike surge of fantasy.

6.11(a)

6.11(b)

In the introspective essay entitled 'The Trout and the Mountain Stream' (1947) Aalto describes something very like this dialectical tension in his own design process:

> Architectural design operates with innumerable elements that internally stand in opposition to each other. They are social, human, economic, and technical demands that unite to become psychological problems with an effect on both each individual and each group, their rhythm and the effect they have on each other . . . The large number of different demands and sub-problems form an obstacle that is difficult for the architectural concept to break through. In such cases I work – sometimes totally on instinct.

And here we recall the account and illustration (Figures 2.13–2.14(a)–(e)) of his working method as set out in Chapter 2.

The references to the subconscious and to methods akin to the 'écriture automatique' of the surrealists are very pregnant and lend some support I think to my introduction of explicitly psychoanalytical factors. We notice here also the introduction of the notion of 'play' (a central theme in the cultural theories of his friend Yrjö Hirn) for what Corbu called 'the deadly serious game'. In addition, there is of course the conscious play of allusions, the element of acknowledged artifice that permits things to be said and things to be read into them that could not otherwise be permitted or acknowledged. (Here the parallel would be with Freud's analysis of the tendentious joke.) We have allusions to other buildings, Siena, Romana Minora and Pompeian courtyards, Greek theatre and mountain sites (Figure 6.12), encrusted Byzantine walls and spolium architecture.

It is a further characteristic of the ideograph that I have proposed that it has an open linear form of binary nature, and Aalto will occasionally use this fact as in the façades at Wolfsburg Cultural Centre (Figure 6.13) to allow two forms or two adjoining façades to enjoy a quite disparate character or even a deliberate discontinuity. In this it differs from the language of Le Corbusier, for which I offer this other ideograph in which a fixed rectangular framework withstands erosion by violent subforms (Figure 6.14).

6.13

For Corbu there is always this tension between the pragmatic components of brief and site, on the one

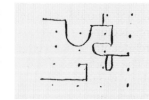

6.14

hand, and some glittering diagram or haunting memory of the Acropolis, on the other. This is the unique drama of his architecture and its formal dialectic. Aalto is wary of the diagram, of any proposition that is schematic. It is significant, for instance, that, except in the case of the Paimio Sanatorium (in which he may well have been influenced by Duiker), he never indulges in any exhibition of the structural frame. His dialectic is more subtle and for its working out demands a suppleness and an ability to change pace; it needs also the freedom of a less demonstrative tone in order to pursue his close reading of the working requirements of a brief.

Nevertheless, the language of Aalto and Corbu has more in common than with, on one side, the abounding fluidity of Scharoun's a-formal inventions, which scarcely admit to the existence of an autonomous architectural language, and, on the other side, the strict framework and pure externality of the Miesian temple form.

In one sense we are here rehearsing the range of what Stokes meant when he said that the generic difference in styles lies in the varying combinations by which the two poles of aesthetic experience are conveyed to us. We might even conceive of a form of architectural horoscope by which to define the predominance of one or the other sign at different times in history. Were we to do so we would notice the uncanny way in which Aalto seemed time and again to be offering the counterbalance to a dominating trend. It is with difficulty that one recalls what a shock it was, in the early 1950s when the first photographs of the town hall at Säynätsalo appeared (Figure 6.15); it hit the bland imagery of the Lever House like a bulldozer. In much the same way the massive containment of the courtyard there challenged the fashionable fluidities and elisions derived from the ITT Campus. Baker House at MIT had of course appeared even sooner, while, by comparison, a few years were to pass before the images of Ronchamps, Villa Shodan and La Tourette were to be published. At this time therefore Aalto's work was at the forefront in shattering the elegant mould of the International Style 'White' architecture. As in his earliest industrial buildings, architecture regained lost robustness.

6.15

The other, gentler, characteristic of Aalto's language which separates it from all of his peers is his use of images and metaphors from nature rather than machinery, and of materials that weather to maturity;

and this relates also to his sense of time and endurance. Impatience is not consonant with a feel for nature. Both the farmer and the sailor know better than to try to call the tune, and we sense the same wariness in Aalto's anticipation of growth and change, both in the form and the fabric of his buildings. He is said to hold that it will take 50 years before his buildings can be judged properly.

He shared with the Japanese a reverence for the variations and recombinations that flow from nature's continual change. And by these means he gives us the sense of a building perceived as a shimmering structure of transformations, responding to the light and weather and colour and smell of each season always changing and, in itself, weathering and changing colour: not as Platonic form in immutable Mediterranean light but as man-made fabric enduring time. He knows what it is like when sunlight refracted from rippling water dances on the bulkhead of a yacht (and he seeks to build this into the clerestories at Aalborg (Figure 6.16), of which he said 'light is to the Art Gallery what acoustics is to the concert hall') and how in the courtyard of Muuratsalo (Figure 6.17) the glow from a winter campfire creates with its reflections from the surrounding snowbanks an almost mystical feeling of warmth. All in all, it was a language of unprecedently wide range and stylistic diversity at a time when a narrow strictness was all the cry; and in its sense of presence, it has more in common with those painters of our time who call for a renaissance of the figure after an age of drained abstraction. This quality tempts one to revive the concept of 'character' in assessing his buildings – that quality of figure or image through which Ruskin and Stokes can suddenly deepen the game. Certainly, one is provoked to treat seriously again the question of ornament, for many of his buildings evoke an almost Byzantine glitter, through surfaces and details that answer to myriad demands of use, yet still remind us that Helsinki lies on the same line of longitude east as Tirgu Jiu and the birthplace of Constantin Brancusi.

But above all, this virtuosity and diversity served a working theory of open torm that demanded on behalf of the range of its subjects an equally wide and generous implementation; for when architecture serves life rather than just itself, its means must be prodigious.

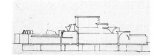

6.16

6.17

Aalto and the present State of 'Modernism'

To acknowledge the significance of this Other Tradition is of great importance today. We have seen that that tradition has, from the first disagreement at La Sarraz in 1928, been critical of the 'established' values and strategies of the International Style. In recent years much of that same criticism has come home to roost in a spate of journalism announcing the 'death' of Modern architecture.

But evolution is of the essence in authentic Modernism, and we have seen how Aalto himself in 1940 referred to 'the first (and now past) period of modern architecture'. But one thing is quite certain, and that is that the tradition of which I speak requires neither funeral rites nor expiation in the much abused ashes of Pruitt-Igoe. And what are the alternatives?

Only two of any substance, and both hinge on the issue of the 'missing language'. On the one hand, we have the claims of technology 'transcending', in the famous phrase of Mies Van der Rohe, 'into architecture'. To Aalto himself this is an overreaching – the raising of both the products and the intellectual values of technology to the level of idolization. One senses in Aalto a sort of physical repugnance towards objects and surfaces that exhibit a polish too cold and glossy and dandified to be touchable. At a deeper symbolic level, it is relevant to record Adrian Stokes' quotation from 'The Delay of the Machine Age' by Hanns Sachs: 'The Ancient world overlooked the invention of machines not through stupidity nor through superficiality. It turned them into playthings in order to avoid repugnance'.

It is clear that, to Aalto, technology raised to the level of importance at which it drains attention from the objects it was created to serve, in order to focus attention upon itself, indulges in a sort of blasphemy. We could exemplify this concern by taking three recent art galleries, each a miracle of technology, but each using that fact to frustrate our attempts to look at the works of art by thrusting to the forefront of our attention, in each particular case, some aspect of itself, either the structural system, or the bits and pieces of the constructional 'kit', or the servicing entrails. This kind of technical obsession is not just a question of an innocent desire to please through the excellence of the 'well-made thing', it is the deliberate and aggressive narcissism that motivates the whole Modernist aesthetic in its drive towards the purification of means, to the exclusion of all content, all subject matter but itself, in a frenzy of self-exposure. In terms of what Aalto stands for, this subversion of aim has rather the same effect (though far from the same cause) as the grounds of inauthenticity of which we spoke earlier – things seeming to be what in truth they are not, a show of freedom that proves in the event to be a bondage: bad faith.

The second alternative is of a different order, since it represents a point of view which, paradoxically, is both more novel and very much older. I refer to those claims on behalf of architecture as an autonomous discipline proclaimed most poignantly by Aldo Rossi. If this were no more than a criticism of the International Style, on the grounds that architectural language has been trivialized by reducing it to forms that are born solely out of service to use or structure, then we would simply be back with Aalto's story of the student and the lion. But it is much more than that. In the first place, from an impatience with what is claimed to be the banality of the everyday, it has moved towards a kind of estrangement from reality that is surreal in nature. It is not just a flight from reason (though in my view it is that), it is also a poetic complaint of some force, telling of a torn and unassuageable need for a long-lost world in which massive forms might assert order once more, imperious geometry take the place of panic, astonishing presences repeople the void in order to humour positivism's dread of the Sphinx (Figure 6.18(a)). This is the world of Giorgio de Chirico (Figure 6.18(b)). The cry is to get straight back to something like Summerson's language of antiquity, whose unarguable authority established the necessary plane of phantasy upon which much of our subliminal and conventional coding can be played out.

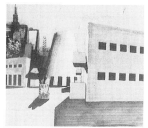

6.18(a)

6.18(b)

It is to the echo of these ancestral voices that Rossi is listening. It is, however, one thing to be the inheritor of a vast and undispersed iconography (that is indeed the virtue of working within a tradition – you are not on your own), but it is another matter to re-invent that lost world overnight. For although we are not asked to return to the classical forms literally, something is wrong with the argument from the start. Where the prototype evolved as the transformation of use and structure into poetry, we are now invited to short-cut straight to the poetry and to cut out the banalities of use and structure. This is Art for Art's sake again, and it is one of the oft-noted characteristics of aestheticism that its most favoured phantasies revolve around the idea of death (take the writings of Walter Pater as a supreme example). It is no coincidence, therefore, that Rossi's most poetic project is for the cemetery at Modena. Borrowing de Chirican images of ambivalence and impotence, it achieves a haunting evocation of death. These are images of power, but it is a power that oppresses; and those unframed and windowless apertures that no one will ever look through remind me of the advice that Aalto once gave to a student, 'When you are designing a window imagine your girl-friend looking out of it.'

6.19

That thought in turn recalls to mind another surrealist image, only this time the surrealism of life: it is a photograph by Picasso's friend Dora Maar (Figure 6.19). It comes as a timely charm or benediction to guard us from the hypnotism of that death wish; for the only thing that can save us from the bewitchment of poetry is another poetry. Here we are offered a composite emblem of architecture, nature and woman – a florilegium to Eros. And, after all, what I have tried to convey from the start is that the probity of Aalto's life work lies precisely in the way that, in an age of terrible violence and bad faith, he preserved a vision of architecture as a celebration of life, of a power that does not oppress, but sustains.

Thus we can admire the way in which he invented a world of forms, and we can be deeply moved on occasions by the way those forms are assembled to create a presence and a place that, like a human face, have the memorability we do not normally enjoy in our daily commerce with the man-made world. Now, unarguably, much of that grace is a pure gift (from the Gods), personal, rare and inexplicable, which pours through one person and becomes a sort of blessing on us all. What is not so personal, and is, indeed, available to any of us who wish to learn from it, is the probity that launched and informed that world of forms – I mean that very down-to-earth humanity that addressed itself with what Leonardo da Vinci called *ostinato rigore*, obstinate rigour, and a great professional pride, to the tangled web of needs and annoyances, desires and frustrations by which each day we follow our course; and to find an answer to those needs is to give to the individual a kind of self-respect which constitutes a form of freedom that the politicians know nothing of, because it has nothing to do with dogma, but all to do with how each person (Aalto's 'little man') is helped to be at home in a world that can be marvellous in unison, but terrifying in alienation. Aalto was one of the rare architects in our time who could make monuments; but much rarer was this other gift, which could make poetry out of the everyday, which could, in the words of the painter Vincent Van Gogh, 'give back to ordinary men that something of the eternal that the halo used to represent'.

References

All reference to Aalto's writings are to page numbers in 'Sketches' published by MIT Press, 1978, a substantial but by no means complete selection of Aalto's writings and lectures edited by Göran Schildt. (A.A.'s writings have been variously translated and versions differ significantly; eventually an 'authorized' version must be produced.)

1 'Sketches', p. 31: 'The Dwelling as a Problem', 1930. 'We have certainly had enough examples of such a minimal line.'
2 'Sketches', p. 116.
3 'Housing Construction in Existing Cities', 1930 ('Sketches', p. 5).
4 'Building Heights as a Social Problem', 1946 ('Sketches', p. 92).
5 'Rationalism and Man', 1935 ('Sketches', p. 47).
6 Adrian Stokes, *The Invitation in Art*, p. 52.
7 Hitchcock in 1952 stigmatized Aalto's Baker Dormitory as 'expressionist'; and Giedion when he, at last, in the eighth printing of *Space Time and Architecture* introduced a chapter on Aalto, set it under the rubric of 'the irrational'.
8 *RIBA Journal*, June 1957.
9 'Art in Technology', 1955 ('Sketches', p. 128).
10 Speech at the Centenary Jubilee of the Jyväskylä Lycée, 1958 ('Sketches', p. 164).
11 'The Humanizing of Architecture' 1940 ('Sketches', p. 77).
12 The handling of contradicition here is something very different from the use of the term by Venturi for whom its connotation seems to be purely stylistic – a sort of mannerism employed to attack the 'boredom' that is presumed to be the price of conformity.
13 1947 ('Sketches', pp. 96–8).

7

Hans Scharoun

'Significant irregularity – in Gothic for instance.' LUDWIG WITTGENSTEIN

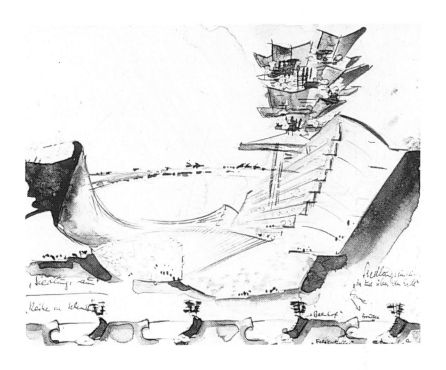

In the Tiergarten in West Berlin, two buildings have stood for 10 years in amicable contention: *inter se disputando* as Panofsky once described to us the debate between two High Gothic masters. The Philharmonie of Hans Scharoun and the Nazional Galerie of Mies van der Rohe confront each other like demonstrations of an argument that started between friends in Berlin 50 years ago. Minimalist abstraction: pluralist actuality. Nowhere else in the world of building is there a debate of such intense polarity nor exemplars of such authority.

What is remarkable about this confrontation is the silence with which it is greeted. But then such silence has largely been the case in the reception of Scharoun's work.[1] Reproof for this fact must lie at the door of the established historians, who for 50 years have either disregarded or misrepresented Scharoun's work. Now I do not dwell upon this sorry fact out of any pleasure to be derived from attacking the historians but because the core of all that Scharoun stands for lies right at the centre of what Banham in another context once called a 'zone of silence'. I hope to show that much of the sillier confusions of our time were born out of that same *trahison des clercs*, but first it is necessary to start by clearing away the misrepresentation of Scharoun's work that has arisen from it. In the first place we must clarify the relationship of his work to Expressionism. Certainly in 1919 at the age of 26 Scharoun, no less than his elders Gropius, the brothers Taut and Luckhardt, Mendelsohn and Mies, was inflamed by the post-war vision of an Utopian community living in glass houses, and his drawn images of burgeoning symbols are now the classic emblems of that period; but within a year, when that vision had passed for him as for the others, these forms were turned to a very different use. What he did not do, however, was to conform to the tactics and the new canon of those who formed the hard core of CIAM; indeed all his sympathies lay with Haering's opposition to that conformity at the very first meeting at La Sarraz in 1928.[2] Nor did he join the diaspora to America in the mid-1930s. From that time on when his work is mentioned, it tends to be identified pejoratively as a late survival of Expressionism, and it is interesting to note the way that this term is used as a sort of euphemism for any nonconformity to the established CIAM line.[3]

What all these historians have failed to observe was the transformation that had taken place in that language which they labelled Expressionism. The first

of my counter-claims on Scharoun's part is to point out
that it was precisely the achievement of a handful of
architects (Scharoun, Haering, Duiker, Melnikov and
Aalto) to discern in the explosive and bewildering
richness of the Expressionist vocabularies, modes of
order that could be brought to bear on quite other
issues, serving quite other intentions and making
possible a completely different order of functions than
the mere will to 'express' forms of energy that first
brought them into being.

Louis Kahn once said that 'some functions suggest
forms and some forms suggest functions'. Many of the
shape devices of the Expressionists (simple and double
curvature, stepping in plan or section, dihedral angles,
polyrhythms, contrasted materials, sharp changes in
scale and formal juxtaposition) were taken over to
make possible complex functional configurations not
available to the International Style canon. Hitchcock
wrote at the time (1929) that 'each real style of
architecture is able to express (*sic*) certain functions
perfectly . . . Only by a loss of perfect integrity . . . can
a style succeed in giving the most adequate expression
to all the functions'.[4] And for those who were less
content to protect the 'perfect integrity' of the
International Style and were impatient of the restraints
it laid upon their freedom of search for functional form
the lexicon of Expressionist form must have suggested,
in Kahn's terms, many fruitful applications.

I find this transformation very clear when comparing
the extraordinary group of watercolour drawings that
Scharoun made between 1939 and 1945, though these,
too, have been advanced by our conventional historians
as evidence of Scharoun's continuing adherence to
Expressionism. They are nothing of the kind. It is true
that they share a certain ecstatic quality, but that is all.
Unlike the early drawings, they swarm with people;
and what they deal with are the two things that
mattered most to Scharoun at a time in his life when he
was utterly deprived of any chance to do anything
about them but draw – spatial experience and its
relation to human activities. Their 'irregular' geometry
may be alien to Roman order but not to the Greek
(Figure 7.1).

They are daring attempts to depict what he, more
than anyone, knew could only be *built*. As drawings
they are bound to fall short, because neither graphics
nor photography can render the kinds of a-perspectival
space with which they deal; but construed properly they
are a stunning insight into what could have been built in

7.1

Stuttgart, in Kassel (Figure 7.2), in Mannheim and was at last built in the Philharmonie. These are the drawings of an imagination that feeds upon sensations of spatiality and of movement ordered in relation to foci of enormous concentrations,[5] and whose interest in constructional elements and their figurative disposition in façades (all the things that we *can* draw, the elements themselves of *disegno*) is of a secondary order. They are very moving, yet they must have been drawn under agonizing conditions and it is painful to recognize in them an awareness that they are substitutes, at best secrets to be nursed for another day.

7.2

The drawings were made when Scharoun was deprived of building work altogether; but there had been a time before when he had had to practise a different kind of substitution. With the coming to power of the Nazis his work was identified as that of a 'culture-bolshevist', his Academy in Breslau closed and all possibility of public work cut off. Nevertheless he yet managed to carry out a number of private commissions for very remarkable houses. Blundell Jones has pointed out that 'all of these houses were built in traditional materials with pitched roofs and relatively ordinary street elevation (Figure 7.3), the result of restrictions imposed by the Nazi building authorities who vetoed absolutely the architectural vocabulary of the Modern Movement. The fact that Scharoun could work under these conditions is significant: they would have been fatal to Mies . . . whose architecture would have lost its meaning if forced into the mould of traditional construction'. Scharoun, whose White Period architecture (Figure 7.4) was superbly detailed, fluent, original, stopping just short of the mannerism that came through in the hands of his successors (such as Terragni), dropped the whole paraphernalia almost, it seems, without a moment's regret.

He could do this because his passionate concern was with space as the essential moulded substance besides which the vessel that contains it is of secondary order. The essence of what Scharoun was after could survive in spite of prohibition upon technical innovation and upon Modernist 'good taste'; on both those fronts it could go in disguise. Now this is extraordinary enough: no other of the masters (except perhaps Melnikov) was put, by the tyranny of his political masters, to such extremes of deviousness. But we have to notice certain characteristics and results of this encoding. In the first place the transformation in Scharoun's style was in part

7.3

7.4

a reversion to the stylistic phenomena of his youth, the ripe and popular taste of the followers of Muthesius (Menzel, Fischer, Mohring and Schmoll), born out of the English Free School. In the second place his weapon against sentimentality in such revivalism is irony. But, more fundamental still, he did not return, when the Nazi ban was lifted, to the language of Modernism, as did, for instance, the Luckhardt brothers or (the younger) Eiermann. Instead, in a series of truly astonishing school and theatre projects Scharoun develops the essence of the free style away from traditional references into a freewheeling vocabulary of great vitality. In the competition for the Marl Town Hall (1958), the contrast between the majority of pseudo-Miesian schemes (Figure 7.5(a)) and the jolting energy of Scharoun's project (Figure 7.5(b)) speaks for itself.

7.5(a)

Among its characteristics we note first the extraordinary independence of the parts both in their intensively developed particularity and in the means of their association into a whole complex. No regulating lines, no *ordonnance* of the frontal plane, no grid, no canon establishing hierarchies of structural, spatial and servicing elements. Instead, the technique of collage – elements overlaid, dovetailed, juxtaposed; sometimes the 'cutting' is drastic in its change of scale, material, rhythm, idiom. Detail ranges from a relaxed use of the most conventional (even banal) of 'contemporary' motifs and popular elements,[6] through the one personal leit-motif (the circular window) to original inventions drawn straight from the exigencies of function – for instance, the catenary (acoustic) roof or the luminous stair balustrades of the Philharmonie. Yet the sense of order is there and it grows upon the vitality with which the very order of things themselves is rendered; the individuality and therefore the identity of each functional element is made manifest. The evoked analogy is that of the medieval town. Since scale is established by the operational dimension of the parts: the size of even a very large building is mediated down to human scale.

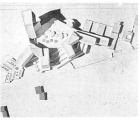

7.5(b)

There is also most clearly at work a mode of inflection and adjustment to site conditions of all kinds and explicit acknowledgements to neighbouring structures.[7] The impact of the anti-aesthetic is baffling yet strangely liberating. It recalls Brecht's alienation effect, which says 'You're not here to sit passively on the axis of the proscenium and clap at all the right moments. You are involved.' There are distinct elements too of humour and irony, and the spatial organization within the buildings is unrivalled in its richness and diversity. Here Blundell-Jones in his book is very good at walking you around the plans and compelling attention to the techniques used to develop each episode.

Now we must inquire into the theoretical basis of this extraordinary evolution in style. Clearly we are presented with a radical change in building language. The architect who, in the Breslau flats and the Schminke house, proved himself a master of continuity, of the flowing surface, now confronts us with calculated discontinuities, even discords. Here it is helpful to have recourse to the writings of his friend Hugo Haering. 'We want to examine things and allow them to discover their own images. It goes against the grain with us to bestow a form on them from the outside.'[8] This 'examining of things' concentrated upon 'the form arising out of operational performance (*Leistungs-form*); and the clarification and articulation of *Lei-stungsform* would in turn 'lead to every object receiving and retaining its own essential shape'.[9] Scharoun's application of these principles is well illustrated in the Philharmonie,[10] which he describes as 'a hall not motivated by formal aesthetics but whose design was inspired by the very purposes it serves' (Figure 7.6(a)–(c)).

7.6(a)

7.6(b)

7.6(c)

The stunning invention of the valley-section, present-ing 'music in the centre', is reciprocated acoustically by the catenary tent of the roof structure and the many-faceted galleries. Architectural envelopment becomes live music. And in the foyers the staircases, galleries and bridges by which the public are led in the round to their seats is itself an astonishing piece of topological orchestration that, when the interval bell goes, has to be seen to be believed. As to Expression-ism, I leave the last word to Scharoun. When pressed by a student to say whether or not he was really satisfied with the façade, he replied 'Has it got one?'

When, in 1951, at the Milan Triennale in describing his school projects he emphasized that 'my efforts are not concerned with the aesthetic nature of the problem', we must inquire more closely what lies behind his attitude to aesthetics. It is not a rejection in favour of technology (as Mies in 1923) or 'scientific design' (as Hannes Meyer in 1926) or the 'false trickeries' of style (as Gropius). For instance, he went on to say of his school projects that they must 'not be the expression of a political platform nor primarily the product of a technical or aesthetic perfection'. Here we are confronted with a triple exclusion that seems to sweep aside symbolic representation, technology and aesthetics alike.

Instead Scharoun takes as his text a quotation from Kant – *Raum ist bewustseinsform* – which I interpret to mean that 'all experience is grounded or manifested in forms of space', and we are then presented in his Darmstadt school project (Figure 7.8(a)) with an extended 'performance specification' for the various activities that take psychological terms, defining the characteristics of contrasted territories, of 'tension' between the public and private realms, and between the characteristics of home-bases for the three different age groups of children.

All parts of the school (Figure 7.8(b)) are connected by a common winding 'street', widening here and there into a 'meeting cloister', to overlook a courtyard or playing field. Each of the three 'school-hoods' has its 'gatehouse tower' containing cloakrooms, WCs and wet services. The Lower School (Kindergarten, Figure 7.8(c)) is characterized as a 'warm nest', with an emphasis upon protective enclosure both indoors and out, south exposure, warm colours. The Middle School (Figure 7.8(d)) provides for a more disciplined aura in which two enclosed spaces, each with three classrooms sharing a common patio, face east and west respectively so that the direction of sunlight in the patios changes significantly throughout the day. In the Upper School (Figure 7.8(e) the emphasis is upon self-discipline; the external spaces are no longer enclosed but open up to the outer world. Orientation is to the north and the four classrooms share a common debating chamber ('parliament'). In short, Scharoun is claiming to match the imputed psychological context of each set of activities to an equivalent range of physical characteristics in a sort of psychological topology: the Leistungsform becomes architecture.

It is at one and the same time a deeply original as well as deeply traditional pattern of relationships (cf. the African village Figure 7.7); and at its core we come face to face with a challenge. For while Scharoun satisfies abundantly our appetite for spatial enclosure, inventing forms of envelopment of astounding power, he denies us its twin pole of the self-sufficient and independent object, distanced from us and emblematic of stability. The language of form is no longer part of the Cubist tradition but belongs in the organic field of forces that we find in the pictorial world of Paul Klee (Figure 7.9(a)). Mies and Le Corbusier present us

7.9

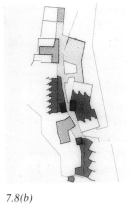

7.8(b)

7.8(c)

7.8(a)

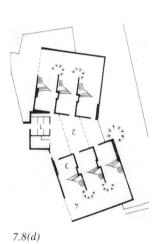

7.8(d)

7.7

7.8(e)

frontally with images of affirmation, and these we may gratefully incorporate in our need for reassurance; but this mode of appraisal too easily shifts into the game of visual aesthetics which Scharoun, who in the 1930s had been a master of it, now rejects. Ernst Kris has pointed out[11] that the aesthetic stance only emerges when the viewer becomes an onlooker rather than a participant in the function (of ritual, religion or politics) that the art is serving. My hunch is that Scharoun, like Brecht, like Butterfield, not only denies us the comforts of conventional rhetoric but deliberately used many of the devices I have described (banality included) to prod us out of relapsing into the aesthetic trance.

In Chapter 2 I have argued at length that 'the programme' as generating agent was the one new proposition that modern architecture has added to the traditional body of theory. Suffice it to say here that in developing such a case the work of Scharoun would be adduced as extremely powerful evidence. There are, however, those who find the case to be untenable, and this includes the majority of historians, whose values appear to be exclusively formalist.

In 1964 I attended a symposium in New York on the architecture of the 1930s and sat in some bewilderment as one speaker after another padded out the Hitchcock/Johnson paradigm of the International Style.[12] Not only were Le Corbusier and Wright excluded on the grounds that their work was too various to conform to that canon, but there was no mention of Aalto, let alone Scharoun, Haering or Duiker. Given that interpretation of what 'Modern architecture' represented, it was no surprise when, 10 years later, these people pronounced Modern architecture to be dead. Nor is it surprising that at the funeral rites of this fiction it was found necessary to invent the birth of another – Post-Modernism: *parturient montes nascetur ridiculus mus*.[13]

The architecture of which I write, of Scharoun as of Duiker, Aalto and others, is untouched by the birth and death of these fictions, and requires no expiation in the ashes of Pruitt-Igoe. And it is time that it was acknowledged.

References

1 This chapter was provoked by the close coincidence of the opening of the Berlin State Library and the publication of Peter Blundell-Jones' exemplary reading of Scharoun's work in his monograph (published by Gordon Frazer in 1978), which was described as 'The first critical monograph in any language on Hans Scharoun'. But cf. also the collection of buildings, projects and texts by Scharoun put together by Peter Pfankuch, published in 1974 by the Akademie der Kunste.

2 See J. Joedicke, 'Haering at Garkau', *AR*, May 1960.

3 Thus we see Hitchcock in 1952 stigmatizing Aalto's Baker Dormitory as 'Expressionist' and Geidion, when he at last in the eighth printing of *Space Time and Architecture* introduces a chapter on Aalto, sets it under the rubric of 'the irrational'. See also Chapter 11: 'Open and Closed'.

4 *Modern Architecture*, 1929, p. 216.

5 Rudolf Schwarz's contemporary studies of ritual space bear comparison, see his *Vom Bau der Kirche*, 1938, translated as *The Church Incarnate* (foreword to English version by Mies), 1958.

6 See the renderings by Sergius Ruegenberg for the 1951 project for the American Library in Berlin (and just to thicken the plot, remember that Ruegenberg was job-architect for the Barcelona pavilion).

7 The reading room of the library winks at the Nazional Galerie.

8 'Approaches to Architectural Form', *Die Form*, 1925/1.

9 'The House as an Organic Structure', 1932. *Programmes and Manifestos of Twentieth Century Architecture*, U. Conrads, Lund Humphries, 1970.

10 Consider also the fact that the Philharmonie has been a success with its public beyond comparison with any of Scharoun's fellow architects.

11 Ernst Kris, *Psychoanalytic Explorations in Art*, p. 57.

12 See 'Two Letters on the State of Architecture'.

13 Translates: 'The mountains groaned in labour and out popped a silly little mouse'.

8

Sigurd Lewerentz

The Sacred Buildings and the Sacred Sites

A question of paradox

Sigurd Lewerentz, born in the same year as Gunnar Asplund (1885), has not received comparable acclaim although he outlived Asplund by 35 years. International fame came to him when his St Mark's Parish Centre at Skarpnack became identified as a forerunner of the New Brutalism – but this classification was only a half truth.

'It was as if he stood at a slight angle to the world', wrote E. M. Forster of the Greek poet Cavafy; and that image could most aptly be applied to Sigurd Lewerentz. It is said that he could sit for a long time just looking at a common nail and asking himself how many ways it could be used – for 'out of the simple question a surprising answer could come'. We read also of his instruction to a despairing metal-worker: 'All I know is that you are not going to do it the way you normally do.'[1]

It is not that we have to contend with perversity; what is at issue for Lewerentz is the search beneath conventional appearance for the shock of a renewed truth. Christian Norberg-Schulz once described the convention of modular space as *space without secrets*: Lewerentz was able to find secrets wherever he looked because he looked hard. 'If you do not expect the unexpected you will not discover it,' said Heraclitus,[2] and, in so saying, he pointed to much that is enigmatic in Greek architecture. In the architecture of Lewerentz (above all in his sacred architecture) we are confronted as much with a new interpretation of ritual and symbolic form as with the manner of its making.

But above all we are confronted with a major paradox. Whereas in his early work Lewerentz was a master of the classical language of architecture, in his later work (notably in the churches at Björkhagen and Klippan) he totally rejected that language and yet produced buildings of great authority, propriety and emotional impact. Furthermore, whereas in the case of Asplund, his contemporary and sometime collaborator, this transformation was accompanied by some equivocation, for Lewerentz, the 'turn' was extreme, unblinking, absolute. His classicism was more refined, more deeply felt, more original than that of any of his contemporaries; his late work was more austere than any minimalist, more uncompromising than any Brutalist.

At a time of reassessment of the classical language of architecture, the testimony of this man has unshakeable authority, and the grounds for his rejection of that language must be explored; for his work is the exposition of a profound polemic. Henri Matisse maintained that a painter should have his tongue cut out so that he would be compelled to say all he had to say with his brush. Uniquely among architects, Lewerentz elected that silence.

He was a man of few words; all he had to say was said by the way a brick is laid, a pair of beams straddle a column, a piece of glass is clamped across an aperture in the wall, a path is cut through a forest. What for lesser mortals is called 'detail' was for him a means of heightening and transfiguring the day-to-day, and in that he is of the company of Hawksmoor and Borromini.

The Sacred Buildings

Lewerentz was one of the greatest rarities of our times: a master of *sacred* architecture. Where others used their skill to make it a little easier to face death, mixing unfocused sentiment with well-focused clinical detail, Lewerentz did not flinch at the tragic sense. By an architectural alchemy of great intensity he fused the simple elements of construction into metaphors of brooding mystery.

Aristotle, in *The Poetics*, assigns unique significance to the ability to invent metaphor: 'The greatest thing by far is to be master of metaphor. It is the one thing that cannot be learnt from others and it is also a sign of genius since a good metaphor implies an intuitive perception of the similarity in dissimilars.' Lewerentz possessed this unteachable gift to a marked degree. We will see, for instance, how, in St Peter's, Klippan, a painfully evolved solution to the need for central support – a 'technical' assembly of raw steel sections into a column and crossbeam, which thrusts into the centre of the Church – irresistably recalls the central symbols of both the New and the Old Testaments: the tree of knowledge and the cross of redemption. Without any recourse to rhetoric, a way of making has become transmuted into a figure infused with 'terribili-tà'.

Such a gift is rare; what is equally extraordinary is Lewerentz's ability to exercise that magic irrespective of stylistic terms. In this chapter, I have tried to account for the radical transformation in language between the first neo-classical masterpieces (the Chapel of the

Resurrection in Stockholm) and the equally powerful last work (St Peter's, Klippan). A Schinkelesque refinement was abandoned in favour of a poverty of means unique in the history of architecture – an elected 'silence' that is infinitely more moving than the noisy rhetoric that is all the rage today.

His work is fraught with paradox. He was qualified as a structural engineer and for many years divided his time between conventional practice and the design and production (in his own factory) of standard metal windows, doors and partitions. Yet his later buildings had no windows at all. In addition, in a period increasingly enamoured of high technology he turned towards the masonry of ancient Persia as the point of departure for his last inventions (Figure 8.14).

It is a pity that his rightful heir and one-time collaborator, the much underrated Peter Celsing, died comparatively young, pre-deceasing Lewerentz himself. But for the present Lewerentz's work carries great relevance to the current debate about the classical language of architecture; the fact is that its most moving and skilful exponent in our time abandoned that language in its entirety – and did so without any loss of power to move us deeply.

In an early project of 1914 in Helsingborg, Lewerentz explored the theme of the cemetery chapel in a profoundly original way (Figure 8.1). This was in the early days of the practice of cremation, and Maurice Maeterlinck had been drawn in by the town commissioner to help formulate a 'programme'. It was proposed that the mourners should not exit through the door by which they had entered, but instead pass through a progressive 'rite of passage', from the chapel where the funeral rites are enacted into a place of memory or celebration and thence out into the graveyard itself.

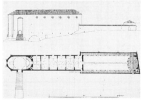

8.1(a)

In the case of the Helsingborg project Lewerentz invented an extended narrative in which building and landscape are drawn together as one continuous theme (Figure 8.1(a)–(c)). The sloping contours and presence of water on the site are developed into a moving and lyrical analogue. The water is channelled (as a metaphor for the River Styx) into a dark vault under the entrance façade of the building. In the ceremony itself the mourners move from the dimly lit Hall of Death up a staircase to the Hall of Life, whose high windows receive the dance of sunlight reflected from the waterchase passing beneath. Overhead a choir sings, concealed in its gallery. The mourners then pass

8.1(b)

8.1(c)

into an arcaded cloister, lined with urns and closed at its western end by a memorial pavilion from which, by a small door, they may either walk into a Grove of Remembrance or return to the world of the everyday. The brook that passes like a millrace beneath the chapel emerges on the far side, renewed as the Waters of Life, in a steep cascade that returns down towards the tree-lined avenue to the south.

This rite was not merely the contrivance of a 'promenade architecturale', but the enframing and sustaining – through architecture – of a common experience of great poignancy: the necessary acceptance of death, the decent rituals of mourning.

Like so many of Lewerentz's major inventions this project was, alas, never built. Fortunately his design, conceived 10 years later (March 1922), for the Chapel of Resurrection in the Woodland Cemetery of Stockholm was carried out. Here Lewerentz extended this experience of the confrontation with death to a much larger canvas, beyond the isolated building and out into the landscape at its more sublime. The design of the whole Woodland Cemetery itself was won in competition in 1915 in a joint submission with Asplund and went through a number of evolutionary stages that are explored later in this chapter.

8.2(a)

The particular sequence in the plan that forms the approach to the Chapel commences from the raised Grove of Remembrance, a paved square with fixed seats surrounded by elm trees (Figure 8.2(a)). From this vantage point of rest there lies straight ahead a long pathway cut through the dense woodland forest of tall pines (Figure 8.2(b)), a thin shaft of light parting the blackness. This is the Way of the Seven Wells, crossed by pathways into the forest, where groups of gravestones are sprinkled at the feet of the trees. Here and there a solitary figure tends a grave. Gradually a white glimmer at the end of the forest path comes into focus (Figure 8.2(c)), announcing the presence of a tall limestone portico; we are about to arrive at the Chapel of the Resurrection (Figure 8.3).

8.2(b)

The first thing we notice is that the portico closing the view of the forest path is not only disengaged from the megaron form of the chapel but is, ever so slightly, set at an angle to it. It is as if a wedge had been driven between them. This departure from the orthogonal draws with it the plane of the west gable wall of the chapel itself (Figures 8.4).

This disengagement is enigmatic. It is a condition present elsewhere in the building at the scale of detail.

8.2(c)

8.3

8.6

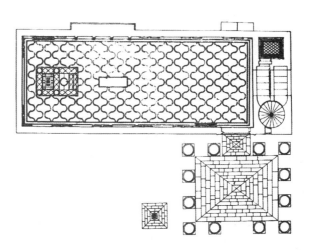

8.4

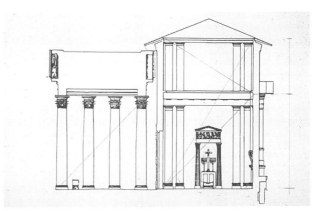

8.5

For instance, just as we see daylight between the roof of the portico and the eaves of the chapel, so too at the eaves level of the chapel there is a deep undercut between the roof slate and the stone cornice, as if the plane of slates hovered above the body of the chapel itself (Figures 8.5 and 8.6).

I know of no precedent for such independence between portico and sanctuary; not even the Erectheion has this freedom. But then, wherever we look in the chapel, things are not quite as we are led to expect. This ramifying strangeness takes hold of the attention in a way that seems to address the visitor personally.

The entrance to the chapel stands behind the north-facing portico. The chapel interior is dominated by the presence of a tall aedicular baldachino over the altar, strongly lit from the southern window (Figure 8.8(b). The exit is a separate, minor doorway in the west-facing gable. It is clear therefore that Lewerentz is applying the principles of the 'rite of passage'. The exit opens towards a flight of steps that leads down into a sunken graveyard, surrounded by trees but also flanked along its northern edge by a range of cells in which coffins awaiting burial can be housed. It is in this sunken court that the journey that started at the northern entrance comes to its terminus (Figure 8.7).

8.7

I suggest that the freeing of the portico is to compensate for the weakness that would result from locating it at the far corner of the chapel, a location necessary to the proper sequence of the 'rite of passage' procession; for this sequence would clearly require that the entrance door should be located as far away from the east end as possible without actually being in the west wall, which is to be reserved as location for the exit. To have simply attached the portico to the corner of the chapel would have been formally banal.

The 'Corinthian' order of the chapel is an original invention in which memories of the Tower of the Winds in Athens are compounded with the Theban bell-capital, which, like the plane of the roof slates, is deeply undercut at the plane of connection to the square abacus. Setting this carved elaboration of limestone against the sheer rendered surface of the chapel, with its plinthless wall, transmits the emotional charge from the whole into the detail of the part.

8.8a

Although some of the strangeness in this interior is of a conventional mannerist nature – recalling in its distension and structureless 'wall paper' of pilasters the stair-hall of Michelangelo's Biblioteca Laurenziana – the real strangeness lies in that transposition whereby

8.8b

the powerful aedicule, whose presence outside dominates the chapel, is recalled within by the stiff tall stance
of the baldachino (Figure 8.8(a)–(b)). There is
something haunting about this insistence, its juxtaposition and transformation that hints at some metaphor we
cannot grasp – a quality to which de Chirico ascribed
the status of the 'metaphysical'.

There presides in both part and whole a Grecian
canon of proportion, founded on the square, the golden
section and their compounding in the square-root-of-
five relationship. The application here is rigorous and
confirms my belief that where this is so, the presence of
a building becomes charged with 'gravitas'; constant
relationships are perceived simultaneously or in time,
in the way that verse is measured out by rhyme, and
this insistence builds up to a persuasive authority.

At about the time of the construction of the Chapel
of the Resurrection Lewerentz was also engaged in two
major competition projects at Malmo – a new theatre
(Figures 8.9(a)–(b)) and a project for the Eastern
Cemetery (Figures 8.23 and 8.24(a)–(d)). They were
designs of extraordinary elegance in the manner of
Schinkel. In fact the projects are equal to anything that
Schinkel himself produced; the theatre is richer in ideas
than Schinkel's Schauspielhaus in Berlin and the
cemetery project is the most haunting celebration of
mortality in our time.

Be that as it may, the drawings, which are now the
unchallenged masterpieces of their kind, demonstrate a
finesse in the invention and manipulation of classical
themes that is truly remarkable. They establish a
position of such perfection that the reasons for
subsequent rejection of this language must have an
exceptional urgency.

8.9(a)

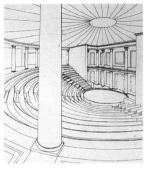

8.9(b)

Transition

Many others, including Asplund, made the shift shortly
afterwards to the 'white' architecture of the 1930
Stockholm Exhibition. The building for the Social
Security Administration in Stockholm of 1930 was the
major work of this period. However, the austerity of its
façade reveals Lewerentz's fundamental kinship to the
ethos of Adolf Loos and it is a signal of further austerity
to come. The Johanneburg Church project of 1933 for
Gothenburg was his most original work during this
period and is discussed in the argument below. It is,
however, at this time that Lewerentz' final collabora-

tion with Asplund on the last, and most important, building for the Woodland Cemetery took place. There were disagreements and Lewerentz was dismissed. The affront, after almost 20 years of profound collaboration, was wounding and perplexing.

Nevertheless the war-time extensions to the Malmo cemetery with the Chapels of St Knut and St Gertrude (see Figures 8.33(a)–(b)) carried further Lewerentz's 'turn', only this time it is not merely a reaction against the classical mode but also against the 'white architecture' itself. No one carried that 'turn' to the pitch that earned Lewerentz the reputation by the late 1950s of being a godfather to the Brutalists, and which is most dramatically demonstrated in his last building: the Church of St Peter, Klippan, in southern Sweden. 'Swedish grace' was a thing of the past.

In the Church of St Peter, 1962–5, sited on the outskirts of Klippan near Helsingborg, an unprecedented austerity of means prevails. But this austerity is not an end in itself – it is the means by which the tragic aura of the mass envelops us with a breathtaking primitiveness. Once again there is the element of strangeness that we found in the Chapel of the Resurrection, though it is of a different order. It does not lie in the reinterpretation or distortion of ancient themes; there are no orders, no portico or pediments or symmetry to be subverted, and therefore the building does not lend itself to description in conventional terms (Figure 8.10).

8.10

The building's mystery lies in the discrepancy between its apparent straightforwardness and its actual obliqueness. The harder you look, the more enigmatic it becomes. In the age of rationalism and 'the new objectivity' Lewerentz had the reputation of being exasperatingly private and disdainful of explanation.

8.11

The competition design for the Johanneburg Church of 1933 (Figure 8.11), carried out during Lewerentz's 'white' period in the 1930s, prefigures a major issue in the design of the Klippan Church. As so often with Lewerentz, the great virtue and subtle originality of his thinking was instantly grasped by the most intelligent of his architectural contemporaries, but was not understood by the members of the jury.

The point at issue is the rethinking of plan-form for the performance of the liturgy. This subject is now well rehearsed and Rudolf Schwarz's *Vom Bau der Kirche* of 1938[5] stands as a remarkable document of exploration at that time. The relocation of the altar was a prime consideration. Instead of being sited at the far end of a linear (basilican) space so that the officiating priest stands between the congregation and the altar and performs the office with his back to the celebrants, the altar was now to be moved into the heart of the congregation. The term that Schwarz used, 'the open circle', corresponds closely to the term used by Lewerentz, *circumstantes*. By this conception, the celebrants 'stand round' the performance of the sacraments, which are therefore carried out in full view of the congregation. This re-interpretation of the Lutheran mass recalls the practices of the primitive church before the time of Constantine, when the sacraments were performed secretly in the catacombs or the family dwellings – in a state of utter simplicity.

Although at Skarpnack Lewerentz adopted the linear basilican form, with the church in Klippan he returns to a forceful application of the principle of *circumstantes*.

Just as the Chapel of the Resurrection grew from a reinterpretation of the ceremony of the commital of the dead, so here the new principle of *circumstantes* lies at the heart of a new plan-form (Figure 8.20; page 123).

It shows the altar surrounded (counter-clockwise) by the bishop's seat, pulpit, organ, choir, font, congregation and lay-clergy. The priest's point of entry is immediately from the sacristy to the north; the congregation has two points of entry (from west and south) directly outside, and one (from the north), through a protected entry porch to which is attached a small wedding chapel. There is a bell-tower over the sacristy. The other elements of the church centre – meeting-room, communicants' classrooms, parish council, children's club and pastor's office – take the form of an enclosing L-shape lying to the east and south protectively against the prevailing wind and forming a communal 'street-court' as an extension of the meeting rooms and the children's club. The children's club, in turn, has its own sunken courtyard at the centre of the 'street'.

In proposing the square plan-form required by the principle of *circumstantes*, Lewerentz was confronted by the need to reduce the span of his roof members by some form of intermediate support. In this case, as at Skarpnack, the roof elements take the form of vaults. But, whereas at Skarpnack the vaults invariably ran laterally to the nave axis, in St Peter's he ran them along the main axis towards the altar – though they required some form of intermediate support to reduce the length of the span across the entire church (18 m, approximately 60 ft). This could not be achieved in the masonry structure used elsewhere without massive invasion of the central zone of the church. Lewerentz was thus led to adopt some form of columnar support. At first he divided his space by a pair of columns (Figure 8.12). Later he proposed a solution that not only reduces the degree of interrupton to a minimum but also (as we shall see shortly) imparts a symbolic gesture which is as profoundly apt as it is original. A single column supports a short cross beam that in turn supports at each extremity a pair of lateral beams, whose outer support lies in the east and west side walls (Figure 8.13(a)–(b)).

8.12

At this point we have to note that strange instinct by which Lewerentz, apparently concerned only with a dogged working out of an issue in terms of building construction, in the end arrives at a figure pregnant with symbolic meaning – its form irresistibly evoking the form of the cross with a harshness for which we are quite unprepared. It is almost as if the ancient legend of the Discovery of the True Cross had happened here, and these rough walls had been erected to protect the discovered object. I know of no precedent in the architecture of our time for the sheer impact of a way of building transformed into symbolic statement.

It seems worth while therefore to look closer at the building rules that Lewerentz set himself. In the first place we find that the use of brick is subject to three propositions stringently applied in the teeth of commonsense compromise. First, Lewerentz proposes to use it for all purposes: wall, floor, vault, rooflight, altar, pulpit, seat. Second, he will use only the standard, full-size brick; there will be no specially shaped bricks. Third, no brick is to be cut. The only way these conditions can be met is by a very free proportioning in the ratio of mortar to brick; to achieve such jointing (often very large) a very dry mortar mix that included ground slate was employed.

The effect is of a surface in which bricks appear to be embedded in a matrix of mortar rather than laid up in bonded course work of conventional joints. It brings with it memories of ancient brickwork, Byzantine and Persian (Figure 8.14), as well as the indigenous vernacular of farm buildings.

Heating and ventilation are incorporated in the brickwork such that the cavity walls of the church serve as a plenum, acting through a pattern of open perpend joints or through open channels at window sills. The refusal to cut brick produces some startling results; for instance, in the window openings to offices in which the

8.14

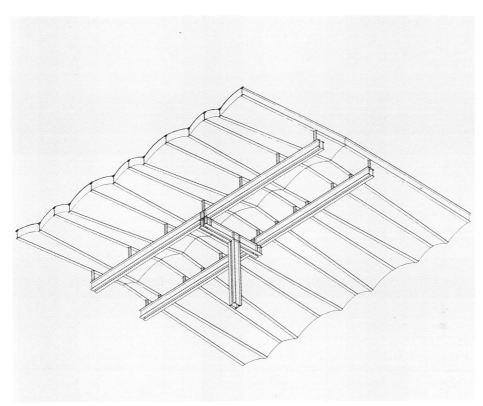

8.13(a)

8.13(b)

cavity between inner and outer leaf is kept open as just such a channel for warm air, the toothwork of the outer leaf stands exposed (Figure 8.15). A similar serration occurs at the springing of each vault (Figure 8.16) and at each end of the fissure in the floor created by the font (Figure 8.18).

8.15

Similarly, floor tiles are never cut, whether they be brick or the wider range of Hoganas tiles of different colour and size. Their pattern is frequently eccentric, and width of joint random, but all such work was carried out to the on-the-spot instructions of Lewerentz who apparently spent three entire days a week on the site.

Openings, be they for door or window, are never framed *into*. Closure is effected by applying an element across the opening to the face of the wall. Thus, both door and doorframe, or glazing element, sit *on* the face of the wall, not *in* it (Figure 8.17). The surfaces of the wall and its openings are massively complete irrespective of all trim or services.

8.16

As with the Chapel of the Resurrection, we are once again confronted with the unexpected. It were better that nothing be taken for granted, whether it be the detail of window, vault and door or the layout of the whole. A square plan seems simple enough; but let the floor as it slopes down to the altar swell into a shallow mound and burst open to reveal a well for the baptismal shell (Figure 8.18), and let a raw steel column crowned with a crossbeam stand like a crucifix off-centre of that space to vie with pulpit and altar as a centre of focus, and a certain drama enters in.

The column itself is not what it at first appears to be: split in two from top to bottom, its twin cross-trees, which are not symmetrical, carry at their extremities yet further beams, which are also split into pairs (Figures 8.19(a)–(b)).

8.17

On these beams stand steel struts to support the metal ribs that support the brick vaults at both springing and ridge lines alternatively. Then again, these ribs to the vaults are neither horizontal (they pitch gently to the 'centre' of the church) nor do they run parallel but expand and contract as they run from wall to wall. Lewerentz speaks of the vaults as a recall of the ancient symbol of the heavens, but here his treatment of them is strangely moving and insinuates into the mind a closer analogy to the rhythm of breathing – the rise and fall, the interlocking of expansion and contraction (Figure 8.21(a)). Lewerentz worked closely with the project engineer and proposed

8.18

8.19(b)

8.19(a)

Key to 8.20
 1 Infants Room
 2 Interview Room
 3 Interview Room
 4 Pastor's Room
 5 Playroom
 6 Lobby
 7 Kitchen
 8 Lobby
 9 Administration Office
10 Archive
11 Council Chamber
12 Meeting Room
13 Confirmation Classroom
14 Lobby
15 Toilets
16 Toilets
17 Kitchen
18 Lobby
19 Meeting Room
20 Open Fireplace
21 Stage
22 Choir
23 Vestry
24 Sacristy
25 Organ
26 Pulpit
27 Bishop's Throne
28 Priest's Bench
29 Altar
30 Choir
31 Sanctuary
32 Font
33 Waiting Room
34 Wedding Chapel
35 Porch

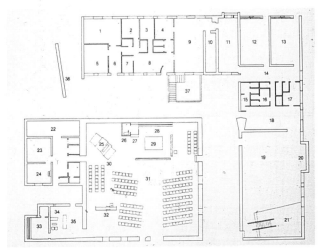

8.20

the use of smaller steel sections, paired, rather than large single sections, so that light could shine through the middle of the structural assembly.

To what extent these shifts and discontinuities are brought about for visual reasons or to compensate for the difference in physical performance between steel section and brick vault I do not know. The fact is that a technical requirement is transformed into a haunting metaphor and how this is brought about is unfathomable.

Lewerentz's handling of light deepens this quality. Instead of the coloured radiance of the Gothic or the dazzling luminous white of the contemporary tradition from Bryggman to Leiviska, we are invited into the dark (Figure 8.21(b)). Enveloped in that heart of darkness that calls on all the senses to measure its limits, we are compelled to pause. In a rare moment of explanation, Lewerentz stated that subdued light was enriching precisely in the degree to which the nature of the space has to be reached for, emerging only in response to exploration. This slow taking possession of space (the way in which it gradually becomes yours) promotes that fusion of privacy in the sharing of a common ritual that is the essence of the numinous. And it is only in such darkness that light begins to take on a figurative quality – the living light of the candle flame or, as at Klippan, the row of roof lights that forms a Way of Light between sacristy and altar (Figure 8.21).

8.21(a)

8.21(b)

This invitation to explore is further induced by the way the floor (which is not level) seems to move beneath your feet: at one point as we have seen the brick surface swells up into a mound and then breaks into a fissure to form the baptismal font (Figure 8.18) – an astonishing metaphor, which hints at the idea of the water of life bursting from the living rock. Then there is the gentle inclination of the floor from the entrance towards the altar, inducing the experience in the visitor of being drawn into a presence. This 'movement' in the floor combines with the action of the vaults above, which seems to expand and contract with a 'breathing' rhythm to create a certain charge in the air that recalls the interior of St Mark's in Venice. Such space can be activated by the disposition of lights into the focused spaces of church ritual or can recede into isolated centres of solitary inward focus.

Finally we notice that in his handling of the façades Lewerentz is cryptic to a fault. The only rhetoric left is the peal of the bells. But this too recalls Byzantine practice: just as the rough brick shed gives way to a

dark interior shimmering with oriental blue and gold in
the tomb of Galla Placidia, so, at Klippan, it is within
that the building comes to life. Here we have not only a
recollection of Adolf Loos but, more aptly, of Le
Corbusier, who said of the monastery at La Tourette –
the one building that most closely approximates
Klippan in its concentration, its passion and its
austerity – '. . . it does not talk. It is on the inside that it
lives . . . that the essential lies'.

So to what end did Lewerentz, the most poetic
master of the classical language of architecture in this
century, abandon that langauge? As a student of
Schinkel, Lewerentz would have been aware of that
master's own conviction that the means of architecture
would have to be 'created anew. It would be a wretched
business for architecture . . . if all necessary elements
. . . had been established once and for all in antiquity';[7]
but Lewerentz's concern lay at a much deeper level
than the pursuit of novelty.

In a remarkable chapter on Greek architecture in
Lisle March Phillips' book *The Works of Man* we read:
'Every shed builder who lays a stick on two uprights has
mastered the structural principles of a Doric temple:
but the Greeks alone have comprehended the inward
significance of the act.'[8] In Phillips' appraisal of the
unprecedented ends to which the pursuit of optical
corrections were carried, he advances the notion that
what started out as optical rigour became transformed
somehow into an ethical obsession:

> Visual perception passes into ethical conception. The
> two are fused together. We think with the eye and
> see with the mind . . . A Doric temple is saturated
> with ideas that were not put into it as ideas at all but
> by another faculty (that is, sight).
>
> It is, indeed, difficult to speak for a moment of
> Doric construction without being led insensibly into
> the language of ethics, for the suggestions of the eye,
> which that construction everywhere obeys, turn of
> their own accord into ethical ideas directly they take
> shape in stone . . . We find the Doric temple
> penetrated and, so to speak, suffused with slight
> imperceptible inflections of line and contour, involv-
> ing incalculable extra trouble and expense in the
> building, and we find that the object and aim of all
> these expedients is to adapt the outlines of the
> temple more perfectly and accurately to the laws of
> sight (Figure 8.22) . . .

8.22

Equal columns which appeared unequal would be made unequal to appear equal. A level floor which looked unlevel would be made unlevel to appear level. Vertical lines which appeared to slant would be made to slant that they might appear vertical . . .

Nothing in this strange art is what it seems to be. The most obvious facts turn out not to be facts at all. And the closer we carry our examination the more the mystery spreads and deepens. It infects the whole temple.[9]

What we are offered in this description is a search for the truth of a certain kind: 'to see with the mind and to think with the eye'. In that moment, aesthetics and ethics become one. What was required of the Greek temple was that it would stand as the utterly self-sufficient and visually inviolate sculpture to house and to celebrate a god or goddess. Propriety would ordain which of the prescribed and unchangeable orders should be adopted. Within that symbolism, cosmic order was to be transcribed and embodied as visual order. A building language for the sacred was born.

This insight into a paradox matches very closely the quality of experience provoked by the buildings of Lewerentz. At a time of 'isms', of *l'architecture à thèse*, of buildings required to be no more than demonstrations of some narrow issue, here was an architecture of extraordinary directness, utterly transparent to the functions it was created to serve, uniquely concrete in setting forth the substance and the manner of its making.

In developing the design of St Peter's, Lewerentz spoke of two things only: the interpretation of the brief (there was a consultant on liturgical matters, Lars Ridderstedt) and questions of building construction (he and the foreman, Sjoholm, are said to have worked very closely together – often far into the evening planning the next day's work). But throughout the evolution of the design there were endless alterations and on-site revisions. This arduous search reminds me of a statement by the painter Michael Andrews: 'Painting is the most marvelous, elaborate and complete way of making up my mind.' At Klippan we become witnesses of the extraordinary process by which Lewerentz, at the age of 80, slowly made up his mind.

An eloquent passage in Heidegger's 'The Origin of the Work of Art' describes how a Greek temple 'does not cause the material to disappear but rather causes it to come forth for the very first time'.[10] Just so in Klippan: brick was never more brick, steel more steel, glass more glass, wood more wood. In that attention to the essential nature of materials there lies a quality of respect that has its own morality. Ethics and technique become one. It is not surprising therefore that the language of classical forms was no longer viable for Lewerentz. For that language was born out of an order of construction, transposed from timber and finding its final and essential refinement intrinsic to stone.

When Lewerentz built the Chapel of the Resurrection, the stonework of the portico was cut from the solid Ignaberga limestone. At that time in Sweden such technology was in no way abnormal; it was not so in 1960. The sort of equivocation that satisfied a Lutyens – rolled steel columns encased in masonry 'orders' – was beneath contempt for a man for whom the spirit of Greek architecture was far closer to his heart than the law. It is perhaps both chastening and reassuring to recall that the very foundation of Western culture is grounded on something that is as simple and austere as it is difficult: the spirit that created the original and imperative ethos of the Doric out of the technology of its day.

At a time when the fashionable madmen seek to revive the notion of 'ritual' to give 'meaning' to the pursuit of aesthetics, and seek to reinstate the classical language to indulge in the shifts of rhetoric, it is salutary to do honour to the opposite mode, the true and humble process by which a new poetry was hammered out of the endless wrestle with worn-out forms. In doing so it won back a long-lost authenticity and a profound reinterpretation of the place of sacrament.

John Ruskin said: 'No one can be an architect who is not a metaphysician,'[11] and certainly there is in the 'argument' of St Peter's at Klippan much that reminds us of the way in which the philosopher lays down his proposition, brick by brick as it were, each with its own integrity, but nevertheless bonding into a whole wall. Lewerentz was the contemporary of Samuel Beckett and Giacometti, and he shared with them an unflinching acceptance of a poverty of means. But he did not share their despair. Rather it is as if, like the inventors of the true Doric, he had to find his truth by embracing utter simplicity. 'Greece and poverty have always been bedfellows,' wrote Herodotus.

When all is said and done, it must also be recognized that St Peter's is an old man's building. Although nearly 80, Lewerentz spent many days of the week on site interpreting and revising his intentions. While the compression of ideas is enormous, it recalls late Cézanne or the Rondanini *Pietà* on which Michelangelo was working when he died, and which, unfinished and bearing the scars of numberless changes, has the quality of immediacy as if we could still hear the blow of the hammer, as if thought itself were being carved before our eyes. Here too in Klippan, the making and the thought are one.

The Sacred Sites

Monumental landscapes

Lewerentz's power of metaphorical interpretation was brought to bear with equal invention upon the wider theme of landscape in a series of projects of exceptional beauty (Figure 8.23). Here the marriage of building to earth, sky and water sustains a dominant theme across a large range of episodes. This is *architecture parlante* on a grand scale. Four examples will suffice to show Lewerentz's range.

8.23

In each case, the theme is the elegiac celebration of death and memory in the presence of nature. Adolf Loos wrote: 'When we come across a mound in a wood, six feet long and three feet wide, raised to a pyramidal form by means of a spade, we become serious and something in us says: "Somebody lies buried here." This is architecture . . . ,'[12] and in the same piece: 'Only a very small part of architecture belongs to art, the tomb and the monument'. Whether or not Lewerentz took such thoughts to heart, he did undertake some twenty-eight projects for cemeteries, chapels or churches, one-third of which were carried out – a preponderance in his work the more remarkable when compared to the predominantly secular work of his famous contemporaries. Clearly he was choosing the themes most removed from the everyday and most demanding of metaphoric interpretation.

We saw earlier how Lewerentz engaged in two major competition projects for Malmo at the time when the Chapel of the Resurrection was under construction; and that one of those projects was for the Eastern Cemetery (Figures 8.23 and 8.24(a)–(d)). Of this scheme we have only the drawings, but, executed in the manner of Schinkel, they rival in both form and metaphor anything that the German master ever invented himself.

The scheme encompassed detailed designs for a main chapel, a crematorium and a circular ceremonial plaza. The main chapel took the form of a rectangular cella with two shallow hexastyle and two deep tetrastyle porticoes on a raised podium; the columnar order was Corinthian. The bell-tower was to be located within one of the porticoes. The tripartite crematorium consisted of a central cella (for the reception of coffins and caskets and the exhibition of urns for sale) with a conical structure to house two furnaces to the east and a similar structure as a sepulchral chamber to the west. For this building, whose forms were apparently based upon the Etruscan Necropolis at Tarquinia, Lewerentz studied many variations (with and without paired obelisks). The circular ceremonial plaza was surrounded by a wall broken by four entrance porticoes, with a single column in antis. A small circular chapel also appears in some versions.

8.24(a)

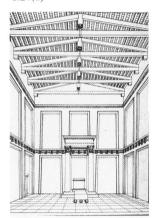

8.24(b)

Lewerentz's details were very rigorous, his forms very demanding, and when in 1926 the bid for the construction greatly exceeded the proposed expenditure, the project was put off until its resurrection in a very different form much later. However, the drawings, executed by Artur von Schmalensee are remarkably haunting. Modelled on the engravings in Schinkel's *Architektonische Entwürfe*, they equal the work of the German master in the quality of both design and draughtsmanship. Indeed these projects and the Chapel of the Resurrection together form a body of work that makes a unique contribution to the tradition that it salutes. It is significant that in his use of the classical language Lewerentz stayed close to the subject matter out of which that language arose – the sacred, the funerary and the monumental – unlike those who elsewhere have abused it, to lend cachet to such themes as banks and the houses of stockbrokers.

8.24(c)

The Woodland Cemetery at Enskede, to the south of Stockholm, is the largest of these projects, and its design evolved through a number of stages, from highly elaborate beginnings to a monumental simplicity. In its final form, it is one of the great epic landscapes of all time; indeed it may be said that in its primal elements – forest, cropped mound, water, low sun – it is the archetypal embodiment of the North, just as the horned mountain, rock and blazing sky of the ancient

8.24(d)

temple site of Greece is the embodiment of the South
(Figure 8.25).

The design is the fruit of a collaboration with Gunnar
Asplund that lasted for nearly 20 years, until
Lewerentz's shameful dismissal by the Cemetery Board
during the evolution of the last chapel group in 1934.
While the work was a genuine collaboration, I believe
that the greater responsibility for the landscape design
rests with Lewerentz – a claim strongly supported by
the fact that, of all the buildings on the site, it is his
Chapel of the Resurrection that is most at one with the
gravitas of the landscape.

The original cemetery design of 1914 (Figure 8.26)
won the competition by responding closely to the
pre-existing spirit of place (the Nordic forest of tall
pines and gravel pits) (Figure 8.27(a)) with the least
possible violation of its intrinsic qualities. Conceived in
the vernacular of the National Romantic movement,
the devices employed for the inhabitation of the forest
were numerous and inventive – the Path of the Seven
Wells, the Seven Gardens, the Way of the Cross, the
Path of Urns – but they were too liberally dispersed,
straining to create identity and orientation by episode
rather than overall plot (Figure 8.27(b)). The scheme
then underwent a number of stages of development. A
stronger and more detailed scheme of 1917 was
supplanted a couple of years later by a powerful
invention in geometrical order, in which Lewerentz
deployed more conventional uses of axis, symmetry
and orthogonal grids. In 1922 it too was changed by a
sweeping gesture of simplification in which the eastern
sector of development was reduced to a straight road
running directly to (and through) the portico of a single
Chapel of the Holy Cross. From this simplicity, a great
drama unfolds (Figure 8.28).

Opening in solemn mood, a semicircular propylaeum
of massive masonry converges upon a narrow Via
Sepulchra, whose walls, embedded with columbaria,
frame a landscape that is as haunting as it is beautiful.
The axiality of approach suddenly dissolves into an
apparent irresolution –– a device that would be
dismissed in conventional Bleaux-Arts terminology as
an 'unresolved duality'. To the right, the eye is drawn
towards a close-cropped mound that recalls the Bronze
Age burial mounds of Agri (known as the Maiden
Mounds) and into this is cut a broad flight of steps
ascending to a tree-lined platform marked out with a
group of stone seats – the Grove of Remembrance

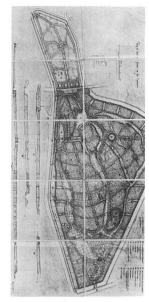

8.26

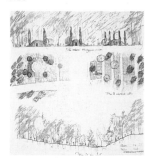

8.27(b)

8.25

8.28

Key to 8.28
1 Main (north)
   entrance to the
   Woodland
   Cemetery
2 Grove of
   Remembrance
3 Way of the
   Seven Wells
4 Chapel of the
   Resurrection
   (Lewerentz)
5 Woodland
   Chapel
   (Asplund)
6 Chapels and
   crematorium
   (Asplund)

8.27(a)

(Figure 8.2(a) on page 114). Straight ahead lies the long dark Pathway of the Seven Wells, which slices through the dense forest of tall fir and spruce to arrive at the portico of the Chapel of the Resurrection (Figure 8.29(a)). To the left, the Way of the Cross ascends to the grand portico and impluvium of the chapel group (Figure 8.29(b). The path is firmly defined along one side by the low white wall of the graveyard, but throughout its entire length it is transfixed by the presence of a huge freestanding stone cross. Just as Lewerentz's image of the cross was the imprimatur of the original competition scheme, (see Frontispiece) so the presence of the monumental stone cross silhouetted against the sky gives tragic meaning to the whole landscape. But what of the centre. Bare sweep of the plain, a sheet of unruffled water, a glimpse of dark forest beyond, huge clouds piling up in the sky – this 'biblical' landscape is shot through with a very modern disquiet, a focus on the void (Figure 2.25(a)).

8.29(a)

8.29(b)

Stuart Wrede has traced one element of the chemistry of this haunting place to the Romantic landscapes of Casper David Friedrich, and there is no doubt that a source of inspiration lies there. But this is no painting. It is a world that you walk into – plain, mound, water and dark forest. Death in the hubbub of the city is different. Compare this place with the Modena Cemetery of Aldo Rossi. There all is geometry and the melancholy of repetition, of the pathetic mass-produced columbaria in metal racks, row upon row. Here, where the headstones stand between the trees in the silence of the forest, the rhythm of the seasons mediates a very different mood.

The second example of Lewerentz's mastery of landscape is the design of the Rud Cemetery in Karlstad of 1917 (Figure 8.30(a)). This scheme is small, but none the less offers a dramatic composition of considerable power. Once again, a heavily wooded landscape is the basic theme, but this time focused on an artificially formed valley below. Water cascades down a central flight of steps that leads down axially from the square necropolis above, enclosed within a high wall of pruned trees. Here nature is strictly marshalled into a geometry of the sublime in which the imagery, with echoes of Italian rhetoric, is of a more conventional kind. The view from the valley up the cascade to the tall cleft in the trees is carried off in the high manner of Boullée (Figure 8.30(b)). Unfortunately, this design was never carried through to completion.

8.30(a)

8.30(b)

Lewerentz's other major built landscape design was the revised version of the Eastern Cemetery at Malmo of 1943 (Figure 8.31) with the chapels of St Knut, St Gertrud and St Birgitta, the circular plaza of remembrance and the bell-tower. The landscape composition is utterly different from the Rud or Stockholm schemes. Here there is little enclosure; all is exposed along a ridge that runs east-west at an upper level the full length of the site. The first chapel (St Birgitta), a traditional Nordic burial mound and a bell-tower are distributed along the northern part. At the western end, the twin chapels of St Knut and St Gertrud were added to an existing crematorium.

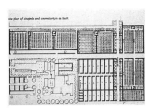

8.31

The landscape is remarkable enough – laid out like the excavation of a Hellenistic city – but it is around the forecourts and porticoes of the two chapels that the visitor is arrested by certain unfamiliar traits. The ground surface is raked gravel. The imprint of footsteps disturbs the even grain spread out to receive the ritual procession of mourners (this is no place for tourists). Stone slabs are laid in the raked gravel, whose plane of arrival is warped up to meet the threshold of entry. Overhead, the portico takes the form of a sequence of discreet monopitch canopies (Figures 8.32(a)–(b)) – an aura of the shrine sites of Shinto is provoked by this play of roofs and raked gravel 'landscape'. A shared instinct for the irregular rhythms of nature prevails, together with a reverence for the simple shifts by which they are manifested.

8.32(a)

8.32(b)

The crisis of Classicism

It has become apparent in recent exhibitions and publications that the one original contribution during this century to the classical language of architecture lay not in the last rites proposed by the Ecole des Beaux Arts on behalf of spokesmen of the 'master race', but in certain austere monuments of the Nordic Classicists; and in that achievement, Lewerentz was an undisputed leader. It could even be claimed that some of his work enlarged our understanding of the original Greek. This is a large claim, but at a time when so much work is signally failing in the professed attempt to extend that tradition, a claim that justifies further explication.[15] It is based on T. S. Eliot's celebrated formulation in *Tradition and the Individual Talent* of the relationship between novelty and tradition as a reciprocal exchange – a two-way relationship in which not only is the new influenced by the past, but the past is 'if ever so slightly altered' by the introduction of 'the really new'. It follows from this formula that a simple test can be devised. On the one hand, it is axiomatic that the new, in so far as it derives from the past, gains in status. But what is difficult is to repay that debt, and I suggest that the failure to do so – the failure, that is, to deepen our understanding of the past by a contribution in the present – is the mark of *kitsch*. For it is the mark of kitsch that it borrows indiscriminately, but never repays. Has the AT&T building deepened our under-standing of Chippendale cupboards or the Paternoster 'Development' led us to think anew about the Rome of Pope Julius?

Lewerentz, by his neo-classical work, has 'if ever so slightly' altered our perception of both classical and Byzantine Greek architecture: both the Erechtheion and Hosias Lukas take on an extra depth in that historical perspective. How, then, could such a master come utterly to reject that language, and then go on to make equally powerful and equally mysterious build-ings out of that rejection?

Modern architecture is a critical movement; that is, it is founded upon a criticism of life, and therefore by definition contains a large component of self-criticism and polemic. The present debate is fuelled as much by this internal criticism as by external criticism. The possibility of a revival of classical forms exists only as an episode within that debate; it does not exist as an alternative source of authority. It is to be entertained as one influence among many, within a debate whose terms are forever in movement. It is in this sense that Nordic Classicism (whose formal roots lie in the works of Boullée and Ledoux) has differed from the Beaux Arts or revivalist nature of classicism elsewhere. For in Scandinavia, classicism was not merely an escape from National Romanticism, but a step towards Modernism. There was not a shred of nostalgia about it – it was for the most part forward-looking, not a style but an escape from 'the Styles'. Far from wishing to turn the clock back, there was a feeling that through a return to the true origins (not the Beaux Arts but the purgative spirit of the Doric Greek), a new start might be made. The aim was not revival, but renewal.

Lewerentz had made a contribution of complete authenticity to a programme that lay close to the meaning of the Classical origin – the sacred and the funerary – and within a building method that lay equally close to its original inspiration – masonry. But from now on, both programme and technical possibility were to be utterly changed. The old language could no longer take the strain.

The 'turn'

The architecture of the chapels of St Knut and St Gertrud marks the moment at which Lewerentz spoke out with a voice entirely his own. Up to that time, his invention had gone into the manipulation of a received language, be it neo-classical or, from the time of the 1930 Stockholm Exhibition, Rationalist. But at this point we can speak of a 'turn' or fundamental shift in his work. One of the perspective studies (Figure 8.33) seems to be his swansong to the forms of classicism carried to a fine level of abstraction. Then, quite suddenly, forms are invented and materials put together in ways that had never been tried before. And yet (and this is the most extraordinary characteristic of his late work), this newness reverberates with remote affinities to Persian antiquity and to the early Byzantine. The spirit of that which is most ancient hovers over structures of perplexing novelty. Lewerentz never spelt out the ethos that bound these themes together, but clearly there is an affinity with just such values as were spelt out by Adolf Loos.

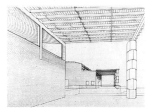

8.33

As to that new programme to which his friends in Sweden responded with the manifesto *Acceptera* – the broad social and technological revolution of our time – Lewerentz made little direct contribution. His building programme was still in the realm of the sacred. What is remarkable, however, is that even there he found the classical language no longer able to carry meaning as before. So what is at issue in his late buildings is not the inadequacy of the classical language to deal with *functionalism*, but rather the exhaustion of its powers to deal even with its original province – that realm of building that Loos defined in terms of 'the tomb and the monument'. In that exhaustion, it had become a language that can only tell a lie. Another truth had to be explored: a secular truth, to exist in parallel to the sacred and to be evolved through the same rigorous search. The *fin-de-siècle* had made many efforts to obscure the issue by compounding secular needs in a fancy dress borrowed from the language of the sacred, and to that form of aestheticizing pretension a growing disgust began to be voiced: 'We have had enough of the extraordinary: what we need is the self-evident' was a typical cry. So the classical sense of truth as a reality to be dug out from the world of appearance – a stripping bare, an absence of rhetoric, an illumination – was revived.

It is an idea that is both very old and also very new, in the true tradition of Modernism. One of its clearest expressions lies in James Joyce's use of the words *entelechy* and *epiphany* in forming his own working method. The word *entelechy* in Aristotle's usage relates to the condition in which a potentiality has become an actuality by achieving a perfection of form. And Joyce uses the word *epiphany* to denote those moments of *showing forth*, in which a remark or gesture becomes a sudden revelation in depth of a state of affairs hitherto concealed or unacknowledged – a reality that lies beneath the veil of conventional discourse, the small talk of *partly living*, suddenly acquires a shape and therefore an identity. The same terms are used by Heidegger, again with insistence on the roots in Greek thinking, in explaining the meaning of truth as revelation (*aletheia*), the laborious uncovering of that which lies concealed: light and attention are directed upon a problematic area until a form of language permits at last the recognition of a true state of affairs and the possible terms of its embodiment. It is in its failure to respond to this test that the capacity and propriety of the old language came into question.

Lewerentz both in his buildings and in his mastery of place, of that 'Topos' in which building and nature and symbolic narrative are locked together in one inscrutable gesture, has conjured up a world that is as ancient as it is modern and in whose spell we enjoy at last the conviction that 'the really new' has been presented to our view.

References

1 Janne Ahlin, *Sigurd Lewerentz*, Byggeforlaget, Stockholm, 1985 (English trans. 1987).
2 Heraclitus, *Fragment*, 18.
3 Ten years later Asplund borrowed the same motif for his version of the large Chapel of the Holy Cross constructed on the eastern part of the site. This was after Lewerentz had been dismissed from the project.
4 The intervals between the antae are irregular and their distribution on the north wall is not recalled on the south wall.
5 Published in translation as *The Church Incarnate* in 1958, with an introduction by Mies van der Rohe.
6 Lewerentz drew the setting out of every brick at a scale of 1:20 and then demanded that the bricklayers should use neither plumb-line nor spirit level.
7 Schinkel, Karl Friedrich. *Tagebucher Briefe Gedanken*, Madowski, ed., 1922.
8 Lisle March Phillips, *The Works of Man*, Duckworth, 1911, p. 113.
9 *Ibid*, pp. 117–18.
10 Heidegger, Martin, *Poetry, Language, Thought*, Harper, 1971, p. 46.
11 J. Ruskin, *The Poetry of Architecture*.
12 Adolf Loos, *Architecture*, 1909.
13 S. Wrede, *Landscape & Architecture in Perspecta* No. 20.
14 *Classical Tradition and the Modern Movement*: The 2nd International Alvar Aalto Sympsoium, 1982. 'Nordic Classicism', 1910–30: Museum of Finnish Architecture. Exhibition and catalogue, 1982.
15 See discussion in Chapter 4 'The historical sense'.

9

GUNNAR ASPLUND
and the dilemma of Classicism

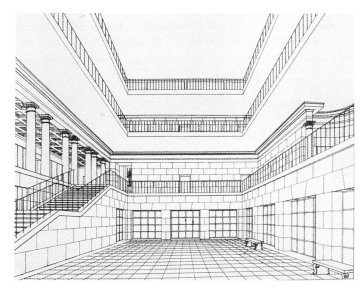

Modernism and modernismus

Gunnar Asplund claims our attention now not only because of the celebration of his centenary, but also because his great talent was shot through with hesitations and reservations that reflect, in a unique way, upon the debate in architecture in the late 1980s. Certainly the two poles of that debate are graphically summarized within the scope of a single project; the now familiar pairing of the 1925 and 1937 versions of the Gothenburg Law Courts (Frontispiece). These images (both of which are exemplary of their kind) all too easily suggest that the debate can instantly be reduced to a question of style alone. 'Taste,' said Degas, 'is a vice,' but there are many who are happy to indulge in it and a few (including Asplund's son) who are convinced that Asplund made the wrong choice.

Now that may make a good chapter in the conspiracy theory of history, which in 1932 defined the nature of Modernism as the 'International Style', pinpointed its 'death' in the demolition of the Pruitt-Igoe housing in St Louis in 1972, and discovered the 'birth' of Post-Modernism in the Chippendale cupboard that crowns Philip Johnson's AT&T building of 1975. To the contrary, I would argue that the briefest reflection upon the work of Asplund raises a fundamental challenge to that theory, and it is no coincidence that neither Giedion in *Space Time and Architecture* nor Jencks in *Modern Movements in Architecture* make any mention of Asplund at all – in other words, at both ends of the historical survey of the Modern Movement, the true significance of Asplund's work has been tacitly ignored.

In his 1940 obituary 'Asplund In Memoriam', Alvar Aalto put his finger on the crux. He wrote of Asplund's attempt 'to tie together the threads of a living future with those of the living past. In the creation of forms, pastiche and copying were as alien to him as rootless technocratic constructivism'.[1] If we associate this reminder with Aalto's own crucial article of the same year, 'The Humanizing of Architecture', we get a critical insight into the whole project of Modernism, which turns the Pruitt-Igoe incident 3o years later into insignificance. In that piece, Aalto refers to the 'first and now past period of Modern Architecture', and pursues a critique of the naive, interpretations of 'function' and 'rationalization' which 'have not gone deep enough'. Remember that Aalto had only the year before completed the Villa Mairea, which, in the words of Juhani Pallasmaa, seems 'to question the basic stylistic attitudes of Modernism . . . by creating impure collisions of motifs, and by fusing together items of separate intellectual categories (such as modernity and folk tradition).'[2]

In both Asplund and Aalto, we have come a long way from the prescriptions of the International Style, that first stage of a Modernism, which, in the phrase of Gropius, 'is not built from some branch of an old tree but is a new plant growing directly from roots'. Whatever it was that is supposed to have gone up in smoke in the demolition of Pruitt-Igoe had already been condemned over 30 years earlier by the work of Asplund and Aalto – and not by them alone. What of the other witnesses, at this same time? What of the 'living past' of Terragni's Danteum, the 'living future' of Wright's Johnson Wax headquarters, the decorative symbolism in Bryggman's Abo crematorium? What of the widespread progeny of Berlage, Mackintosh, Loos, Van de Velde and Wright, whose work never rejected association with the past, never lost the will to respond to context or climate, or to the desires of its inhabitants, and never lacked the quality of figurative power? Never, in fact, took the route to Pruitt-Igoe at all?

The distinction has been lost between the caricature of Modernismus and the authentic grounds for the impulse of Modernism. On the one side is ranged the aggressive Modernismus of the Brave New World, of the International Style, of the rejection of ornament and of history (history was not taught at the Bauhaus), and the promotion of system building with mechanization in command, of the planning by four functions. On the other side is ranged the critical and broad-based Modernism that is epitomized in other disciplines by Joyce, Eliot, Picasso or Mahler, with its common vision (for which a heightened relationship to the past is intrinsic to the invention of the new). Inevitably the hasty 'philosophers in action' required propaganda, which in turn required the simple statement, impatient of the complexities of authentic evidence. We know the outcome only too well. But the conclusions now drawn have once again dismissed that evidence, and by stupidly confounding authentic Modernism with the disgrace of Modernismus, they have compounded the error by conflating and condemning the whole project. All the talk now is of revaluation, of a concern for links with the past. If that is the order of the day, better by far a hard look at the authentic strain of Modernism that was overwhelmed by the hollow victory of Modernismus. It is precisely such a revaluation that is provoked by an examination of Asplund's work.

The issue of Classicism

Let us first take the question of the death or rebirth of Classicism, an issue on which Asplund's testimony has great authority, for a number of reasons.

In the first place, Asplund, like his contemporary Lewerentz, was a master of the neo-classical school in the true sense of the term, grounded in traditional masonry structure, in that extraordinary Indian summer known as Nordic Doricism. As an example, one could point to his 1922 competition design (with Ture Ryberg) for the Royal Chancellery in Stockholm (Figure 9.1 and its further description in Chapter 13, Figures 13.1–13.5). It would be tedious to spell out the many strategies employed to cope with the shifting axes on the site – deflection, inflection, variants on the circle and semicircle – in a running exchange between specific circumstance and ideal prototype. But note the always positive use of in-between space in the *poché* of encircling geometries. Just to look at the plan is like reading music. It is only by such means that a huge, official building is mediated to proportions that invite the observer to a balanced and empathetic relationship to it.

9.1

Furthermore, the spirit that informed Asplund's approach was grounded in a rigorous and sensitive interpretation of context. The way in which the strands of a formidably orchestrated order are woven from the grain of the surrounding fabric is truly remarkable. For instance, the use of subsidiary levels that fall gently from the main datum through the lateral courtyards to arrive at a waterside promenade is effortlessly contrived. It is as if the architect were merely the midwife to a deeply desired and inevitable flowering of forces inherent in the situation as found. Asplund once described the Gothenburg Exhibition complex by Ahlberg and Lewerentz in terms of 'forms which do not threaten but invite'. No better phrase could describe his own achievement with this project, so utterly free from the rhetoric and bombast of late Beaux-Arts composition employed by his contemporaries in Hitler's Germany, Mussolini's Italy and Stalin's Russia.

Indeed, there is no better way to confirm Asplund's mastery in this mode than to compare his Chancellery

with Speer's Chancellery built for Hitler in Berlin; for
in that clumsy piece of black theatre, every attempt was
made to use the apparatus of Roman authoritarianism
and Beaux Arts devices to intimidate and undermine
the self-possession of any visitor to the Führer.
Associated with the bombast is a stylistic incompetence
that I have explored in some detail in Chapter 13. But
my choice of Speer's incompetence (see Figures
13.6–13.14) as foil to Asplund's mastery is of course
not innocent, for one of the least comprehensible
episodes of the current architectural debate is the
attempt to dig up the unquiet ghost of this bungler and
present Speer as the great talent martyred by the
uncultured brutes of Modernism. The whole venture
cries out for the derision that Chaplin directed at it in
The Great Dictator.

The second aspect that lends authority to Asplund's
witness is that for him the decision to abandon the
classical language was not easy. Between winning the
competition for the Gothenburg Law Courts in 1913
and completing the final design in 1937, he produced at
least six alternative schemes (see Frontispiece). De-
layed by economic crises, harassed by changes in the
taste and values of the client committee, but spurred on
by the slow evolution of his own convictions, Asplund's
proposals ranged from an early evocation of the
National Romantic mode through numerous variations
on the neo-classic to the final, exemplary Modernist
invention. One has simply to observe the successive
stages of this scrupulous development to be made
aware of a unique search for authenticity. What had
served well the wit of the Lister Court-house and the
light-hearted fantasy of the Skandia Cinema could no
longer bridge the gap between.

In Eliot's famous essay 'Tradition and the Individual
Talent' he propounds a dynamic view of tradition as 'an
easy commerce between the old and the new', which
operates both ways, so that the new is modified by the
past and the past modified, seen anew, by the
introduction of the new (see Chapter 4). He emphasized the point that the really new meant an extension
of the language to embrace an extension of sensibility,
of awareness, of experience. Wittgenstein said: 'The
limits of my language are the limits of my world.'
Certain things can be thought in one language only and
not in any other.

So it is with the Classical language of architecture.
There are things that it cannot say and there are things
so entrenched within it that it cannot shed them. We

have seen that for a Speer (or a Piacentini, or an Iofan), the language lends itself all too easily to assertions of power and authority. Herbert Read said: 'In the back of every dictator can be found a bloody Doric column.' Wittgenstein observed on the completion of Canada House in Trafalgar Square that it proved that we are no better than Hitler or Mussolini, for words used quite correctly in one age can in a later age 'become the words of a cheat'.

As part of his inaugural lecture as professor of the Royal Institute of Technology in Stockholm (1931), Asplund remarked that 'our understanding of architectonic space has changed so much that the supremacy of the rules that formerly governed architecture has been destroyed'. And so he came to break the mould of the classical language with a conviction unanswerable in its authority. His challenge was immediately established in the variety of invention of the 1930 Stockholm Exhibition, which, unlike the Stuttgart Exhibition of 1927, was not confined to the theme of housing but played upon urban themes – places of public gathering, recreation and communication. In this sense, it has claims to a priority of its own.

To extend the language of the tribe

We could characterize Asplund's special gift as the ability to extend the language of architecture in a very rich way, with a range of vocabulary by far exceeding that of any other architect. Each building is thought out anew right down to the use of unique detail, all at the service of the central impulse in his work: to establish a narrative out of the operational, contextual and figurative requirements of each situation.

Every building is conceived in terms of such a narrative, and a wide repertoire of architectural means is deployed with astonishing inventiveness and precision. The phrase *promenade architecturale* is too peremptory to cover the range of experience offered – the change of pace, the shifts of scale, the alternations of envelopment and exposure, expansion and contraction, passage and rest, light and dark, natural and man-made. The word *theatre* more nearly approximates to the refinement with which each episode in the sequence is elaborated. An exhaustive inventory of relevant detail – the colour and tactility of surface, the delight in the polished and the woven – is pursued with an almost Proustian indulgence, and not without the hint, at times, of an overripe elegance inherited from Art Nouveau. This indeed is the transformation of the abstract reading of space into the spirit of place. It is as if each design is built up like a portrait, so that each building has its own unique set of forms.

The realism of such a portrait also requires its own form of freedom and can only be achieved by close attention to operational criteria. This is illustrated by the account of one of Asplund's assistants that, when overwhelmed by the number of factors they were required to take on board, only Asplund himself was allowed to suggest elimination, and then of one factor only. This compares significantly with Paul Rudolph's praise of Mies's reductionism. 'Mies makes wonderful buildings only because he ignores many aspects of a building. If he solved more problems his buildings would be far less potent.'[5] So it was that, to take aboard all his problems, Asplund needed a range of language far beyond the limits of the classical.

One quite explicit example of the deliberate employment of shifts in scale and sequences of inside–outside–inside is corroborated by the descriptive text of Asplund himself for the Skandia Cinema of 1922 (Figure 9.2). In this case, he found the classical language very appropriate to the world of phantasy he had been asked to provide. Simo Paavilainen, describes this well:

> It is profitable to examine how richly and abundantly Asplund in the Skandia Cinema (Figure 9.2(a)–(c)) builds houses within interiors or exteriors within houses, how he enlarges corridors and shrinks halls. The cinema is also a beautiful example of interlacing an existing old building into a new theme. In the street there stands a grey, weathered neo-renaissance façade. The grey asphalt of the pavement extends into the portico, linking the lobby to the street. In the middle of the lobby there stands a rectangular colonnade. First one comes from an exterior to an interior, but still as to an exterior. Then one descends a flight of stairs to the foyer (Figure 9.2(b)), whose walls and ceiling were originally dark green. In the middle of the greenness stands a brightly-lit, white-walled building with cornices and red velvet doorways – a white building in a deep green space. The visitor believes that he is entering a building, but inside he finds a moon and a deep blue arch of sky. The visitor is surprised three times with variations of the same theme on his way from the sooty façade to a

9.2(a)

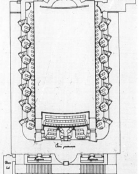

9.2(c)

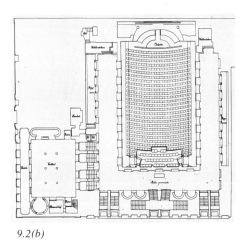

9.2(b)

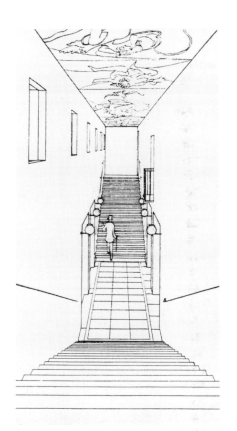

9.2(d)

9.2(e)

seat in front of the glimmering silver screen. Upstairs the spectator's sense of scale is confused: the entrances to the boxes have the appearance of a row of stately façades (Figure 9.2(e)); whereas in the auditorium the giant ornament of the balcony's front wall gives the impression of a smaller space than the actual dimensions of the auditorium.

9.3(a)

In particular, the nesting of the circular upper-level boxes, replete with intimate double seats, tucked in two steps above the balcony edge – a loggia in a balcony overlooking an auditorium – is a delicious play upon the Pompeian aedicule, which Asplund had noted on his trip to Italy.

   Each of Asplund's buildings invites an account of this type of spatial narrative. For instance, the entry sequence to the Stockholm Library (Figure 9.3(a), (b) and (d)) contains a typical instance of counterpoint, in which the direct axial entry is subjected to the *interference* of the side stairs – the tall, exciting shaft of space that ascends in a gentle curve between the enclosed drum and its protecting cube (Figure 9.3(c)).

Acceptera

Asplund never allowed detail from one building to be used in another, an approach which clearly separates him from the heroic goal of the modern masters to establish a new canon replete with universal rules, standards and building types. The title of the only polemic to which he subscribed was *Acceptera* – an acknowledgement of the pioneering groundwork carried out by the Dutch, the Germans and the *Genie of the Lamp*, as Ahlberg called Le Corbusier. Except for the brief and brilliant fling of the 1930 Stockholm Exhibition (Figure 9.4), he never concerned himself with the sort of polemic developed by the participants of CIAM: all that he had to say was said in the language of building. Within that language, he focused not upon *le problème du grand nombre* and the general laws that would provide the framework for mass production, but on the unique.

   In fact, this unprincipled freedom from established norm is the very condition upon which the range and variety of Asplund's architecture is grounded, together with a concern with orchestration, for which the precedent was his former mentor Ragnar Ostberg – above all where the distortions in plan suggest

9.4

9.3(d)

9.3(c)

9.3(b)

analogies with natural form. It is with the mention of nature that one recalls another extension to Asplund's palette or repertoire of means – landscape. Setting aside for a moment the tragic and sublime landscape of the Woodland Cemetery (for which Lewerentz was the prime mover), we see in all Asplund's later ground plans a *poché* in which the order hinted at is drawn from the irregular rhythms of nature.

The relation to nature in Scandinavia is highly charged for a number of reasons. The long dark winter invests sunlight with mythical powers (Orpheus and Persephone could well be the presiding spirits). There is always a certain drama – white nights, low sun, snowscape, dark woodland, islands in lake water – and when the ice breaks, there is good reason to celebrate. What Asplund and Aalto brought to the vision of an organic architecture is too familiar to need discussion here. Let it suffice to say that whereas to Frank Lloyd Wright the organic was manifested for the most part by a shift in geometry, for both Asplund and Aalto it injected a whole repertoire of forms and processes of Leonardesque ramification, often drawn from the unique qualities of a particular region.

Connections and collaborations

Asplund's connection to Aalto has been fully recounted by Göran Schildt – the close friendship and the running exchange of ideas, each taking turns to take the lead. What is less familiar is his relationship to Sigurd Lewerentz – exact contemporary, fellow-student in rebellion, collaborator, rival. Neither wrote much, although Asplund was for some time editor of *Byggmästaren* and, for the last 10 years of his life professor at the Royal Institute of Technology in Stockholm. Neither showed any interest in joining CIAM in its programme of propaganda, in working outside Sweden, or in projecting their work out to an international audience. Their relation to the architectural revolution of the 1920s was that of late-comers (1930), responding to an invitation born under another sky.

Our perception of that response has been obscured by the general impression projected by the work of the other signatories of *Acceptera* and their followers. The philosophical grounding of that work was heavily sociological and its stylistic nature rendered down to a blandness so banal and cosy that in the form of the New

Empiricism it became a major provocation of the New Brutalist movement. Aalto enjoyed telling the story of the man who started out of his sleep, shouting: 'Who can save me from Vallingby?'

The themes addressed by Asplund and Lewerentz were of a very different kind – the sacred, the institutional, the monumental – and their collaboration over 20 years and more on the Woodland Cemetery produced the greatest monumental landscape of our time (see Chapter 8, p. 114). There is nothing to compare with this sublime work except the great temple sites of Greece; to the southern acropolis of stone, addressing its horned mountain and clear blue sky, this haunting landscape responds with the natural forms of the North – the narrow path through a tall forest, clipped grass on the burial mound, still water shimmering in the raking light of a low sun. Here the physical and the metaphysical are folded into one – straight ahead the huge empty sky; to the left the cross, plunged like a sword into the rising ground: the tragic confronted by the indifference of nature.

From the time of their joint victory in the 1915 competition, Asplund and Lewerentz had worked together closely and amicably. Each had built a chapel in the grounds of the cemetery, and it had always been supposed that the large central Chapel of the Holy Cross would be an extension of that collaboration. Many joint studies were done right up to 1934, against the background of Lewerentz's principal responsibility for the landscaping. The main bones of the idea were worked out: the chapel shifted off-centre to the east of the axis of entry, the free-standing cross, a major portico. The portico is an extraordinary invention, in which the tall cube of the chapel is hollowed out to allow the north-south route of entry to pass through and is then reformed by two sets of clustered fins enclosed at ground level. These tall and austere forms are original and oddly disturbing; I sense at this stage the dominating hand of Lewerentz.

Then, out of the blue, Lewerentz was dropped by the cemetery authority and Asplund had the whole job to himself. The programme was enlarged to embrace two further minor chapels. The final result is a strange composition in which these are set back behind courtyards and the main chapel thrusts forward the famous impluvium portico. This acts as the primary focus for the ascending Way of the Cross leading up from the main entrance. One paradoxical feature, the disengagement of this portico from the chapel itself

(Figure 9.5(a)–(b)), is not, however, without precedent. Fifteen years earlier, Lewerentz had not only
disengaged the portico of his Chapel of the Resurrection, but had set it a few degrees askew of the main axis
of the chapel, and in so doing had allowed it to pull the
west façade askew to align with it (see Figure 9.5(c)). It
is a measure of the difference between the two men to
compare what is achieved in each case by this move. In
the case of the Chapel of the Resurrection, the part
played by this inflexion is crucial in compensating for
the *incorrect* (non-axial) location of the portico – a
location required not only by the axis of arrival through
the forest, but also by Lewerentz's adherence to the
principle of *passage*, which required that the mourners,
instead of leaving by the same door through which they
had entered, should make a ritual passage through the
chapel to exit into a garden of remembrance (see
Chapter 8, p. 116). There is an intensity in Lewerentz's
wrestle with this conflict that recalls the part played by
distortion in a work by Cézanne – a distortion that is
not an end in itself, but the by-product of the
conflicting forces at work.

In the case of Asplund's chapel, there is not the same
intensity: formal relations are ever so slightly diluted by
the pragmatic. For instance, although the portico is
apparently in a normal relationship to the axis of the
chapel, the chapel is in fact shifted off-centre to the
portico to allow the cortège to drive through (Figure
9.5(b)). It accordingly corresponds to only four of the
seven bays of the portico, and even then, the column
that corresponds to the central axis of the chapel is
simply removed to accommodate the required breadth
of entry. Centrality is assigned to the impluvium and its
expressionist sculpture.

The achievement of effects here is obtained in ways
that the stricter Lewerentz would have rejected, a
compositional dilution which reflects a comparable
softening in the treatment of thematic material. In the
competition drawings for the original Woodland
Cemetery design, the now famous image of the Way of
the Cross was made by Lewerentz. Asplund's many
studies for the final version of the chapel were evasive
on this theme, omitting the Cross altogether (Figure
9.6) or substituting an obelisk, and it seems that he
resisted right up to the last moment the return of the
cross as proposed by Lewerentz. In the end, its
presence was reaffirmed, and its free-standing confrontation with the portico – a stripped form of the pagan

9.5(a)

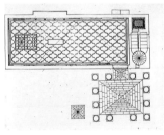

9.5(c)

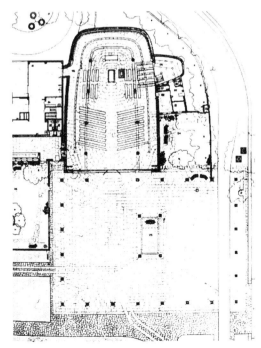

9.5(b)

temple – recalls in a new mode Alberti's daring conjunction of these themes (Figure 9.7).

Perhaps, after all, the mystery of the Woodland Cemetery lies in the tension between Lewerentz's strict and tragic vision and Asplund's sensuous manipulations.

The dilemma

When Asplund died at the age of 55 in 1940, Alvar Aalto wrote: 'the first among Architects . . . has left us'. Aalto was never quick to praise, so this accolade is all the more remarkable when set against the baffled silence with which the historians of our time have treated Asplund. On the other hand, death robbed him (as it did Duiker, Terragni and Bryggman) of the chance to deepen the game during the period of post-war reconstruction – the biggest building boom in history. With a cut-off point of 55, a comparison could be made with Le Corbusier without any work from the Unité onwards, or Mies without his work in the USA.

What is called for now is a much broader presentation of work, particularly of the later, unbuilt projects – Bromma Airport, Stockholm Tower, Stockholm City Archive, and above all the superbly orchestrated Stockholm Social Welfare complex (Figure 9.8). On the evidence so far available, these projects were developed in considerable depth; they certainly belie any impression given by the bungalow at Stennäs that Asplund was retreating back into the woods.

9.8

Of more general and topical concern is the need to expose the nature of a working theory that grew from much reflection and self-criticism to produce a body of work whose excellent condition 50 years later is testimony enough to its validity. The fundamental grounding of that theory, and its equally fundamental vulnerability, were clearly exposed by two arguments in John Summerson's 'The Case for a Theory of Modern Architecture':[6]

We have explored at length in Chapter 2 the first of these arguments proposing the programme as the new source of unity; and Asplund's diligent interpretation of need and context were exemplary in this respect. But then Summerson raises the question of the capacity for such an approach to import a corresponding building language.

9.7

9.6

Secondly, Summerson went on to say that:

> The crux of the whole matter . . . lies in the fact that
> the conceptions which arise from a preoccupation
> with the programme have got, at some point, to
> crystallize into a final form and by the time the
> architect reaches that point he has to bring to his
> conception a weight of judgement, a sense of
> authority and conviction, which clinches the whole
> design, causes the impending relationships to close
> into a visually comprehensible whole. He may have
> extracted from the programmes a set of interdepen-
> dent relationships adding up to a unity of the
> biological kind, but he still has to face up to the
> ordering of a vast number of variables, and how he
> does this is a question. There is no common
> theoretical agreement as to what happens or should
> happen at that point. There is a hiatus. One may
> even be justified in speaking of a 'missing architectu-
> ral language'. Gropius has stated the difficulty as the
> lack of an 'optical key' . . . as an objective common
> denominator of design – something which would
> provide 'the impersonal basis as a prerequisite for
> general understanding', which would serve as 'the
> controlling agent within the creative act'. That is a
> precise description of the functions served by
> antiquity in the Classical centuries when it 'provided
> something which is essential to the creative designer
> – a bulwark of certainty, of unarguable authority on
> which his understanding leans while his conception of
> the building as a whole . . . takes shape', and it is
> very much to the point that that 'bulwark' was not
> just a formal grammar, but a highly charged system
> of metaphors, a sort of collective memory that was
> yet available to manipulation. The dilemma is really
> an enlargement of the flaw already apparent in
> mid-eighteenth-century theory – that while antiquity
> was eliminated as an absolute, nothing was intro-
> duced which took its place as a universally accredited
> language of architectural form. The flaw seems now
> to have widened into a veritable dilemma.

This passage is important for two reasons. First, it holds
out the challenge to those who, like Asplund, have the
resources to take it up, of the existence of authentic
potential *life forms* that can only come into being
poetically if they can be interpreted and embodied in
the kind of narrative depth central to Asplund's vision.
The *programme* conceived of here is not to be confused
with one of those exhaustive Alexandrian checklists,
though it will more likely than not evolve its generic

form around a pattern of use. Secondly where it differs from the remit of a functionalism limited to the pragmatic fulfilment of operations alone, is in the powers of interpretation that set its use-patterns into the context of their historic type, expose their lineage, and comment on their meaning by overlaying an analogous storyline, as Asplund proposes in the Stockholm Library, the Woodland Cemetery chapels, the Skandia Cinema and both of his Law Courts. As to technical innovation, it will certainly not allow any pre-existent rules of language to get in the way of its right to adopt whatever advances in technology it deems fit.

The alternative to which Summerson only faintly hints in 1957 has now grown to a rival proposition. For those who do not have any conviction in the existence of such a social reality, or the tenacity to draw it out of obscurity into recognition – for those, in other words, who do not feel the authority of an authentic situation demanding realization and commitment – there is the fall-back option: surrender to a pre-existent authority. In Asplund's time, that authority was the established language of CIAM, the International Style. In our day, it is not so much Summerson's 'authority of the Ancients' as a return to the fold of the Beaux Arts. Art for Art's Sake, Amen! The attempt to invest this last enterprise with the aura of authenticity has drawn from Jurgen Habermas the withering description of 'the avant-garde of the reversed fronts'.

'The Modern Movement has died many times,' said Giancarlo de Carlo.[7] We are at a moment of great perplexity, and certainly cannot afford to throw away any of the rare victories that have been won since the great Modernist venture was launched. To look again and hard at the goals and their achievement in the work of Gunnar Asplund is both to criticize the critics and to lift the spirits a little once more.

References

1 Alvar Aalto, 'G. E. Asplund in Memoriam' (1940) in '*Sketches*'.
2 J. Pallasmaa and Y. Futagawa, 'Villa Mairea', *Global Architecture*, No. 67, 1985.
3 T. S. Eliot, *Burnt Norton*.
4 Translated in *International Architect*, Vol. 1, No. 8, 1982, p. 40.
5 See discussion of this point in *The Ethics of Architecture*.
6 *RIBA Journal*, June 1957.
7 Giancarlo de Carlo, 'Reflections on the Present State of Architecture', Thomas Cubitt Lecture, 1978.

10

GERRIT RIETVELD:
in memoriam (1964)

'It is essential for us to create not with an aesthetic purpose . . . but only to provide us with a more direct experience of reality. RIETVELD

In 1917 Gerrit Rietveld made a chair, and with it he signalled the most radical change in the language of architecture for 500 years (Figure 10.1). Following a period of intense development with his friends Van Doesburg, Van Eesteren and Schröder-Schräder, he completed, 7 years later, the first house in Europe to demonstrate an absolutely rigorous and novel plastic system 'free' (in his own words) 'of associations',[1] and unprecedently free also in its interpretation and provision of flexibility for use, the Schröder House in Utrecht of 1922–4 (Figure 10.2(a)–(b)).

10.1

So he made the first chairs, the first light fittings, table, cupboard (Figure 10.3), radio-set, desk, flexible walls – in short, the first house and all the equipment in it to match the dream of a world in which only the New could be marvellous and desirable. After 40 years it is still the youngest house in Europe.

10.2(a)

We are shamed today by an imagery so intense, so innocent and so defiant; and the further miracle is that two such small and unremarkable things as a chair and a house could condense such potential energy. One clue to this is given by the revelation it brought to an early visitor, El Lissitsky, who wrote of the open plan that 'cupboards, sofa-beds and tables are arranged like houses in a town in such a way that there are areas for movement and use as if they were streets and squares.'[2] As a world can be seen in a grain of sand, so may a house evoke a city.

10.2(b)

It was this carrying-power of the new system that raised it above the level of personal licence to the status of a new canon; and it was Rietveld's unique contribution to the invention of this canon that puts him in the rare class of those whose work has renewed the powers of architecture itself.

10.3

The force of that canon lay not merely in the rigour of its syntax but in the inseparable rigour of its philosophy. Its forms were intellectual forms, and Morton Shand, writing in *The Architectural Review* 30 years ago, rightly called the Schröder House 'ideologically modern'. Its plastic rules were few and were formulated like a set of philosophical propositions about elements and their relations; their aim was to celebrate a way of life in which clarity and simplicity were articles of faith as much as they were constructive means; they were tools of a positivism claiming mystical insight. Rietveld wrote that this clarity was to be experienced 'not with an aesthetic purpose but only to provide us with a more direct experience of reality',[3] and again, 'We used only primary forms, colours and spaces because they are so fundamental and so free of associations.'[4] It cannot be overemphasized that this has nothing whatever to do with aestheticism.

It is not necessary to spell out at length the metaphysics of de Stijl, but it is vital to realize that we are here confronted with an indivisible body of passionately held ideas and not just a set of elegant forms. The bond between image and intention was a metaphysical one.[5] It was over the precise nature of this bond that Van Doesburg and Mondrian fell out (Figures 10.4(a)–(b)), and over his refusal to accept the necessity for any such bond that Oud severed his relations with the group. De Stijl was, in Van Doesburg's phrase, 'conviction in action'; its 'translation of reality into constructions controlled by reason'[6] was going to create a New Society by creating new possibilities for living. That image (most familiar in the work of Mondrian) of a spatial field traversed by orthogonal lines of force was an icon (*werelbeeld*) common to all members of the group. Here it is idle to speak (as so many have done) of architecture 'imitating' painting or sculpture; all concretized in their mode a central principle by which opposing forces could be brought into resolution.

It is vital to stress this point because the failure to understand its significance has led the historians to create a false impression of Rietveld, which must be eliminated before one can hope to appreciate his true significance. Encouraged by the contemporary propaganda of Oud, Lissitsky and Van Doesburg himself, early assessment of both the Schröder House and the Rietveld furniture interpreted them as attempts to turn de Stijl painting into architecture. This view very soon rigidified into a cliché that passed unquestioned by any historian until Theodore Brown pointed out that the red-blue chair anticipated by nearly 2 years the Mondrian paintings it was supposed to have 'imitated'.[7] Open-minded study of both house and chair reveal how obviously and purely spatial the conjugation of elements is. Nothing could be more essentially architectonic, and it is easy to understand that Rietveld's method of work was immediately three-dimensional, either by making very small working models (Figure 10.5) or by folding paper upon which adjoining plans and elevations had been roughly

10.4(a)

10.4(b)

10.5

sketched. It is significant that he shared with Loos and Duiker the remarkable fact that his drawing was seldom more than notational and certainly never 'pictorial'.[8]

Such weaknesses as the canon may have contained were not the weaknesses of painterliness but of a structural ambiguity arising from a stress upon spatial properties at the expense of all traditional associations of substance. While both the ideological incentive and the restriction of means brought great intensity to the early exemplars of the canon, they were not perhaps in themselves sufficient nourishment upon which an architecture might mature. The 'freedom from association' had been won (as it had with twelve-tone music) at the price of a certain flattening, a reduction in levels of reference, a self-sufficiency that lacked resonance. It was not only a freedom from history, it was also a freedom from nature.

The architectural consequences of this 'denaturalization' were of mixed value. The concern for smooth and brilliant surfaces and the suppression of natural materials helped to provoke a healthy impatience at technological delay; but taken in conjunction with the desire 'to destroy natural structure',[9] to create the illusion of weightlessness, this 'dematerialization' reveals two characteristic weaknesses in the schema. First, an almost casual attitude towards structure. Rietveld wrote 'weakening and defects always result when colour of material and form of construction influence the space',[10] and at the conceptual level, structure is significantly omitted altogether from Van Doesburg's famous 16 Points of 1924.[11] Second, the resulting ambiguity incorporated into the very syntax an impulse towards mannerism at the level of *trompe l'oeil*. This is already present in the Schröder House in the device by which the red and yellow transoms are 'stitched' through steel stanchions; but what is 'true' in the world of its inventor becomes in the work of lesser men short cuts to an imagery without substance. I suspect that the polemic about 'formalism' which built up at this time in Berlin was largely brought on by the Schröder House, not only because, like all poetry, it provoked uncritical imitation, but more generally because it brought to focus sooner, more concretely and more uncompromisingly than any other building, the complex 'linguistic' problems bound to be faced sooner or later by the common pursuit of 'a New Architecture'.

It is not enough that a system be syntactically complete; the meaning of an architecture lies in its use and in the manner of its making. By 1925 rapid developments technically, analytically and formally had almost overwhelmed Rietveld's initial achievement. Of these, two were important. First, the establishment of the structurally robust and analytically diversified canon of Purism in a position of international supremacy; neutrality of elements gave way to hierarchy of components and the range increased to embrace Urbanism. Second, within Holland itself a slight shift in attitude (parallel with the Sass Group in Russia and the 'G' Group in Berlin) hardened into the *nieuwe zakelijkheid* mode, in which analytical, technical and structural factors were advanced under the banner of 'Functionalism', and all formal factors ostensibly sent to the decompression chamber. In the words of Van Loghem, the new basis and its methodology could hardly ensure an 'automatic' origin of architecture but from it architecture might come as a 'reward'.

Rietveld's reaction to this turn of affairs has not yet been satisfactorily accounted for. Like all true inventors he scorned to value the canon for its own sake when in his own words, 'excessive rules of the game threaten to crush the game of life'.[12] He kept moving; and we begin to see that the unifying principle behind all his work was not a formal notation but the belief that the task of the architect was to 'help to simplify life and rid it of its superfluities',[13] to achieve immediacy of experience. He said later that architecture was a 'tenuous equilibrium in a life which, as a whole, is like a balance eternally looking for its centre of gravity'.[14]

Although it was Mies who wrote at this time, 'My attack is not against form but against form as an end in itself . . . Life is what is decisive for us',[15] it was Rietveld who acted upon the premise; and we begin to see that this in fact always had been the springboard for his work. Even his most 'abstract' devices were, in a later terminology, 'concrete' mechanisms both as practical equipment affording freedom and economy of energy and as sensory stimuli to 'the immediate life, the ordinary, simple, direct experience of reality'.[16] Certainly when Mrs Schröder showed me around the house she accounted for the spatial arrangements entirely in terms of their response to the way of life that she and her three children wanted to live (Figure 10.6). Accordingly she walked around nimbly sliding partitions to subdivide areas for individual privacy. This point has to be stressed in opposition to those who will

10.6

persist in seeing the elemental forms merely as 'abstract relationships'.

It is my claim that this attitude had been and always remained the constant factor throughout Rietveld's life. But whereas up to 1929 his genius had invented the system through which this attitude could be made concrete in canonical works of art, we find that during the late 1920s he is beginning to lose the initiative to others. Under new circumstances, which brought dramatic technical advances and a great increase in the size and complexity of architectural assignment, that system had either to be radically extended or else scrapped and another formulated in its place. It was Duiker (Figure 10.7) and Van der Vlugt who forged the new canon of 'functionalism', while Rietveld, in his next group of buildings, seems to have become the follower. He began to share the new concern with structure. And in the first Erasmuslaan group of terrace houses of 1930 in Utrecht we have not only a broadening of content into a whole series of housing projects and buildings (which remind us that Rietveld was a founder member of CIAM) but a new laconic regularity, born from his appraisal of the 'unknown client' of mass society and here embodied in the planning module, the sliding partitions and the grouped services.[17] Certainly in its own way this building was a masterwork of the new canon.

10.7

The fact remains, however, that the great poet of that new school was not Rietveld but Duiker, in whose Zonnestraal Sanatorium at Hilversum of 1926–8 the concrete frame became a 'witness of potent means' unrivalled in precision and intensity anywhere in the world. Here we seem to be faced with some puzzling questions. For instance, need Rietveld have abandoned the neoplastic system when he did? After all, Mies's whole corpus of work has been the slow magisterial exploration of it. Was Rietveld unwilling or unable to make such an extension? Was he seeking something else, or was he simply a miniaturist?[18] Or did he, like de Chirico, lose some inner grace?

The more one learns of Rietveld's character, the more do such questions appear too crude. The answer lies in the region of 'something else', but until his later work is given the attention it deserves we cannot define this quantum. Before I am accused of over-compensating for the historians' neglect, let me add that I do not think Rietveld ever again attained the universal pivotal significance of his early work. Nevertheless the cumulative effect of his later work seems to build together (where the individual works do not do so) into a deliberate and unique whole whose value we have yet to judge: experimental, anti-monumental, unerringly scaled to human activity, deliberately casual often with an almost Butterfieldian inelegance. 'Each work is only a part of the unending constructive possibilities: and an attempt towards completeness in a single work would injure the harmony.'[19] Extraordinary innovations like the early shop designs, the series of moulded ply (and aluminium) chairs from 1927 onwards, the do-it-yourself boxwood crate furniture and the famous zig-zag chair of 1934, the Vervijn-Stuart summerhouse (Figure 10.8) and the Arnhem pavilion are interspersed among works of a deliberate 'ordinariness'.

10.8

We are reminded more of Duchamp than of de Chirico. Among architects one is reminded of that other 'outsider', Schindler, of California, before whose Pueblo Ribera houses in La Jolla (also 1924) we feel the same tingling excitement that a simple zest for life could inspire such plastic invention (Figure 10.9). For both men architecture was a spontaneous improvisation to serve the occasions of life, not a monument to conserve values. Both of them travelled light, abhorring the tie of supporting a large office. It is typical of Rietveld and of Mrs Schröder that shortly before he died they were working out a means of altering the house radically in order to counter the effects of the new highway in course of construction alongside, and never gave a thought to the idea of preservation of the house for its own sake. He saw all his work as expendable, and happily destroyed drawings and past records as superfluities.

10.9

Finally one cannot speak of Rietveld's work without acknowledging the significance of his collaboration with Mrs Schröder. This was not so much a technical collaboration (for which she was not trained) as an interpretative one, and it points up the phenomenon which gives the Dutch contribution its unique significance in twentieth-century architecture. Behind each of the great seminal buildings there stands a client as original and adventurous as the architect. For the Van Nelle factory and the Spangen housing it was van der Leeuw, for the Zonnestraal Sanatorium it was van Zutphen (Figure 10.10), and for the Schröder house it was of course Mrs Truus Schröder-Schräder.

Later perhaps we shall see a larger pattern in his work. But for now we value most that marvellous moment when a stubborn search for a simple thing

10.10

turned everything to magic, enlarged the powers of life by renewing the powers of architecture and transformed the framework for the common acts of men so that they could become again vivid and immediate experience, 'each time renewed, creating, continuing and expanding our being'.[20]

References

1 Rietveld in *Schröder Huis*, published by Steendrukerij de Jong & Co., Hilversum, 1963.
2 Lissitsky, 1926. Quoted by Theodore Brown, *Rietveld*, p. 58.
3 Rietveld in *Insight*, 1928. Brown, *op. cit.*, p. 160.
4 Rietveld in *Schröder Huis, op. cit.*
5 A theosophical interest seems to have been in the air. Brinkmann and van der Vlugt were interested in Krishnamurti (who was quoted by Le Corbusier); Van Doesburg and Mondrian studied Schoenmakers and fell out over a disagreement about Mondrian's contention that the archetypal lines of force in Nature were the vertical and horizontal absolutes. Rietveld, no great reader of books, knew Schoenmakers personally but rarely spoke of him, whereas, according to Theodore Brown, he would occasionally quote Rabindranath Tagore.
6 Schoenmakers, quoted in Jaffé, *de Stijl*, p. 56.
7 I am not concerned with questions of priority except to exclude them from misleading intrusion.
8 The famous drawings of the Schröder House were not made by him but by others in 1951 for exhibition purposes.
9 Mondrian in *Home–Street–City*, 1926.
10 Rietveld, *Insight*, 1928.
11 See 'Tot een beeldens Architectuur', in *de Stijl*, 6, 6.7.1924. Quoted in Theodore Brown, *Rietveld*, pp. 66–9.
12 Rietveld, *View of Life as a Background for my Work*, 1957. Quoted by Brown, *op. cit.*, p. 162.
13 Rietveld, *Insight*, 1928.
14 Rietveld, *View of Life*.
15 Mies van der Rohe, 'A Letter on Form', 1927, quoted in P. Johnson's monograph, p. 187.
16 Rietveld, *Insight*, 1928.
17 He had already projected the first 'service-core' houses in Europe in 1929.
18 Unfortunately his League of Nations project cannot be found and he was generally starved of larger-scale commissions until the last years of his life.
19 Rietveld, *View of Life*.
20 Rietveld, *Insight*, 1928.

I am particularly indebted to Theodore Brown's *The Work of G. Rietveld Architect*, published by Bruna & Zoon, Utrecht, 1958.

Part III
POLEMIC, 1960–91

11

Open and Closed

It is a long-professed claim that the New Architecture, having freed itself from the closed system of the Styles, would break through to an unprecedented mode of action constantly open to every challenge of developing circumstance and demand. Contrast that claim with the following statement in 1957 by Alvar Aalto: 'The architectural revolution is still going on but it is like all revolutions: it starts with enthusiasm and it stops with some sort of dictatorship.'[1]

Of the general nature of that recurrent symbiosis, revolution/dictatorship (so dear to Europe), all that needs to be said is that it is as true of the world of ideas, of science, of art as it is of politics. The power of novel and aggressive ideas to sustain themselves against the entropy of systematization or the subtleties of perversion is put to the grinding test of time. In both politics and architecture, the happy determinism of the 1920s, which believed perpetual revolution to be not merely desirable but historically inevitable, today looks badly bent after collision with the facts of 30 years. Architecture too has its iron curtains.

To understand that predicament today both in America and Europe it is essential to examine certain issues raised in the formative period of modern architecture. Two significant proposals emerged in the early 1920s as possible strategies for the development of architecture.

One stressed the formation of an explicit language of forms. The old chaos was to be superseded by a New Order replete with its own laws for implementation and symbols for public communication. It is not surprising that those groups intimately connected with the constructive avant-garde of painting (constructivism, de Stijl and Purism) should find such a language most readily available.

A quotation from Le Corbusier writing in *L'Esprit Nouveau* best illustrates a tendency common to all these groups:

> An aesthetic and a work of art are, above all, systems.
> An attitude is not a system.
> Genius is personal, decided by fate, but it expresses itself by means of system.
> There is no work of art without system.[2]

It is important to note that although, for Le Corbusier, the invention of a new language of form was a public necessity, it was in practice bound to be a personal and heroic task of elected individuals: seer, poet and lawgiver in one. Stress is laid upon generality, a typology of forms; the tone is authoritarian.

The second method of attack was proposed by Hugo Haering (Figure 11.1). Opposing the approach of Le Corbusier (*Gestaltwerk*) as premature, he advocated what he called '*Organwerk* – the task of developing the architectural organism' through a study of function: 'we want to examine things and allow them to discover their own images. It goes against the grain with us to bestow a form on them from the outside'.[3] It is important to realize that here the emphasis upon the 'organic' relates to the proper ordering of functions and their plastic organization and not to any naturalistic analogies.

GUT GARKAU

11.1

Again personal involvement is implied, but here the stress is laid not upon generality but upon the spirit of particularity. Functional analysis demanded that solutions could only be discovered *en route*: any predetermined set of relations would inevitably inhibit their organic development. Given talent, an adventurous and unpredictable poetry might emerge.

This was not an approach calculated to make life easy for either architect or public. It is the lore of the Lone Ranger.

With the best will in the world, the contribution of the Bauhaus seems, in retrospect, to have largely confused the issue. For Gropius the search for form was something nasty that took place in the woodshed of the nineteenth century. To avoid the recurrence of this offence, the new designer must be 'purged of all subjectivity', becoming thereby a fit vehicle through which an improbable 'Spirit of the Age' would pour forth the true blessings of The Machine, whose inherent characteristics were prejudged to be standardization, platonic purity of form and above all impersonality. This curiously mystical assumption that forms are invented by sleepwalking exposed its victims in the worst way to enchantment by the poets of what Le Corbusier calls 'system'.

Forms are made not by the Zeitgeist but by men.

Here the subtlest form of dictatorship emerges: poetry. The effectiveness of any plastic system is to be measured by its capacity to attract, to communicate, to capture. To this end poetry is veiled but ruthless; when victorious it blinds its victims to all but itself.

What N. W. Pirie has said of the world of science is true here also. 'A cynic can assess the eminence of a scientist by the length of time for which his theories are able to hold up the development of science after his death.'

The only weapon against such poetry is another poetry.

The forging of any such weapon was precisely what Bauhaus theory refused to permit. As Plato exiled the poets from his Republic, so Gropius, in the celebrated skirmish with Van Doesburg (Figure 11.2) at Weimar in 1922, sought in vain to exterminate the 'formalistic perversions' of de Stijl from the Bauhaus. The integrity of this decision is clear but the infection of poetry had taken hold. The full irony of his failure was revealed by his own essay in the manner of de Stijl, on the Dessau Campus, 4 years later (Figure 11.3).

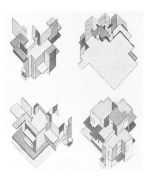

11.2

The real struggle for power lay between the protagonists of *Gestaltwerk* and *Organwerk*. The historian Joedicke reports that at the first meeting of CIAM in 1928 precisely such a contest did take place when Haering protested that Le Corbusier's insistence upon *Gestaltwerk* was altogether too premature. He was outvoted, and it is important for us today to be clear about the reasons for this. Certainly it was not for lack of poetic force: buildings by Haering himself, Bijvoet, Duiker (Figure 11.4) and Aalto were as eloquent and plastically intact as any.

11.3

But they did suffer from being associated in the minds of many with the superficial excesses of the Expressionists, which was precisely the stigma that would offend most the minds of Gropius and others. This was a serious misjudgement, and we shall find a similar misreading of certain tendencies in criticism today. In fact political expediency would appear to have been the real cause of this defeat: the members of that congress were rightly searching for a principle of unity, and the propaganda of unity demands not only clear and persuasive symbols but also the suppression of uncomfortable contradictions. It would be absurd and ungrateful to deny its proper glory to the CIAM Group but it is well time to realize that its passionate exclusivity did tend to stifle the development of diversified advance, which is the very essence of adventurous radicalism.[4] Today, in our appraisal of how we ourselves should act in a situation that is largely the inheritance of yesterday's decisions, we are compelled to critize even those whom we readily acknowledge to be Masters. Not the least reason for our scepticism is that these Masters accompanied their inventions by theses in which poetry and logic, invention and self-justification were shuffled about in maddening ambiguities.

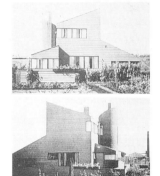

11.4

There emerged from that first meeting of CIAM the beginning of an institutionalized set of ideas. Somehow the mysticism of the Bauhaus was grafted upon an imagery derived from Le Corbusier, Mies and the Van Doesburg models of 1920–3. These latter projects and their partial fruition in the Rietveld house of 1924 had, before any other, proposed an architecture of extreme abstraction of form, the appearance of levitation and dematerialization of substance; to achieve this, structure was reduced to a series of subterfuges. The image of The New as pure, magical and defiant was struck. This was the 'cardboard' abstraction that Frank Lloyd Wright denounced. On that tight wire only the great poets, Corbusier and Mies, could preserve their balance; lesser architects were compelled to resort to *trompe l'oeil*, even at the same instant as they protested in print against 'lying façades and false trickeries' (Gropius).

The one subject upon which there had been decreed a conspiracy of silence had started to work its way through the system: the old paralysis of style was closing in fast. In 1932 three men in search of a 'style' (Johnson, Hitchcock and Barr) toured Europe and came up with a formula called 'the International Style'.

In this context the post-war development of architecture in the United States takes on a special meaning in European eyes, resuming and extending the same paradoxical themes of rule and misunderstanding and defiance.

It would certainly appear that by the mid-1950s the poetry of Mies van der Rohe had attained 'dictatorship' through an elite, over a wide field of American building. Now some of those who had at first most willingly submitted appear to have made an uncomfortable discovery: the space between Miesian principle and Mies' own projects does not leave much room for lesser talents to manoeuvre in. A 'discipline' had been assumed too smartly; certainly a glance at the plans convinces one that the understanding had not penetrated far beneath the surface. Such facility was bound to grow impatient with Mies' own private obdurate and almost Bramantesque concern with the grammar of his system, the conjunction of elements, the turning of corners, the minutiae of being 'correct' (Figure 11.5(a)–(b)).

Those who had blossomed in conformity now contorted themselves in promiscuous postures of escape. From gullibility through disenchantment to the dull hope that salvation might lie merely in being

11.5(a)

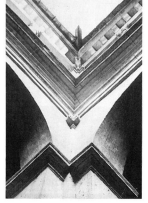

11.5(b)

anti-Mies, one whole exercise has come full circle, only
to give birth to the Neo-Hysterical Styles (Figure 11.6).

It is disastrous that in this case criticism and revolt
have expressed themselves solely in terms of surface
style. At the formal level it is unprofitable, to say the
least, to attack Mies; but in the fundamental organization of a building, the true heart of architecture, his
decisions are quite properly open to attack, for they can
be breathtakingly wilful. To sink one whole half of a
building into the ground as a podium so that the other
half can look like a temple is bad enough (Figure
11.7(a)–(b)) – establishing the iceberg principle, by
which some followers (such as Philip Johnson) have
obtained licence to evade all functional representation
whatsoever (Figure 11.8). But to make an art gallery as
at Houston, in which the visual conditions are such that
it must be impossible to see an exhibit silhouetted
against a glass wall, is to take the concept of 'universal
space' to the point of outright obstructiveness.

To react to this situation merely by saying, as
Saarinen has done, that the way out is to extend the
alphabet of architecture beyond A and B is to miss the
essential point altogether.

One is compelled to recall Haering's distinction
between *Gestaltwerk* and *Organwerk*, and two buildings at MIT can serve as illustrations of the distinction.
Professor Russell Hitchcock has suggested that Aalto's
Baker Dormitory (Figure 11.9(a)–(b)) could be seen in
retrospect as the unacknowledged turning point in
post-war American architecture. Certainly it is interesting to note that in the 1952 edition of *Built in U.S.A.*
this building was referred to as 'Expressionist' and 'the
most strikingly mannered building of recent years'.

Now maybe it is a strange and imperfectly executed
building but emphatically it is not 'mannered' in the
sense that Saarinen's Auditorium on the same campus
is. Its forms may be unprecedented but they obey the
internal law of an architectural organism in Haering's
sense. Possibly Aalto himself was surprised at the form
this 'law' disclosed in the course of its development.
But conceptually it was entire and, once embarked
upon, quite unalterable; all this has nothing whatever
to do with expressionism. Conversely Saarinen has
merely shown that you can cram anything, even two
Auditoria, under the dubiously structural form of an
eighth of a sphere, if that kind of thing appeals to you
(Figure 11.10). One is reminded of Mendelsohn's
Einstein Tower, which started life as a sketch for twin
concrete towers, semi-detached and labelled 'Optical

11.6

11.7(a)

11.7(b)

11.8

11.9(a)

11.9(b)

11.10

Factory', only to hive off a few years later as a spectrograph tower, built in brick and with the real works tucked well underground (the iceberg principle once more). A moment's reflection must reveal the absurdity of hailing as 'constructive experiment' a mode of procedure that works backwards from a foregone conclusion by the ingenious manipulation of a shoehorn. Nothing is evolved or discovered through analysis of the requirements; the organization is trumpery and nothing remains to consummate the farce but the dreary chore of 'making it work'. That truly is 'expressionism'.

It is not necessary to dwell on further examples. However brilliant technically, this 'new language' is a string of adjectives; the absence of verbs (of plan, of thought, of organization) makes the construction of intelligible sentences impossible. It is as though the decisions taken are starved of the nourishment of *thought* and serve only the exasperations of *fancy*. The symptoms of dissociation reappear, and one closed system has been avoided merely to embrace conceptual vacuity. Time and again one sees specific devices of the genuine innovators turned overnight into decorative 'features'. Sun breakers, beton brute, the glass curtain, pre-cast concrete are treated in the spirit of Art Nouveau devices, and the iceberg principle of organization, which permits maximum licence for these 'effects', threatens to become endemic. Will 'servant-spaces' be the next form of decoration?

Fortunately there are clear exceptions to this current of trivialization. Chief among these is ironically, the one architect whose work has borne the least superficial resemblance to that of Mies but whose fundamental understanding must have been most rigorous and passionate; for the architecture of Louis Kahn bears most strikingly the mark of principle. The plan generates its own laws of continuity, the anatomy of spaces, structure and organs is exact, thematically related, astonishingly frank. The work has grandeur and yet, unlike the work of the European masters Mies and Corbusier, does not condense into symbols of generality, into archetypes. It has the sharp rigour of rationalism, drawing upon new facts and lyricizing them. Above all its conceptual scope suggests a range of possibilities and an unexpected energy that could inspire many and various talents to fill it out.

It has its own discipline but its system is not closed.

Postscript

This chapter (1960) is the earliest in the book. In so far as it marks out the span that has been traversed, it invites some second thoughts.

Firstly it anticipates by many years both the attack on Historicism by David Watkin and others and foresaw the invention of Post-Modernism. References to the 'Neo-Hysterical Style' and the question: 'Will servant-spaces be the next form of decoration?' were greeted at the time by Reyner Banham with elation.

Conversely it has been heartening to read in Giancarlo de Carlo's journal *Spazio e Societa* (No. 18: 1982) of the extraordinary vitality of Aalto's Baker House at MIT. 'If the design was that of a master the result has been active participation.' In Volume III of Goran Schildt's life of Aalto there is an analytical diagram illustrating how twelve alternative layouts were explored and tested against the desired parameters of privacy, view, sunlight and shared amenity space. (So much for the charge of 'Expressionism'!) What is significant is that the parameters as well as the performance were shown to have survived in the view of the inhabitants over 40 years; for when, in the interests of packing more students in, some of the shared amenity space was taken over (and rent costs proportionally reduced), the students soon demanded reversion to the original layout. Aalto's concern with the habitability of his buildings was very down to earth. 'True architecture is only where man stands at the centre' was his message to the students. His test was to ask: 'What does the building look like thirty years after it was built?' Both the concern and the confidence to accept the challenge of time are virtues that, unfortunately, few of his fellow masters can boast.

References

1 I have since come across Jurgen Habermas' withering phrase 're-enchantment' – a new dope for the middle-class masses purveyed by 'the Avant garde of the Reversed Front'.
2 *L'Esprit Nouveau*, ed. Le Corbusier, Ozentant, Dermée, Vol. 1, No. 1 (1918).
3 Hugo Haering, *Wege zur Form*, 1925.
4 It is no coincidence that *Space Time and Architecture* that brilliant piece of special pleading for the CIAM group, virtually excludes the contributions of Haering, Scharoun, Duiker etc. When, in later editions, a chapter on Aalto is added, it is to present him as the champion of irrationalism!

12

TWO LETTERS on the state of architecture: 1964 and 1981

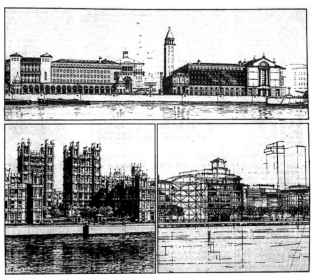

When I was invited to contribute to the *Journal of Architectural Education* in its (1981) collection of writings by architect–teachers, I interpreted the task to be an assessment of the state of play at that moment; and it seemed to me worthwhile to compare the position in 1981 with my last attempt at such an appraisal in 1964. The best way to do that seemed to be to represent by a contemporary document the state of mind that prefigured the turbulence and rebellion of the late 1960s and thereby to ask whether or not anything had really been changed in the meantime.

Letter to an American student

('Program', *Columbia University, School of Architecture, Spring 1964*)

Dear R [Robert von Zumbusch]

I do not wish to go on raging at the latest phase of architecture in the United States. It seems that by now the conflict in judgement between European and American critics upon this subject needs understanding rather than exacerbation; and certainly as I sat and listened to the contributors to the Columbia symposium ('Architecture in the 1930s', Columbia University, School of Architecture, Spring 1964), I began to understand for the first time that there is a fundamental difference between the American and the European interpretation of the role of architecture in society; for the modern architecture of which these contributors spoke was almost unrecognizable to me. It was supposedly defined by some point of purely stylistic maturity called 'the International Style', deeply indebted to neo-classicism and quite detached from the problems of its society. No Athens Charter, no *îlot insalubre*, no echo of the cry 'architecture or revolution', nothing of the search for new standards, of the fervour of groups such as CIAM and MARS to bring architecture to the attention of the people: art for art's sake, amen.

Now in Europe, the notion of a new architecture was always a polemic one, in which, for better or worse, a whole body of ideas was at stake – social, technical, and formal. In this body of ideas, all elements from door-handle to city plan were so bound together that the form of a chair could even project implications for the form of the city. Stakes of this order demand a kind of Hippocratic oath, and this is to be exercised in a realm hard to define, which borders simultaneously upon aesthetics, morality, and politics, and can best be described by the word 'probity'.

From this point, the misunderstandings multiply. For, whereas the members of the symposium finally agreed to exclude Corbu as typical of 'the thirties' because of his stylistic versatility, I found that I was bound to speak of him as fundamentally typical precisely because of the force with which he converted this probity into an axis of intention that guided and unified two generations of younger architects. His forms were intellectual forms, and projected above all else the image of a new way of living.

This raises a fundamental question in semantics. Since the forms were born from a set of intellectual objectives, is the reverse also true? Namely, that the forms so clearly carry information about their origin that they may be said to represent a culture, to enable a society uniquely to recognize itself in them? (Let us agree straight away that this has nothing to do with sentimental notions of imagery, such as 'the style for the job'.) Certain kinds of originality will be excluded: there will be an insistence upon certain norms. To disagree with the resultant architecture will not be because, as some of my American friends would say, one 'saw through all that talk' to a weakness in the form, but because one felt the intellectual basis to be incorrectly formulated, and that the renewal of concepts must be continued.

Surely it was not on stylistic grounds that the Nazis closed the Bauhaus, and not for nothing did Corbu refer to 'ce futurisme *bien dangereux*'. For Corbu, as for the Nazis, forms contained dangerous implications of a way of life. Probity demands such recognition.

Now I will very soon get out of my depth if I try to account for the anti-intellectualism of the American critics; I simply point to it as the major difference between us. In America today there is no public forum for the exchange of ideas, no group gathered around a common idea (and therefore no rebel groups), no discussion that is more than one man deep, no magazine that attempts to focus upon the state of current polemic. This is the starvation of thought. It has been suggested to me that this absence of intellectual debate is common to all fields of American life, that it stems from the notion that the revolution has already happened, long ago, that ideas are not to be dangerous anymore . . . Of this I cannot judge.

The fact, however, that you and so many of the young architects whom I have met deplore the absence of such debate encourages me to believe that the distinction I have made is correct. Only you can decide what action to take to achieve your object: but as to the nature of the object itself, let me add this. James Joyce once defined the aim of his art in terms of the word 'epiphany'. By this he meant the understanding by which the most ordinary acts of men could be 'shown forth' – a sudden focus into depth, into naked revelation, of what had seemed to be trivial incident. Similarly, van Gogh once wrote that he hoped by his art to give back to ordinary men 'that something of the eternal that the halo used to represent'. It would seem to me that the uniquely American contribution to architecture should be in some such direct confrontation with life, bringing new energy to that architectural moment of realization in which a frame for the actions of men suddenly focuses into a place where those actions are not merely made possible, but are made manifest – are made, perhaps for the first time, vivid and recognizable to themselves, and their meaning preserved against erosion by conflicting actions and occasions. This has nothing whatsoever to do with the search for the extraordinary, nor with the abysmal desire to 'enchant'; it has much to do with the enlargement and the celebration of the powers of life and their embodiment.

Good luck, Yours truly, etc,

Colin St John Wilson
Mexico City/Phoenix: 25 May 1964.

Letter to an architect–teacher

Dear Ray [Lifchez]

You were at the Columbia 'Thirties Symposium' that provoked my outburst and you will therefore recall that at that time to speak up for an architecture that sought to be anything more than an *exercise du style* was to run the gauntlet of ridicule from the elders present. But at least a group of students enjoyed the intervention: hence my 1964 'Letter' to one of them. Anyway, it was not long before students in many places began their own protest against the prevailing indulgence in aesthetics or technology for their own sakes: there were student groups working for deprived communities, there was Earth Day, the Paris '68 revolution . . . And, God knows, one can no longer complain of a lack of journals in the United States offering a platform for architectural analysis and polemic! But, alas, that protest never grew beyond a gesture of defiance, and the polemic has become the platform for an unparalleled narcissism. Both the mandarin and the demagogue are too wet for the job.

So, now, 15 years later, where are we? As the dust of Pruitt-Igoe falls from the air, the mandarins emerge once more from the wings. The mentality that promoted the travesty of 'Thirties Architecture' as 'the International Style', a phenomenon defined by its rejection of decoration, blandly returns to the stage with a benediction upon a new style, 'Post-Modernism', a phenomenon to be defined by its indulgence in decoration; and once again we are left high and dry with the phantom of a style that can only tell lies. Only this time, the product is heavy with intellectual pretension: 'autonomous architecture'. Of itself, by itself, for itself – indeed, playing with itself (*onanismo cerebrale*). Art for Art's sake once more: amen. The 'debt' of Pruitt-Igoe has been wiped out by a Chippendale skyscraper, and there's no business like Beaux-Arts business. Forgive me if once again I forbear to join in the conspiracy of fun, and offer instead yet one more cry of despair.

I understand that one of the unifying themes of this collection of essays on architectural education is 'the return to history'. Setting aside the fact that only a madman would exclude history from an architecture course in the first place (did Gropius *really* import that piece of Bauhaus lunacy to Harvard?), then of course its 'return' would be likely to bring on a certain light-headedness in those with a taste for plunder. But history also has lessons to offer. The lesson that the doctrinaire Modernists ignored was that you can't wind the clock hand forward without blowing fuses all over the network. It's not a natural thing to do, such as adjusting to summertime; it is more like frontal lobotomy – it wipes out. The Greeks, on the other hand, knew what they were doing when they said that the goddess who gave birth to the arts was Mnemosyne, goddess of Memory.

Conversely, the lesson that has to be learned by the fashionable madmen of today is that history can never put the clock back either. For us the simple truth is that there can be no going back on the claims made for architecture by the Modernists in their heyday. Of couse too great a claim was made. 'That Architecture . . . alone could give man the possibility of a new way of life', could lead to the Promised Land overnight. But those claims have now promoted an expectation beside which the 'purer' architectural goals will seem to be trivial; and they did so with an unforgettable generosity and with that particular freshness that only the great revolutions of the imagination inspire. The game has been deepened, and it can never be the same again.

In two ways: firstly, in the relationship of architecture to power. For the first time, an architecture of high ambition was born to serve the aspirations not of the powerful few, but of the underprivileged many, and to do so through the technology of mass production. We should not be surprised that the successes have been few. For, setting aside the brevity of the whole venture so far, there is an enigma at the very heart of architecture, in that much of its hold upon our imagination is embodied in images of power, embodiments that have served so well the cause of princes, popes, and pharaohs. The technology that carries the promise of mass production too easily turns multiplication into forms of degrading repetition. The architecture of democracy has not yet given birth to an imagery of its own to match the assurance, the self-sufficiency, the figurative wholeness of the monuments to power. But we must believe that this quest for another poetry is not insuperable, not a contradiction in terms, but merely a falling short – short of the entirely possible. Indeed when I recall Asplund's reference to 'forms which do not frighten but invite', I am filled with conviction that there is a whole world of imagination to be explored in the service of an architecture that does not compress all responses into a hushed submission, but opens up and enlarges that experience beyond all expectation.

Both in his writings and in his practice, Alvar Aalto is the principal vindication of this possibility. The formalists may sneer at his dedication to the cause of 'man at the centre' as insincere. What they disdain to notice is the track record, the lived reality of the buildings. These have matured with time after 30 years, and, in Alberti's phrase, have become 'embellished by use', where those of the other masters have all too often survived only as museum pieces after 'restoration'.

Secondly, the nature of the Modernist imagination is grounded in a deeply divided intention, and this brings it very close to the dualism that marks the nature of architecture itself. On the one hand, its obligation to the social contract (more widely proclaimed than ever before) and, on the other, its 'immortal longings' for something variously called 'autonomous architecture' or 'frozen music'(!). Much confusion surrounds these cloudy abstractions.

But we are not dealing in a world of tidy logic, and I submit that it is precisely in the impossible fusion of these two disparate responsibilities that the act of architectural invention takes place. It is the hard won point of equilibrium in an unstable relationship of terms. The dilemma of Art vs Life has an entirely different role in architecture than it has in any of the other arts. Born of necessity, architecture can never, by definition, be 'pure', unlike any of those other arts, it exists solely on condition that there is in its very genesis some impulse born outside the autonomy of the discipline itself. (If you don't believe me, just look at what people do to a building if it fails to respond adequately to the conditions that called it into being.) Yet it must endure as a work of art, a Practical Art. This unique and inscrutable paradox is, in fact, architecture's glory, its true bond, its sole source of vitality.

Finally, a comment on the term 'post-modernism'. The first rule in carrying out a postmortem is to check that the subject is dead. Giancarlo de Carlo once said that modern architecture had died many times. In 1928 Hugo Haering claimed at the very first meeting of CIAM that the new architecture had been strangled by conformity. In 1940 Aalto referred to 'the first and now past period of modern architecture'. Indeed it is this creative doubt that is the touchstone of the living movement and that endears Aalto in particular to my generation. For the other early masters of Modernism, the enemy was the dead hand of the past; for Aalto, the enemy took the form of falsification of the present, inauthenticity, failure to live with the paradox: 'bad faith'. For him, architecture was a straight fight in the interests of what he called 'the little man', with constant vigilance against *les deux cochons*: formalism and bureaucratic pseudorationalism.

In the thirties symposium, I spoke of 'probity' in order to focus upon this sense of values, and Philip Johnson nearly fell off the platform at the use of such a word; he clutched his head and wailed 'What a disgusting word!' (laughter in audience . . . as usual). I am now convinced more than ever of the necessity for precisely some such term that will warn us where to make a stand in a time reeking as much with bad faith and misrepresentation as with misunderstanding and simple lack of vision. For the great modernist venture is open to two very different kinds of attack. From within, from the 'creative doubt' of the true nonconformists (in the tradition of Wright, Aalto, Asplund, Scharoun, Melnikov, and Kahn), attacking the doctrinaire and the formalist, the reductionist and the overweening rejec–tion of the past; and from without, by those who wish to write it off, turn the clock back, revel in the fact that a grand aspiration has so far failed to attain its goal and rejoice in pillorying the scapegoats – yet have nothing to offer to take its place but nostalgia.[1] This is once more *la trahison des clercs*, and it must be recognized that the plan of attack draws much of its sustenance from the same poisonous sources that feed Fascism.

I wrote in my last letter to the effect that the Nazis did not close down the Bauhaus on stylistic grounds, but because it was the embodiment of values that threatened their own. Little did I guess that the polemic for which I pleaded would produce as models for emulation Mussolini's Terza Roma or Speer's execr–able Reich's Chancellery.

Yours ever,

Colin St John Wilson
London/Cambridge: 1 August 1981.

References

1 I have since come across Jurgen Habermas' withering phrase 're-enchantment' – a new dope for the middle-class masses purveyed by 'the Avant garde of the Reversed Front'.

13

SPEER and the fear of freedom

'Architecture immortalizes and glorifies something. Hence there can be no architecture where there is nothing to glorify.' This pronouncement by Ludwig Wittgenstein is a hard saying: it hinges, like the thought of Wittgenstein's friend Adolf Loos, upon a dubious distinction between 'architecture' and 'building'. But for those who are currently obsessed by the loudly proclaimed 'Death of Modern Architecture' it sets up a framework within which the vacuum left by a shallow unlamented 'functionalism' might be explored; and for this reason it is a thought beset by great dangers. Quite specifically it focusses attention upon the nature of monumentality, which is of course the sacred ground favoured by those most anxious to fill the vacuum. But it is also the enigma of architecture, for at its heart lies architecture's relationship to power. That is an inherently equivocal relationship, since all monuments are statements about power (the power of Pharoah or Prince, of merchant or State), and the use of power in this way is frequently quite overt. But what if it is the sole object? In an age that has perfected the techniques of propaganda, of calculated perfidy backed by torture and unparalled violence it seems surely irresponsible to separate, as the aesthetes do, the nature of an art form from the kind of message it is conceived to deliver. I refer of course to those who, like Leon Krier, have tried to set up the work of Albert Speer as an indictment of the Modernist achievement. Fortunately, since art is its own lie detector, one need not go outside the textual examination of a specific case to find transparent proof of the underlying motives that inspired it, and if the source of those motives is corrupt, the art will be bad art.

I propose to demonstrate that this is so by a comparative analysis of two buildings. Both are chancelleries. Both purport to be carried out in the language of classical architecture. But there the similarities end.

In 1922 Gunnar Asplund and Ture Ryburg produced a competition design for the Chancellery in Stockholm. Kenneth Clark once said that few people are capable of looking at a painting for longer than it takes to peel a banana: this design rewards a lot more looking at than that.

In the first place it clearly takes as point of departure the shape and grain of the pre-existent context. It is not the imposition of another order but the percipient drawing out, reinforcement and crystallization of something there that is quite positive but not yet eloquent in itself (Figures 13.1–13.5). The propriety of this respect for historical continuity is gently raised in pitch to carry (along the waterfront) reflections of Venice; and the way in which the Classical language is handled is so unstrained and various that it demonstrates once and for all that it was not solely the need for functional flexibility that led Asplund later to abandon that language. It would be tedious to spell out the many strategies employed to cope with the shifting axes on the site – deflection, inflection, variants on the circle and semicircle in a running exchange between specific circumstance and ideal prototype. But note the always positive use of in-between space in the *poché* of encircling geometries. Just to look at the plan is like reading music; and it is only by such means as these that a huge official building is mediated to proportions that invite in the observer a balanced and empathetic relationship to it. Asplund himself spoke of 'forms which do not threaten but invite'; and this whole project is an extraordinary transformation of the most recalcitrant material (government offices) into a rich and varied sense of place. This beneficent effect has a ramifying influence upon its neighbours, with whose form it shares a kinship.

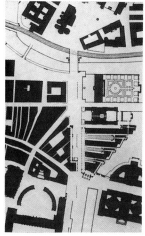

13.1

13.3

Long march to the scaffold

My second example is the new Chancellery (Figure 13.6) built for Hitler in Berlin (1937) by Albert Speer. A rough computation reveals that approximately 85 per cent of the space is circulation; but as we shall see this is no joyous *promenade architecturale*; more like a long march to the scaffold. In an unguarded moment one critic wrote of this: 'The skill and architectural culture with which this structure is planned . . . is beyond dispute, particularly when one considers . . . the architectural promenade which a visitor would have to traverse before having an audience with the Führer.' Now that is surely a judgement arrived at in less time than it takes to peel a banana. Let us look at the evidence of this 'skill and architectural culture'.

The 'architectural promenade' gets off to a poor start. There are two monumental entrances (from Voss-Strasse: Frontispiece), but they are in the wrong place and both lead slap-bang into a lateral sandbank in their attempt to grope a way on to the main 'honorific' axis, which is initiated by a mean entrance from Wilhelm Strasse (Figure 13.7). This leads into an open

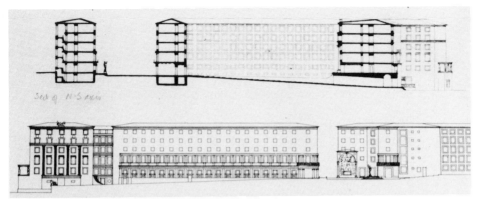

13.4

13.5

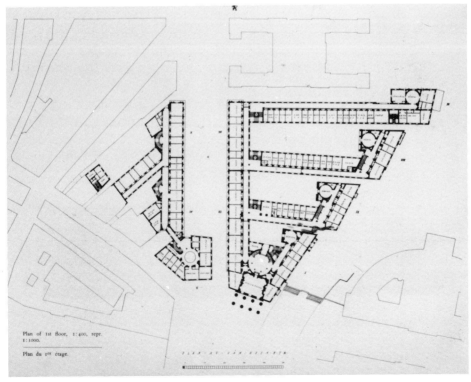

Plan of 1st floor, 1:400, repr.
1:1000.

Plan du 1er étage.

13.2

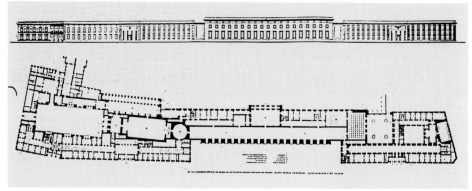

13.6

13.7

13.8

13.9

13.10

13.11

13.12

courtyard whose paving-pattern and relation of ground level to podium are vilely unresolved (Figure 13.8), quickly through an unbalanced vestibule into the glass-roofed Mosaic Room, where everything is the colour of uncooked sausage, (but shiny) (Figure 13.9), and thence into the Round Hall (Figure 13.10). Here the circle as a device to accommodate the slight shift in axis is horribly bungled in detail. The symmetrical floor pattern (wisely not shown on the plan) gives the game away, because it cannot centre upon the slight skew between the two main doors. We would be entitled to believe at this stage both from the form of the room and from the fact that we have already put in a good 200 metres of the march that we have arrived – but no. We are suddenly faced with another 180 metres to go, on the straight this time but with dangerously slippery going underfoot (Jacques Tati would be good on this) (Figure 13.11). We are, however, spared the whole course not by an architectural event but by the noticeable presence of a couple of military gentlemen announcing our rendezvous with the Führer in his living room (Figure 13.12). They stand astride a pair of doors which are, of course 5 m high – just to deliver a final body blow to your sense of self-possession as you set off on the last stretch over a carpet the size of a tennis court to the presence of the Great Man (Figure 13.13).

13.13

Detailing a farce

As to the quality of detail through which this farce is consummated, two observations are surely enough. The attempt to compose the Voss-Strasse façade with a central 'pavilion' is effected by inserting a couple of blanks at each end of the long gallery (Figure 13.14) (poor Schinkel must have turned in his grave at such howlers perpetrated in his name). Secondly, consider the use of *poché* here. With Asplund two geometries are allowed an active presence, and the space between is activated by that dialectic to become a positive third term (Figure 13.15). For Speer *poché* is a way of obscuring the relationship between two geometries: it is merely a kind of inert magma that allows him manically to straighten up the bits that keep skidding out of his control (Figure 13.16).

The primary purpose of the building is of course (*pace* Wittgenstein) to glorify an upstart. We must ask what are the mechanisms employed to this end? Geoffrey Scott's gloss upon the theory of empathy affords some clue:

13.14

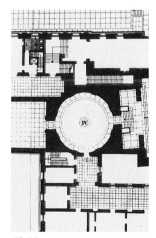

13.16

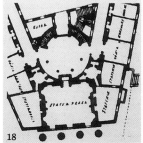

13.15

The concrete spectacle . . . has stirred our physical memory. It has awakened in us, not indeed an actual state of instability or of being overloaded, but that condition of spirit which in the past has belonged to our actual experiences of weakness, of thwarted effort or incipient collapse. We have looked at the building and identified ourselves with its apparent state. We have transcribed ourselves into terms of architecture.[1]

Now the 'terms' offered to the visitor to Speer's Chancellery are framed exclusively in what Asplund called 'forms that threaten'. In Scott's terms your self-confidence is diminished by the massing of forms that threaten to crush you and by the inflation of elements that are familiar (such as doors) so that your sense of body size is disoriented. You are made to feel vulnerable. Awareness of personal identity is drained by a numbing repetition of elements that make it impossible to identify or attribute significance to any one element. Space is manipulated not to shelter and to invite but to expose, to provoke a sense of insecurity. Windows have the blind stare that seems to deny any acknowledgement of your existence. Neither proportion nor detail imply any human presence. All these are the mechanisms of humiliation and intimidation.

It is not surprising to find that this clumsy and banal handling of the elements of each episode in the promenade reflects very accurately the paucity of ideas underlying the whole enterprise. There is no cross-fertilization, no entertainment of contrary or ambiguous ideas, and therefore no dialectic resolved or left in tension to animate the one basic idea.

This is the moment to ask why Asplund abandoned that language, together with such other one-time masters of it as Aalto, Mies, and Lewerentz.

Certainly it was not for the reason that so obsesses Krier – its association with Hitler. It was because it was too restrictive to embrace the enlargement of sensibility and technical compass that are unique to this century; its symbolism was so clogged with dead associations that what T. S. Eliot defined as a *live* tradition ('an easy commerce of the old and the new') was simply not available. To quote Wittgenstein once more, there are times when words that in one age could be used quite correctly can, in a later age, become 'no longer usable'.[2] I deeply sympathize with Krier in his horror at the abuse that that enlargement (because it realises so much freedom) has made possible. But when that horror is transformed into what Erich Fromm has defined as the 'fear of freedom' we know what to expect: only this time there will be an awful lot more books to be burnt . . . Perhaps after all the only sane response to this building is ridicule. In 1937, just when it was completed, Charlie Chaplin resolved: 'Hitler must be laughed at.' The most famous scene in *The Great Dictator* is set in that very living room with the earth's globe in the corner (Figure 13.17).

13.17

About 20 years ago I wrote in protest at the symposium on the thirties at Columbia: 'Surely it was not on stylistic grounds that the Nazis closed the Bauhaus . . . for the Nazis, forms contained dangerous implications of a way of life.' The converse is equally true. Speer, who used a kind of Tudorbethan vernacular (*Heimatstil*) for his residential projects, knew perfectly well that in choosing the classical language for his monuments he had access to a form of rhetoric which could only too easily be inflated to project messages about the *Ubermensch*. No style, ancient or modern, has a divine dispensation to the truth. All can be corrupted, and in its advertence to rhetoric (a Roman abuse of Greek moderation) the Classical language is probably more vulnerable to such abuse than any other. The fact that Stalin, Mussolini and Ceaucescu found that language as amenable to their ends as did Hitler suggests that if you want to stage a brutal lie on a grand scale, the classical language of architecture is replete with persuasive means to that end.

I hope that no one will take what I have written as mere pedantry about that style. What I am concerned about are the forms of thought that are embodied in that language and their corruption when that language is abused. If there is one thing to be learnt from Speer and his kind it is that when that happens, it is already the beginning of the end; it only needs a little fuel from the corrupted intellect, *le trahison des clercs*, to speed the process to its appalling consummation. In the words of one of Speer's other clients, Hermann Goering: 'When I hear the word culture, I reach for my revolver . . .'

References

1 Geoffrey Scott, *The Architecture of Humanism* Chapter VIII (Constable & Co; 1914).
2 L. Wittgenstein, *Culture & Value* (Blackwell, 1980) p. 16.

14

SACRED GAMES:
The urn and the chamberpot

Into the void

Karl Kraus, poet, playwright and editor of the satirical journal *Die Fackel*, wrote: 'All that Adolf Loos and I have ever meant to say is that there is a difference between an urn and a chamberpot: the people of today can be divided into those who use the chamberpot as an urn and those who use the urn as a chamberpot.'[1]

Adolf Loos himself made clear what he considered both 'urn' and 'chamberpot' to signify: 'Only a very small part of architecture belongs to art: the Tomb and the Monument . . . the rest, everything that serves an end, should be excluded from the realm of art. . . .'[2]

Ludwig Wittgenstein, a close friend of both Loos and Kraus, pitched the status of 'architecture' even higher: 'Architecture immortalises and glorifies something. Hence there can be no architecture where there is nothing to glorify'.[3]

Loos and Wittgenstein make a distinction between 'architecture' as art (the art of making monuments and representing ideas) and 'building' (conceived as the production of utilitarian shelter) and thereby point to what they hold to be a division as sharp as that between the sacred and the profane. That I do not hold to this view has been argued in Chapter 2. Nevertheless Kraus blames our culture for an inability to assign to each object its proper working relationship to other objects and therefore its proper place in the world.

It has been said that 'What Kraus, Loos and Wittgenstein have in common is their endeavour to separate and divide correctly.'[4] What concerned them all was the question of normality, a normality that presides over discrete categories of experience and fiercely rejects any spillage across frontiers.

This was the generation that had truly 'wrung the neck of rhetoric', and it is in the terms of their sensibility that we can best appraise the peculiar counter-reformation in the politics of architectural taste that we associate today with the fashionable cry: the Modern Movement is dead. That statement has been mooted many times – not least by Giancarlo de Carlo, who pointed out that it has died many times. What Paul Valéry called 'creative doubt' is inherent in its nature. At all times more cogent criticism raged within the movement than any that was directed at it from the outside. All that is part of a familiar argument.

What is interesting now is that the cry itself recalls that famous cry of Nietzsche's madman, who ran through the market place proclaiming 'God is dead.' It is as well therefore to recall the less celebrated sequence to that announcement. As he ran on the madman cried: 'How shall we console ourselves? . . . what sacred games shall we have to devise?'[5]

14.1

Using Kraus' metaphor, we could crudely illustrate the accusation by saying that an architecture seen to be too committed to 'function' and technology (the chamberpot syndrome) has lost the inspiration and initiative it commanded in its springtime. The pendulum of taste swings back and we are today confronted by advocates of urn worship, with a craving to fill the vacuum with forbidden trophies, to give the home the solemnity of the tomb (Figures 14.1 and 14.2) – or history as decoration, as a return to the Golden Age, as ritual.

Tomb, ritual, return to the womb – are these the games by which we are to console ourselves?

As to the use of history as decoration, all that can be said is that it has produced the unprecedented phenomenon of kitsch taking itself seriously (Figures 14.3 and 14.4) in Paris as in Paternoster. What is altogether more interesting is the underlying anxiety – the sudden panic to fill the void with 'meaning', the nervous symptoms of metaphysical distress.

14.2

Propriety v purity

Every student is familiar with the assumption made by Vitruvius (and sanctified by academic theory ever since) that *firmitas, utilitas* and *venustas* come together as if grown from the same root. The fact is, however, that this is rarely so: for the most part they stand against each other in an unstable relationship, often in competition, and their co-inherence is more the exception than the rule. No other 'art' carries the burden of such an inbuilt contradiction. Since it is the particular heresy of the Modernist sensibility to indulge a passion for extreme abstraction (a yearning for 'purity of means' in all media of the arts), the three components of Vitruvius' formula have been driven further apart than ever before in the history of architecture. Never was *utilitas* more ruthlessly pursued than by the naïve functionalists, on the one hand, and the Alexandrian analysts of 'problem structure' on the other. Never was *firmitas* carried to greater extremes than by the advocates of 'high technology' (Dymaxion or Archigram). As for *venustas*, the early abstractions of the de Stijl group exude a rude healthiness in

14.3

14.4

comparison with the aestheticism of 'de-construction' and *architettura autonoma* – art for art's sake, for itself, of itself, playing with itself.

The key to every one of the architectures of the past that inspire us lies in the varied balance of forces achieved in bringing the three competing elements into resolution; and the agent of that resolution is a missing fourth element. Until that emerges, there can be no architecture – merely technology, sociology or formalism. Vitruvius himself gave it a name when he spoke of propriety – 'decor' or decorum.[6] This, he stated, arises from authority, convention, custom or nature, and decides upon all issues of appropriateness and convention. It is of course precisely the propriety of such acts of judgement that should determine the proper use of urn and chamberpot.

Vitruvius was lucky: all such questions were resolved for him by appeal to a living tradition. We are not so lucky: born into a world torn apart by new and unassimilated demands, demographic and technological, we have not yet arrived at our 'balance of forces'. On the contrary, we have suffered to an unparalleled degree from the over-compensation and sheer intemperance of one-sided and extreme abstraction and for us answers will have to be won and rewon in the teeth of unstable circumstance.

Urn worship

Nietzsche's craving for consolation through 'sacred games' took a rather queer turn: 'Nothing is true: everything is permitted,'[7] he wrote; and concluded, 'only as an aesthetic phenomenon is the world and the existence of man eternally justified'. This mish-mash of spilt religion and art-for-art's sake found its most compelling evocation in the art of Giorgio de Chirico, and it is in turn that work which casts a long shadow across our path, stretching from the Novecento Group to the current work of Rossi and the Tendenza.

On a self-portrait of 1920 de Chirico inscribed in Latin 'And what will I love but the metaphysical?' He declared that his art was 'metaphysical', being based upon Nietzsche's discovery of the 'hideous void' and 'profound non-sense of life', and he extracted a haunting poetry from the depiction of objects (buildings, cabins, toys, biscuits, geometrical instruments) brought together in nonsensical juxtaposition – in relationships that utterly deny their proper nature.

Now it is highly pertinent to our present argument that it was pre-eminently architecture that de Chirico used for his imagery: an architecture which 'had no sense, above all no common sense', and which is the symbol of estrangement. It is a world which is man-made yet unpeopled, and in which space is vertiginous, perspective false, and in which shadows threaten and windows proffer a blind stare. As Freud opened his analysis of the mind by examining states of hysteria, so de Chirico opens our eyes to all that is alienating, threatening and malign by means of architectural forms.

For his successors in the field of architecture it was to be not so much a return to order as the return to rhetoric. Architecture was to be not a search for an enlargement of the powers of life but a mandala for the contemplation of the 'Enigma'.

Currently the most evocative protagonist of this persuasion is Aldo Rossi, whose drawn images of the cemetery at Modena are strangely moving. Rossi is deeply indebted to Argan's revival and reinterpretation of the notion of typology. It is a notion that by definition stresses relationship to the past, to the persistence of forms over time and therefore those aspects of form that are least vulnerable to change (symbolism, ritual, convention) rather than those of an operational nature (which are characterized as 'naïve functionalism'). Furthermore it is a notion that denies to function any significant part in the genesis of the so-called types (Figure 14.5) – and this is then taken as open licence for the formalist and the surrealist to further disengagement from reality.

14.5

Ostensibly Rossi invokes a typology of forms that embody a higher order of activities than 'naïve functionalism' – rejoicing in attributes in which 'the broadest adaptability to multiple functions corresponds to an extreme precision of form'. This happy formula is never developed. One historic example in which it is claimed to work is given – Spalato – and another, the Alhambra, where through over-specificity it does not. The whole theory of ideal forms hinges upon the adequacy of his distinction here, and it simply is not spelt out. More culpably, the theory itself would not distinguish between an urn and a chamberpot, on the grounds that, since they share similar typological properties, they must existentially be the same. One is reminded that Marcel Duchamp, who was also obsessed by objects detached from their proper function, presented to the Independent's Exhibition in

1917 a mass-produced urinal as a work of art entitled 'Fountain', and signed it R. Mutt (Figure 14.6). In his own words, he 'took an ordinary article of life, placed it so that its useful significance disappeared under the new title and point of view' – a deliberate subversion of normality. It is then that we realize that, far from the objectivity and 'rationalism' claimed for his theory, the range of typological forms used by Rossi in practice is not only intensely private, from de Chirico cabins (Figure 14.7) to Morandian coffee-pots (Figure 14.8), but is fundamentally surrealist[9].

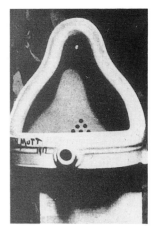

14.6

Nevertheless what is attractive in Rossi's thinking is the importance that it claims for 'the relationship between monument, ritual and mythological elements in the founding of the city and the transmission of ideas in an urban context'.[10] This is close indeed to Wittgenstein's proposition that 'architecture immortalises and glorifies something', and its indictment of city planning in terms of the 'Four Functions' is truly radical. What is disturbing, however, is Rossi's suggestion that clues to the answer can be found in Fustel de Coulange's *La Cité Antique*. This account of the relations between religion and social forms in the cities of classical antiquity clearly depicts the one symbol that dictates order at the heart of *Romanità*: the urn.

14.7

A rigid preoccupation with the daily ritual of obsequies to placate the unquiet grave of ancestors paralysed not only the pattern of family life but the very ground on which the family had settled. The dwelling was a kind of tomb, its hearth a bowl of ashes and a guarded flame. Woe betide you if you did not have a son to perform those rites for you each day when you were dead! The architectural language of that myth is solemn and has a grave splendour. But we must ask are these the 'sacred games' under which 'meaning' is to be restored to our cities? Or are we expected to dump the myth but retain the forms – as decoration for more 'liberated' games?

This line of thought finds an uneasy echo in the *Princeton Architectural Journal* dedicated to 'Ritual' (*sic*).[11] In an open forum whose discussion was haunted by the ghost of Rossi's Modena Cemetery, Alan Colquhoun said:

14.8

One of the things I mean by a building that has ritualistic overtones is that it has a closed form: . . . that the form can somehow be metaphorical: that it doesn't try to imitate but simply says something. It creates a distinctive formal quality apart from the everyday flux of life . . . a world apart from the ordinary world, the everyday world: and that implies some kind of formal closure.

Later on he says, 'a door is a different thing from an obelisk. An obelisk is completely useless. It starts off with a terrific advantage . . .' These are dark sayings. A lot depends on that phrase 'but simply says something'. We are not told what is either 'simple' or 'said' except that it is 'useless'. Nor are we helped when a negative definition is offered – 'the whole thing about de Stijl space is that it is anti-ritualistic'. 'Absolutely,' chips in Michael Graves. 'It's characteristically modern: it's anti-ritual,' pronounces Colquhoun. So we have been herded into a magic circle formed between 'the useless' and (de Stijl) 'abstract space'. What is it that is 'useless' and 'apart from the ordinary world' but not 'abstract' or 'modern'? Ritual? Certainly ritual as the vehicle for the sacramental is not intended (Colquhoun's curt pronouncement 'We are not believers' went unchallenged during the discussion). That dumps the myth all right. *Homo ludens* perhaps?

The painter Francis Bacon has carried the Nietzschean cry even further: 'Man has to realise that he is an accident . . . a completely futile being, that he has to play out the game without reason. . . . Art has now become completely a game by which man distracts himself. . . . It's going to become much more difficult for the artist because he must really deepen the game to be any good at all.'[12] The practical consequences of this avowal are claustrophobic. For instance, the Crucifixion is 'a magnificent armature on which you can hang all types of feeling and sensation'. 'So many people have worked on this particular theme that it has created this armature. . . .'[13] Conclusion: all that we have left from the adumbrations of passionate belief are formal 'armatures', which have been trawled through time to collect interesting sensations that can be played with irrespective of their reason for being.

Lethaby concluded the book in which he traced the origin of major architectural themes to their mythical and religious sources by saying: 'At the absolute end the terror has come to me: suppose that gifted whim-workers should take to putting up sky-ceilings and putting down sea-floors, and call it "The Magic Style". . .'[14]

So here we are back once more at the Nietzschean void, though I doubt very much if we would claim to be fulfilled at last and 'eternally justified' by such an 'aesthetic phenomenon'. Perhaps it is worth concluding this line of thought by recalling that Nietzsche went mad and de Chirico, wary of endlessly repeating variations upon the 'enigma' of things in false relationship, settled for a gladiatorial Mussolini as his Superman instead of Nietzsche (Figure 14.9) . . . It seems that when the passion for transcendental 'meaning' strays too far from the Classical-Christian core of our culture the project tends to become very silly.

14.9

Loos referred to his own writings as being 'spoken into the void'. Where there was 'nothing to glorify' he was content that a building of his should be 'dumb on the outside and reveal its wealth only on the inside'.[16] He was at one with Wittgenstien's admonition: 'Whereof we cannot speak thereof we should be silent.'[17] The sacred, yes: 'sacred games', no. At this time of high kitsch we do well to recall that admonition.

References

1 Engelmann, *Letters form Ludwig Wittgenstein*, p. 129.
2 Adolf Loos, *Architecktur,* 1909.
3 MS167: 1947–8, *Culture and Value*, Blackwell, 1980.
4 Engelmann, *op. cit.,* p. 131.
5 Friedrich Nietzsche, *The Gay Science,* Bk III: 125.
6 Vitruvius, *De Architectura,* Bk I, Chs 2, para 5. He also uses the Greek work *thematismos*, which appears to be his own invention, since the normal Greek word for propriety is *prepon*.
7 F. Nietzsche, *Genealogy of Morals,* III, para 24.
8 Aldo Rossi, *The Architecture of the City,* English translation, p. 179
9 Rossi's expressed sympathy with the working methods described by Raymond Roussel in 'How I wrote certain of my books'.
10 Aldo Rossi, *op. cit.,* p. 24.
11 'Ritual' *The Princeton Journal, Thematic Studies in Architecture,* Vol. I, 1983.
12 David Sylvester, *Interviews with Francis Bacon.* Thames & Hudson, 2nd ed. 1980, pp. 28–9.
13 *Ibid.,* p. 44.
14 W. R. Lethaby, *Architecture, Nature & Magic,* Duckworth, 1956, p. 147.
15 It was in Turin (beloved as much by Nietzsche as by de Chirico) that he tried to make love in the gutter to a broken-down cabhorse and was carted off into total lunacy. As one of his friends said *'Mulierem nunquam attigit'* – he had no luck with women.
16 Adolf Loos, *Heimatkunst,* 1914.
17 Ludwig Wittgenstein, *Tractatus Logico-Philosphicus,* 7, Routledge, 1922.

15

England builds

The building of the Law Courts in the Strand was not only a tragi-comedy of the political and professional behaviour of 100 years ago but also the re-enactment of the archetypal tragi-comedy that is not without precedent when an English government finds itself committed to the building of a monument. Sir John Summerson set the stage in his 1968 lecture on the Law Courts Competition: 'The first point is the obvious one that English governments in the mid-nineteenth century were parsimonious to an almost unbelievable degree; their parsimony being part of a national philosophy which expresses itself from time to time in a horrified contempt for architects and architecture.' Two earlier examples of this 'philosophy' are worth recalling here. During the last 10 years of construction of St Paul's, Wren was put on half-pay before finally being sacked and replaced by a fixer called Benson (soon to be dismissed for sheer incompetence). Secondly, at the opening of the House of Commons the building was deemed 'a complete, decided and undeniable failure', and Disraeli suggested in Parliament that if the government were to hang the architect in public, it would put a stop to such blunders in the future.

It is therefore with appalled fascination but with little surprise that we are brought to realize how all the agonies suffered in the building of the Houses of Parliament were re-enacted in the building of the Law Courts with the crushing fatality of Greek tragedy. The recurrent themes rolled forward. In the first place an ambiguity hovered over the selection of the architect. Then there were the dithering, the second thoughts, the exploration of alternatives. After that the initial impetus slowed down in the losing battle against time, not only in terms of economic inflation but also the shifts of fashion. Inevitably there ensued the customary campaign of misrepresentation and vilification in both the professional and general press. This was followed by the teething troubles of technical innovation (particularly in heating, lighting and ventilation); and finally there were the wrangles about fees, accountability, finishing dates and moving in.

There are of course perfectly understandable reasons why public architecture should stir up such controversy; and paradoxically it is the same reasons that go to explain why architecture, being the most public of the arts, is by the same token so significant. It deals with volatile matter. It deals in vested interests – land (its ownership or its occupation), public money, public symbols, political kudos, success or dissatisfaction in use. It deals in time, which is always running out (like early enthusiasm) and always bringing in changes in taste, technology and practice. Finally, because it is not a science, not amenable to proof or prediction, its results are judged on the basis of precedent and prejudice, fashion and a constantly shifting set of values – and the verdict is given, quite rightly, as much by the man in the street as by the expert. It is answerable to life and indisputably seen to be so in the eyes of both Parliament and the press.

The story begins with the holding of the competition in 1866–7. This epitomized both the high point and the turning point of High Victorian Gothic. The major Gothic architects (George Edmund Street, Alfred Waterhouse, William Burges, George Gilbert Scott) swept the board in dictating the stylistic language of the competition; yet even before construction had started on Street's building in 1874, the design was subjected to the counter-attack of the classical revivalists – a periodic recurrence in the history of taste (Figure 15.1). For instance, Scott's 'Gothic' design that won the competition for the new Foreign Office was rejected by the Prime Minister (Palmerston), who demanded a 'classical' design. Scott supplied a new design ('. . . Italian') but used his old 'Gothic' design as the basis for his winning competition scheme for St Pancras Chambers a little later.

The whole story of the Law Courts competition (Figure 15.2), the pursuit of alternative projects and the construction of Street's final design is patiently and lucidly recounted by David Brownlee[1] in his book devoted to the subject. As an account of a horror story, it is brilliant. For instance, his coolness in letting the facts and behaviour speak for themselves is very effective: he does not let the mounting pressure of protest at injustice leak through his own comment, with the result that it builds up beyond the pain threshold in the reader's head. Street himself remained very cool under attack, only answering back a couple of times – once when he was accused of having bribed all his rivals in the competition with £1,000 each. That was pretty steep for anyone, let alone for a churchwarden.

15.1

On the evidence of his competition scheme (the plan was a mess (Figure 15.3) and he knew it), Street was lucky to get the job. He only did so on the competition jury's preference for his architectural detail and their advice that he should collaborate with E. M. Barry (of whose plan they approved). That decision was then set

15.2

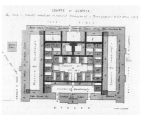

15.3

aside by the judges themselves (after taking legal advice), and they picked not a scheme, but a man – Street. The discarding of Barry's plan was no loss: it was a fussy pin-ball machine of Beaux-Arts provenance dressed up in Horace Walpole 'Gothick' style. But Barry was treated abominably and stirred up trouble whenever the project hit a new crisis.

Of the other schemes, by far the most important was that of Waterhouse, who made a major urban statement at the same time as he resolved the many tactical issues of court-house planning. His project is described in detail in the next chapter.

15.4

The other outstanding scheme was by Burges (Figure 15.4). He and Waterhouse were the only two who really abided by the principal injunction of the competition programme – that the public should be segregated from those engaged in the business of the courts. This he achieved by disposing a number of public access entry points around the perimeter, and each of these was connected exclusively to the public gallery of a courtroom. But it was above all due to the sculptural and picturesque power of his forms and his stunning draughtsmanship that his project won a great deal of admiration.

In the event, however, it is probably true that Street was the best man for the job. In energy, skill, intellect and temperament he was uniquely qualified to survive the assault course ahead of him. Scott said with admiration some time later, 'It is well this . . . load of persecution has fallen upon a man of spirit and nerve calculated to bear it.' It is notable that through seven versions of the project Street continually and imperturbably improved the design, taking account of criticism where it was serious and not just the usual silly invective.

The project had many enemies, most of them the customary cranks, and some who pathetically, in Brownlee's own phrase, tried 'to make a career of criticising Street' – but they are all long since forgotten. Not so Acton Ayrton (Figure 15.5), a destructive sadist of Dickensian proportions. He hated art and was the vizier of the parsimony pinpointed by Summerson and for this reason was chosen by Gladstone to take charge of the project at the midpoint of its evolution in his capacity of First Commissioner for the Arts.

The post was vacant because of the resignation of Austen Layard, a man of great sensibility and the only minister to make positive proposals for the architectural improvement of London. Layard had pressed for

15.5

the relocation of the project to the more noble Embankment site and greatly encouraged Street to produce two schemes for that site. (Street took one of these schemes up to completion of outline working drawings (Figures 15.6 and 15.7).) However, a hard man at the Treasury, called Lowe, and the members of the Law Society, who favoured the original site, sank the Embankment scheme (and incidentally rejected all Street's claims for fees for that project). Layard in despair at the cause of art in such Philistine company chucked his hand in. When, 4 years later, Street's seventh (and final) scheme (Figure 15.8) came back from tender roughly £100,000 above the cost target of £710,000, Ayrton swung into action. (I spare you an account of his earlier dealings with Street.)

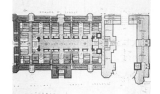

15.6

15.7

Street responded by making three points: £50,000 of the overshoot was due to 15 per cent inflation since the cost target was established; the brief had been expanded to include the lunacy department (badly needed, I would guess); and he could, in any case, whittle away the remaining £50,000 by a listed group of reductions.

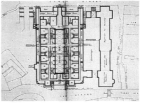

15.8

Ayrton would not listen – he was out for real blood this time. There were two elements of the design really dear to Street's heart. One was the central hall (Figure 15.9), the other was the clock tower. Ayrton said that the central hall could easily be cut out and replaced by a small open courtyard and that the clock tower must go, lock, stock and barrel. In the meantime the flinty-hearted Lowe at the Treasury had conceded Street's claim that inflation had accounted for £50,000 and informed Ayrton that the extra sum would be made available. The perfidious Ayrton did not inform Street of this, but instead demanded a new scheme without Central Hall or Clock and pointed out that Street should not waste further time in writing letters of protest but get on with the job instead. Fortunately Street got to hear indirectly of the Treasury's concession on inflation and Ayrton had to climb down. By this time Ayrton had made a great many enemies and his philistinism had been made the butt of parody by W. S. Gilbert in 'The happy land'. Gladstone finally kicked him out of office.

15.9

The account of the building operations is also fascinating. There were labour problems (the TUC had just been founded in 1871 and the contractor rashly used imported labour to break one strike). The failure of the ventilation system in the House of Commons made the selection of the system for the Law Courts a touchy point (Ayrton tried to make Street design his own system, with full accountability but no fee.) Electric light was just coming on the market after the inventions of Swan in Newcastle and Edison in the US, but Ayrton insisted on belt and braces – the installation of gas supply lines in addition to Street's electrical distribution.

The final building achieved the confident forms and powerful sense of movement that we expect from Street (see Frontispiece and the North West tower, Figure 15.10). However, Street never saw his beloved central hall finished: he died in 1881 before all the scaffolding had been removed. He is said to have done 3,000 drawings and to have draughted all the final working drawings in pencil for his staff to ink in. Special security precautions had to be taken against the Fenian terrorists when Queen Victoria opened the building on 4 December 1882. An address from the workmen was read. It concluded: 'Our one regret is that the great master whose designs we have carried out should not have been spared to see this day.'

All in all the story is a faithful account of the recurrent tragi-comedy that is played out whenever this country tries to build a monument. In the end we got a masterpiece of sorts, but it was a 'damned close-run thing'.

15.10

Reference

1 "The Law Courts: the architecture of George Edmund Street" by David Brownlee. M.I.T. Press. 1984.

Part IV
HISTORY: THE CASE STUDY OF A GRAND PROJECT

16

THE LAW COURTS PROJECT:
by Alfred Waterhouse

Alfred Waterhouse's project for the Law Courts competition in 1866–7 was not only an example of unsurpassed skill in the art of distributive organization (in plan and section) but was also a proposal for an urban event of astonishing originality and aptness, not only to its own time but to ours (Frontispiece and Figure 16.3). It is perhaps too much a *grande machine* for present taste, which has lost its nerve for such things and is inclined to call anything longer than a cricket pitch ''60s thinking'. But it was conceived in the age of the Crystal Palace, the Paris Exposition of 1855 and the Galleria Vittorio Emanuele II in Milan (Figure 16.1). It is not surprising that the Law Courts have never received their due, because Victorian architecture has hitherto been looked to not for planning expertise but for stylistic preoccupation. It is perhaps with less condescension that we should now acknowledge that in terms of functional planning Waterhouse has few rivals. It is also true, however, that some reconstruction is necessary in order to go beyond the various drawings of fragments to a visual presentation of the whole.

16.1

The project was fully set out, as required of all the competitors, in a lithographed report of 93 pages, containing a written exposition, schedules of accommodation, a cost report, drawings and photographs of perspective renderings. The exposition is lucid, the response to accommodation requirements rigorous and the cost report was the only one accepted by the Assessors as accurate; but above all it was unique in having a big idea to which all the parts were answerable.

The competition took a long time to reach launching point because great pains were taken to avoid any repetition of the inadequacies (in either the conditions, the assessment or the final judgement) of the kind that flawed the proceedings of many other competitions, such as those for the Houses of Parliament in 1834, the Royal Exchange in 1839, the Great Exhibition in 1851 and Whitehall, the War Office and the Foreign Office in 1856. As a result, exhaustive documentation was made available to competitors.

The 7¾ acre site lay between the Strand and Carey Street, Clement's Inn Gardens and Bell Yard. The brief set out the accommodation requirements for the Courts of Equity and Common Law in the light of an exploratory project carried out in 1857 by Henry Robert Abraham at the instigation of the Attorney-General, who was his brother-in-law. That project was diagrammatic, with no architectural pretensions, but its topology of inner and outer rings of building was sent to every competitor for guidance and was reflected in most of the submissions. The conditions themselves were daunting, comprising accommodation for sixty departments: the Superior Courts of Law and Equity, the Probate and Divorce Court, the High Court of Admiralty, a bankruptcy court, an ecclesiastical court, an arbitrates' court and a land registry. There were explict requirements not only for good natural light and efficient ventilation of the courts and offices, but also for a circulation system that would separate into discrete realms the judges, lawyers, jurors and various classes of the visiting public. The 'Instructions for competing architects' contained fifty-seven paragraphs and sixty-six schedules, and there were also special reports on fire requirements. A total of £1½ million was assigned for the project, to be split equally between the acquisition of site and the buildings. The assessors were five judges assisted by two architect surveyors (of no great distinction), and there were specialist reports on fire-fighting, heating and ventilation, and of course costs.

Competition fiasco

The competition itself is a *cause célèbre* in the history of architectural competitions. I will examine only the Waterhouse scheme out of the eleven solutions, and deal with it in its own right, rather than in the tangle of politics and personalities thrown up by the actual events. That context was the subject of extended exposition by Michael Port and subsequently at greater length in David Brownlee's *The Law Courts: the architecture of G. E. Street*. Sir John Summerson has also written a fascinating essay on the subject. From these sources I have abstracted briefly what is required as background to the Waterhouse project.

As to that project itself I have worked directly on the basis of a copy of Waterhouse's submission report. Unfortunately all copies of that report known to me lack complete sections through the main Great Hall, although part sections are provided. I have accordingly made good that omission.

The schemes were all publicly exhibited in a special pavilion set up in Lincoln's Inn and received enormous press coverage, and not only in the technical press. The Waterhouse scheme received the greatest support generally and from the legal profession in particular. It was crowded out by some last minute ganging-up of the Londoners against the outsider from Manchester, and the whole deal consummated by the kind of farce that only British competitions can produce. Two totally antipathetic architects were picked as joint winners – Edward Middleton Barry (for what George Gilbert Scott called 'his skill in arrangement') and George Edmund Street (for what Scott called his 'undoubted powers in the higher art', that is, the design of elevations). Scott could not suppress a growl about entering what he thought was a singles competition and then to find himself playing against a doubles team. Protests and accusations were flying. Legal advice was sought and the Attorney-General ruled that:

> The assessors' decision was not a valid award.
> Neither Barry nor Street could sustain any legal right to be employed.
> Although the competitors might claim that no award had been made, they could not compel the assessors to select another architect.

Finally the Treasury Board stepped in and appointed Street as sole architect 'but not as the successful competitor'. Barry, fuming that Street had been selected 'not for what he has done but for what he may yet do – a ground upon which he might as well have been chosen without any competition at all', was then awarded as compensation the first prize in the National Gallery competition (which had also been hanging in abeyance for some time without any decision). Scott commented: 'If it would have been my lot (had I succeeded) to have suffered the bullying and abuse which has been heaped upon Street I cannot say that I regret my want of success.'

Alfred Waterhouse (1830–1905) was placed on the shortlist for the Law Courts competiton as a result of his winning scheme for the Assize Courts in Manchester, where he had set up his practice. That building, constructed during 1859–64, had proved an outstanding success, not only in the view of Manchester's proud citizens (who no longer had to go to Liverpool for transaction of the business of assize), but also in the eyes of the judges and members of the Bar, who, uncharacteristically, sang its praises. It brought Waterhouse national recognition and achieved almost canonical status; so much so that it virtually established that Gothic would be the architectural language of the law.

It was, according to H. F. Lockwood's competition report, 'peculiarly adapted for an edifice containing such vast and varied requirements, and in which a solemnity of character is essential . . . Irregularities which would destroy the symmetry of a classical building, in this style contribute to its picturesque effect'.

The conjunction of notions of functional flexibility, Gothic form and the picturesque were of course to flower in the work of the English Free School and find their way to the USA, Germany and Scandinavia. As to the Gothic component, it is commonly held that while the competition celebrated the high point of Victorian Gothic, the completion of Street's building 15 years later heralded its end. Certainly all the major Gothic architects were (except Butterfield, who would not participate in competitions) on the shortlist – George Gilbert Scott, Street, Burges, Waterhouse and Seddon.

There were eleven chosen competitors. To the above-named were added Edward Middleton Barry (son of Sir Charles), Lockwood, Raphael Brandon, Thomas Deane, Henry Garling and poor old Henry Abraham (who uniquely paid no attention at all to his old diagram but produced instead a layout that resembled a fight between two lobsters). Waterhouse, on the basis of his Manchester experience, was at first asked to draw up a catalogued schedule of requirements, but he withdrew after 3 weeks in order not to prejudice his chances of taking part in the competition.

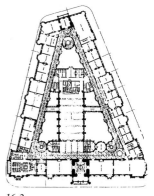

As to Waterhouse's mastery of the plan, we have only to look at his project for Manchester Town Hall, won in competition shortly after the Law Courts (1868) for an example of this (Figure 16.2). A fiendishly awkward site was made to look like a perfectly normal state of affairs, with a neutral centre and well-lit, fluent circulation. His Manchester Assize Court was a much simpler affair, but its apparent simplicity belies a measure of skill in working the section in the cause of natural daylight to the major spaces at its heart.

16.2

The clearest statement of intentions in the Law Courts competition is made by Waterhouse himself in his introductory 'General description', reprinted below.

General description

1 The Buildings specified in the instructions are roughly divisible into – *Courts* (with rooms immediately contiguous) and *Offices*.

2 The first of these, as having the greater claim to quiet and the advantage of a central position, I have massed together in two internal lines of Building running East and West, with a long internal Area or open Court on each of their outer sides, and divided by a large covered Hall, from which access is obtained on the one side (the North) to the Court of Equity, on the other (the South) to those of Common Law (Figure 16.5).

3 The offices I have placed in the external ranges of Building which front respectively to the Strand, Carey Street, Bell Yard, and Clement's Inn. While so arranged as to expose their principal occupants to as little interruption from the external traffic as possible, they form a complete barrier between all noise from that source and the Courts which they shelter.

4 On the Ground Plan are shown stretching across the Building from East to West (1), a range of Offices 58ft wide; (2) an open Court or Street, 53ft wide, (which I would propose in this description to call 'Equity Street') crossed by covered Bridges where needed; (3), a line of Courts and Offices 87ft 6in wide; (4) a great Central Hall 60ft wide and nearly 500ft long; (5), a similar range of Courts and Offices 90ft 6in wide; (6), another internal street 53ft wide, (which I would propose to call 'Common Law Street') also traversed by Bridges where required; and lastly, (7), an outer range of Offices facing the Strand, also 59ft wide.

5 In preference to lighting the rooms within the building by means of several small internal Areas, I have adopted the simple arrangement roughly shown on the annexed sketch as the one which would secure the greatest possible amount of light and air to every apartment.

6 The two internal streets, both of which are on the Strand level, are approached by carriage archways through the outer Strand range of Offices.

7 The best arrangement for the Courts, both *inter se* and with reference to their position in the Building generally, has been one of the chief problems for solution. The following reasons have weighed with me in placing them as shown in my design, that is with little exception, in two parallel lines divided only by a central Hall.

a They are thus brought *as closely together as possible*.

b The greatest possible *simplicity of arrangement* is thus obtained.
c The central Hall affords for Barristers, Solicitors, and, in fact, for all who are within the Building on business *a place of meeting* from which each of the *Courts is immediately accessible.*
d The arrangement is one which secures a certain amount of *elasticity* for any *future modification* in the special purposes to which each individual court is applied. In fact it prevents any group of Courts becoming so crystallised, if I may so speak, as to make such modification difficult or impossible; *eg*, if the Courts of Equity should hereafter increase in number, the Admiralty Court might be converted into a Court of Equity, and the Court shown in the plans under the former name be removed elsewhere, without any detriment to the general scheme.
e A proximity is thus secured *between the Courts of Law and Equity* which may hereafter be turned to account in the event of any further fusion between their respective systems of procedure, or between the Equity and Common Law Bars.

The grandeur of a unifying idea

The most significant characteristic of the project is the grandeur of a unifying idea that not only deals with the operational intricacies of a complex brief with exceptional rigour, but rises above that to address the surrounding city with an arrangement of public routes, places, symbols and structures that belong properly at that scale.

The building, which is itself a 'little city', is connected to its environs by a network of bridges and subways at strategic points, and to the principal streets and carriage entrances and twenty-five subordinate entrances to various offices and departments as follows (Figure 16.5):

A north–south pedestrian gallery running through the centre of the scheme from the Strand and rising at its northern end to the level of Carey Street.
Temple Bar Bridge over the Strand from the existing staircase to the two Temples, with a subway immediately under it.
A bridge across Carey Street in line with the barristers' corridor to Lincoln's Inn.

*16.3   View from the Thames:
the Law Courts seen from a
point at which the composition
could be grasped in its entirety.*

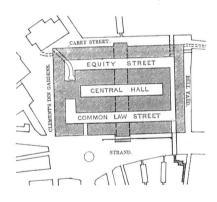

*16.5   Urban context: Plan
showing internal street
connections, by means of four
bridges and three subways, to
associated sites around the
building. It also shows a
proposal for a new street
leading south from the Strand
down to the Embankment with
Temple bar moved.*

*16.4   The strand frontage.
This perspective assumes the
removal of the church of St
Clement Danes (which
Waterhouse recommends as
part of his revised road
proposals). It also shows the
replacement of Temple Bar by
a pedestrian bridge connecting
to the Middle Temple. The
open arcade on the top floor
affords public access to
department offices.*

A bridge across Bell Yard to the proposed new wing of the Law Institution.

A bridge across Bell Yard but further south, to Serjeant's Inn, where further expansion could be envisaged.

As two further subways – one under Chancery Lane from the north-east corner of the building to the Rolls Estate, the other from the north-west corner to a site for accommodation for housekeepers, police, etc.

By the drive-up ramp in the north-west corner that allows judges to be set down at the level of the discrete corridor leading to their private chambers and Court Bench.

The most important elements in the whole composition are the two intersecting galleries. On the north–south axis a pedestrian way (which Waterhouse called a 'Transverse Hall') connects the Strand (Figures 16.8, 16.18–19) to Carey Street, which is roughly 14ft higher in level. It is 64ft wide, 32ft high with a central nave 32ft wide flanked by 16ft side aisles. Over these side aisles run galleries at the level of the main upper level central Great Hall, which lies on the east–west axis at the level of Carey Street. At the point of intersection of the two routes the Great Hall is reduced to a narrow bridge passing over the lower route. This lower north–south route is intended for the use of the general public (Figures 16.7 and 16.8) with access at four points to staircases leading to the two public corridors, which run parallel to, but are completely separate from, the Great Hall. From these corridors, staircases lead up, again discretely, to each of the three types of public gallery that surround, on three sides, each courtroom above: 'general public', 'respectable public' and 'ladies gallery'. These members of the public are deliberately excluded (in conformity with the competition conditions) from access to the Central Hall, but they do get views into it from their staircases.

The total length of this route from the Strand to Carey Street is about 500ft. The Great Hall is 478ft long by 60ft wide and 90ft high to the apex of the roof, and the twenty-four courts are distributed, broadly symmetrically and equally on both sides of the main aixs, except for the Appellate Court and Exchequer Chamber that terminate the west end of the Great Hall. The roof has wrought iron ornamental semi-circular trusses resting on stone corbels and buttressed by the main walls of the courts.

The sides of the hall are composed of three storeys of witness and consultation rooms attached to the general courts, with windows looking into the hall itself, and these correspond to the bays of glazed roof to the hall. Between each set of these ascend the staircase cores, leading from the floor of the hall to the barristers' corridors, and giving access to the witness and consultation rooms themselves. These cores correspond to the sectors of solid roof. The staircases for the general public (referred to above) are interlocked within the same cores but with no intercommunication. Over the three storeys would be a 24ft high clerestory. The gallery behind this would be covered with a glass roof (a continuation of the hall roof), one-half of which would be hung on rollers so as to overlap the other and thus provide ventilation to the hall as desired.

The hall could be warmed in winter by hot water and the staircases would be entirely open, so that fresh air in summer and warmed air in winter would find its way along the barristers' corridors. These two flanking corridors, which run at the main floor level of the courts, are connected at midpoint of the Central Hall by one of two bridges that lie over the line of the ground level north–south route. There is a splendid Bar library (Figure 16.11), as the crowning piece at the eastern end of the Central Hall, while below this, but at 2ft above the level of the main hall floor, is a public refreshment room looking down its whole length. Waterhouse says that the Great Hall is intended for:

a *Salle des pas perdus*: a place of rendezvous for all who have business to transact in the courts, as opposed to the general public who come only to see and hear, and who would have no access to it. This hall I have endeavoured to plan so large, so light, and so attractive, as to make it likely that all whose cases had not actually begun would congregate in it rather than in the corridors and passages leading to the several courts.

The Courts (Figure 16.10) themselves are planned on three levels and served by five corridors so that judges, jurors, witnesses, registrars, shorthand writers and general public would all have their own special entrances while solicitors and suitors would share the entrances used by the Bar. The judges enter at bench level, about 4ft above the court floor, from their own retiring and private rooms. The courts were to be naturally lit through rooflights and also by windows over the bench.

16.7   *The north–south public pedestrian way. Staircases lead to the public corridors giving access to the courtroom public galleries.*

16.9   *Plan of the principal floor (at the level of Carey Street). The main east–west Great Hall is reduced to a bridge at the central point of intersection with the north–south route of the Transverse Hall. The Great Hall is terminated on the east by the stepped refreshment room and to the west by the Appellate Court. Entry point for the ramped carriageway leading to the judges' corridor is shown at the north–west corner. One of the four public corridors leading to courtroom galleries ends in an octagonal waiting room, from which access is also obtained to the Appellate Court Gallery.*

16.8   *The plan at ground floor is at the level of the Strand, but 14ft below Carey Street to the north. The north–south pedestrian access (the Transverse Hall) dominates the centre with four staircase points leading to the public corridors above. Note the location at ground level (as required in the brief) of the Large Appellate Court on the west. In his report Waterhouse described a possible transformation of the lateral spine coal stores into records offices with the area on both sides of the central hall widened to afford necessary natural ventilation.*

16.6(a)   *The main entrance from the Strand.*

16.6(b)   *Carey Street facade. The open arcade on the top floor affords public access to departmental offices.*

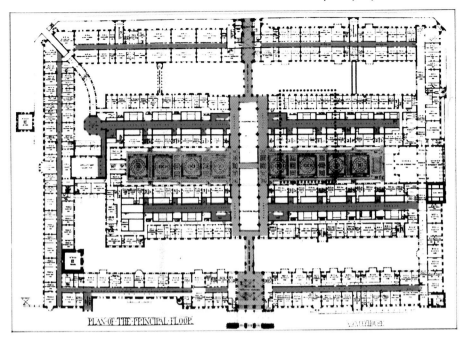

PLAN·OF·THE·PRINCIPAL·FLOOR.   WATERHOUSE

Figure 16.9   Principal Floor

general public   judges

public involved in court   legal profession

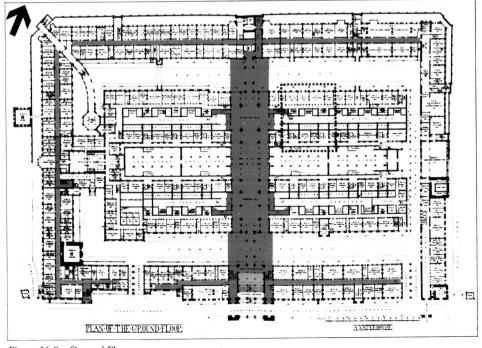

PLAN·OF·THE·GROUND·FLOOR.   WATERHOUSE

Figure 16.8   Ground Floor

16.11   The Barristers' Library at first floor level.

16.13   Plan at first floor level. Note that the Bar Library terminates the Great Hall to the east and the main stair to the Exchequer Chamber to the west.

16.12   Plan of the court floor. The judges' access corridor and chambers are at a level raised above the main court level, which is common to the barristers' chambers and the main north–south corridor, with its bridge connections to the south over the Strand to Middle Temple and to the north over Carey Street to New Square and Lincoln's Inn Fields. Note the bay windows from the consultation rooms that look into the Great Hall. The dotted area refers to Figures 16.14 and 16.15.

16.10   A typical courtroom viewed from one of the three public galleries.

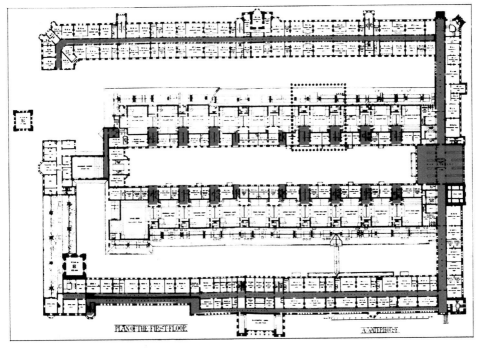

Figure 16.13   First Floor

general public

judges

public involved in court

legal profession

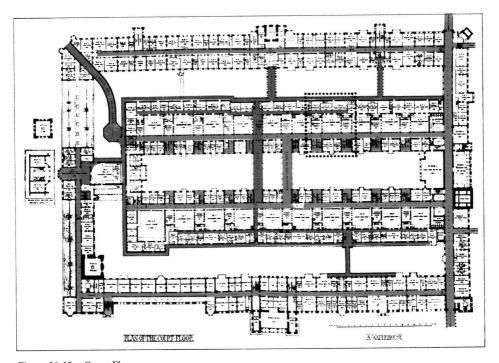

Figure 16.12   Court Floor

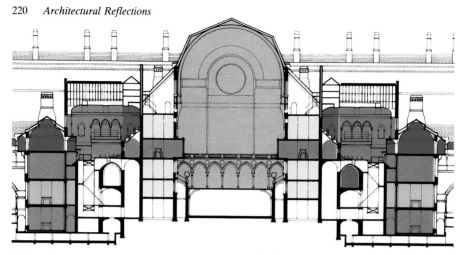

16.16   *Typical north–south section through the Central Hall, showing the relationship of the courts and barristers' corridors to the judges' corridor.*

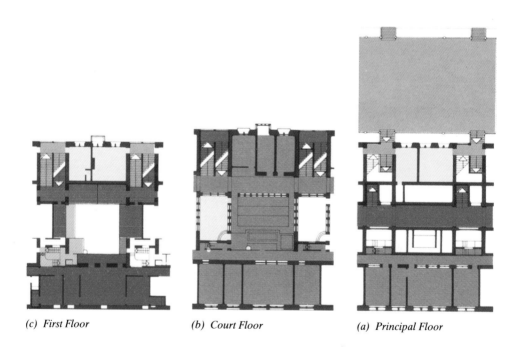

(c) First Floor   *(b) Court Floor*   *(a) Principal Floor*

16.14   *Typical floor plans of zone marked with dotted line on plan Figures 16.8–9 and 16.12–13.*

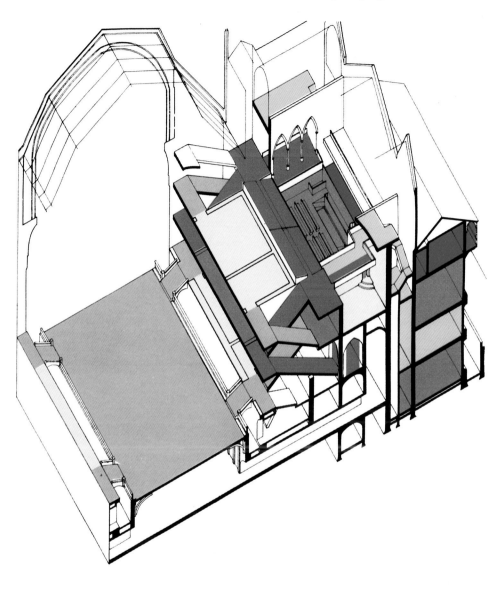

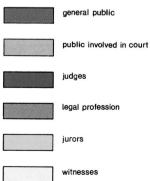

	general public
	public involved in court
	judges
	legal profession
	jurors
	witnesses

16.15   Axonometric of typical courtroom and staircase core indicating, by colour coding, the means of access and space occupied by members of the public and legal profession.

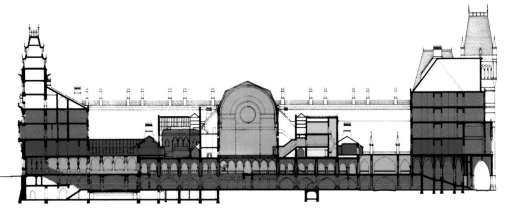

16.18   *North–south section showing the two routes for the public: the general public pass from the Strand at a lower level rising by staircase at the Carey Street entrance to a common level shared with the public involved in the court proceedings whose through-route is at a gallery level above.*

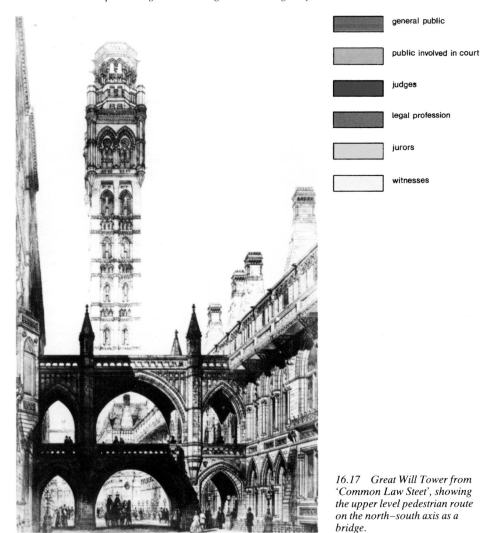

general public

public involved in court

judges

legal profession

jurors

witnesses

16.17   *Great Will Tower from 'Common Law Steet', showing the upper level pedestrian route on the north–south axis as a bridge.*

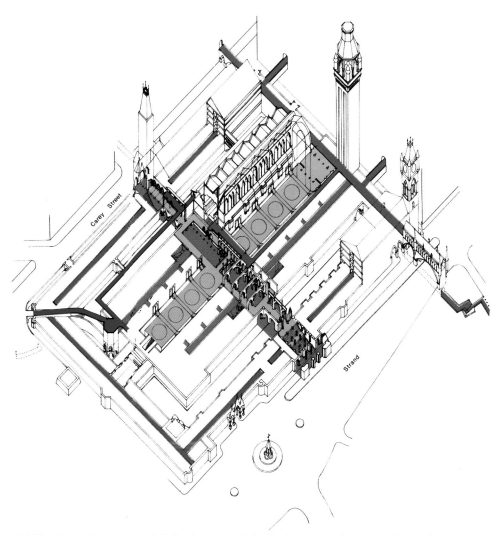

16.19 Composite axonometric indicating principal distribution patterns for means of access for the members of the public and the legal profession.

Waterhouse spells out a great deal more detail to show how his plans respond to the operational requirements of the courts (his report contains over 200 paragraphs on 24 large pages, with a further appendix of 70 pages of schedules of accommodation, comparing the provision for each space to the requirement of the brief). Not only was this working aspect pursued much more rigorously than in other reports that I have seen (Scott's, Burges' and Street's), but it evidently commended itself to the judges and Bar representatives, who favoured this scheme consistently above all others.

Extended sections of the report deal with precautions against fire (fireproof construction and planning by compartmentation with fire shutters to interconnecting ducts and voids); the control of smoke and foul air (drawn to a common ventilating and smoke tower); heating and ventilation (the courts to have a complete air change every 20 minutes); and to an alternaive planning use of the ground floor spaces as records offices.

Tumultuous roofscape

In view of the supposed priority of concern for stylistic matters, the section on style is remarkably brief – one paragraph only. Apparently Waterhouse's adherence to 'the Gothic of the early part of the thirteenth century', on the grounds that it would 'lend itself readily to all the combinations of form, material and arrangement', did not hit quite the right note with the assessors. What is more interesting is that, unlike the other competitors (except Street), Waterhouse grasped the fact that the surrounding context would provide only episodic views of his building, so he retreated to the opposite side of the river to draw a magnificent rendering of his composition in terms of his favoured 'varied skyline', with its tumultuous roofscape, two towers for the deposit of wills (one of them 354ft high), smoke tower and clock tower. Turner could hardly have done it better.

Significant comparisons

The significance of Waterhouse's project is best thrown up by comparison with three other buildings: Street's final building, Joseph Poelaert's Palais de Justice in Brussels of 1904 and Mengoni's Galleria Vittorio Emanuele II in Milan.

Street was understandable apologetic about the plan of his competition submission. The final building was a very different affair; it owed a great deal to Waterhouse's sectional arrangement of access routes and courtrooms to Central Hall, while utterly lacking its scale, complexity and urban significance. However, the dreadful treatment meted out to Street suggests that Waterhouse would have fared no better.

Summerson in his essay on the Law Courts competition made an unfavourable comparison between the products of the competition (which he saw as wrong, insular and riddled with self-doubt) and the success of Poelaert's Palais de Justice (Figure 16.20). 'Placing Poelaert among our 11 London contestants, how does he look? He looks powerful, accomplished, worldly – the confident heir of a great tradition. He is a superb example of success.' I find this hard to accept even in comparison with Street's finished building which had been plagued, strained and dehydrated by governmental parsimony and Philistinism; in comparison with the richness of spatial experience, subtlety and real grandeur of Waterhouse's composition, the Poelaert building suffers from a mindless pomposity and a gross inflatedness, like a glandular defect. Certainly it has assurance: indeed it is one of those buildings 'upon which' (to misquote T. S. Eliot) 'assurance sits like a silk-hat on a Bradford millionaire'. Almost 80 per cent of its space is dedicated to an alarming caricature of the Beaux-Arts *promenade architecturale* in an otherwise purposeless series of set pieces anticipating the dream fantasies of the Surrealist Delvaux. Furthermore the use of bilateral symmetry here simply has the effect of doubling everything without enlarging the experience of parts to the whole. Its contribution to the urban fabric of Brussels results in no amplifying or energizing of its surrounding neighbours, as would have been the case with Waterhouse's project; instead a huge lost object is dumped down to terrorize its neighbours. It is precisely because it differs from this monstrosity that Waterhouse's scheme is rewarding.

There is inevitably something to be said in comparing the Waterhouse project with Mengoni's Galleria Vittorio Emanuele II, built in Milan between 1865 (the year before the Law Courts competition) and 1877. The galleria was a British entrepreneurial venture, and Waterhouse might well have seen some advance notice of it. On the other hand, his use of the galleria theme is much richer, since the side walls are not, as at Milan,

16.20

merely boundaries to an internal street: they are drawn into active engagement in a measured cadence, paced out by the coincidence of solid ceiling over staircase cores, which in turn act as lively viewing balconies into the Great Hall. The passing under of the transverse route and the coincident cross-bridges at court floor level are certainly more dramatic than the Milan central crossing. Had it been built, it would have been a wonder for all time.

Illustrations

Apologia

Figure A1 W. Butterfield: All Saints, Margaret Street, 1849
Figure A2 H. H. Richardson: Winn Public Library, Woburn, Mass., 1876–79
Figure A3 W. Butterfield: Society for the Preservation of the Gospel, 'The Builder', 1871
Figure A4 Viollet-le-Duc: adaptation of Butterfield's syntax
Figure A5 Hugo Haering: Haus von Prittwitz, Tutzing, 1937
Figure A6 P. Lequeue: 'Il est libre', (1798–99)
Figure A7 Leonardo da Vinci: Anthropometric Diagram
Figure A8 Sir L. Martin and Colin St John Wilson: Project for King's College, Cambridge, 1956
Figure A9 Colin St John Wilson: Project for Liverpool Civic Centre, Public Atrium, 1965
Figure A10 Colin St John Wilson: School of Architecture Cambridge, Common Room (1958–59)
Figure A11 Colin St John Wilson: Bishop Wilson School, Springfield, View of Model
Figure A12 Colin St John Wilson: Bishop Wilson School Library, Springfield, 1985
Figure A13 Colin St John Wilson: Bishop Wilson School Library, Springfield, 1985.
Figure A14 Colin St John Wilson: Spring House, Madingley, Cambridge, 1965–1966 plan
Figure A15 Colin St John Wilson: Spring House, Living Room
Figure A16 Colin St John Wilson: Spring House, Dining-place
Figure A17 Colin St John Wilson: Spring House, Portico

1 The natural imagination

Frontispiece Fra Angelico: 'Birth & Vocation of St Nicola', Vatican, Rome
Figure 1.1 Le Corbusier on the Acropolis, 1908
Figure 1.2 Schinkel: Altes Museum, Berlin; painting by C. D. Freydanck
Figure 1.3(a) Michelangelo: 'Giorno', Medici Chapel, Florence
Figure 1.3(b) Hans Scharoun: Schminke House, Lobau, 1932–33
Figure 1.4 Arturo Martini: Tomb of Ophelia, 1932
Figure 1.5 G. de Chirico: 'The Lassitude of the Infinite', 1912–13. © DACS 1992
Figure 1.6(a) Michelangelo: Mother & Child
Figure 1.6(b) H. Scharoun: Concert hall of Philharmonie, Berlin, 1956–63
Figure 1.7(a) G. de Chirico 'The Child's Brain', 1914. © DACS 1992
Figure 1.7(b) Le Corbusier: Villa at Garches, 1927
Figure 1.8(a) Michelangelo Rondanini Pieta, Florence
Figure 1.8(b) Le Corbusier: Monastery at la Tourette, 1953–60
Figure 1.9 Gestalt Diagram
Figure 1.10 Francesco di Giorgio: Turin Codex, Folio 14.V
Figure 1.11 Michelangelo: Esther & Haman, Sistine Chapel
Figure 1.12(a) Picasso: 'Nude dressing her hair', 1940 © DACS 1992
Figure 1.12(b) Le Corbusier: Palace of Assembly, The Capital, Chandigarh, 1951–62
Figure 1.13(a) Michelangelo: Fourth captive, Boboli Gardens, Florence
Figure 1.13(b) Farnese Palace, Rome (Sangallo the Younger and Michelangelo)
Figure 1.14(a) Sigurd Lewerentz: Chapel of the Resurrection, 1922–26, Woodland Cemetery, Stockholm: Interior
Figure 1.14(b) Sigurd Lewerentz: Chapel of the Resurrection, 1922–26, Woodland Cemetery, Stockholm: Exterior
Figure 1.15(a) A. van Eyck: Hubertus House, Amsterdam, 1973–70: Entrance threshold
Figure 1.15(b) A. van Eyck: Hubertus House, Amsterdam, 1973–80: Rear threshold
Figure 1.16(a) Impluvium: House of the Tragic Poet, Pompeii
Figure 1.16(b) Francesco di Giorgio: Logetta balcony, Ducal Palace, Urbino
Figure 1.17 G. de Chirico: 'The Evil Genius of a King', 1914–15. © DACS 1992
Figure 1.18 Piero della Francesca: 'The Annunciation', Arezzo

2 The ethics of architecture

Frontispiece Paeonius and Alcamenes: Fragment from pediment of the Temple of Zeus, Olympus
Figure 2.1 E. L. Boullée: Project for Royal Library, 1785
Figure 2.2(a) C. L. Ledoux: House for Guardians of the River
Figure 2.2(b) C. L. Ledoux: House for Guardians of the Farm
Figure 2.3 E. Brune: 'Stair for a Royal Palace' Prix de Rome, 1863
Figure 2.4 A. Rossi: Project for Sudliche Friedrichsstadt, 1981

3 The play of use and the use of play

4 The historical sense

5 Architecture and the figurative arts

6 Alvar Aalto and the state of modernism

7 Hans Scharoun

8 Sigurd Lewerentz

* Swedish Architecture Museum

9 Gunnar Asplund and the dilemma of Classicism

* Swedish Architecture Museum

10 Gerrit Rietveld: in memoriam

11 Open and closed

* Swedish Architecture Museum

12 Two letters on the state of architecture: 1964 and 1981

Frontispiece (upper) Le Corbusier: 'Des Canons, des Munitions, Non merci'. © DACS 1992 *(lower)* Three projects for office development, London Bridge Site, 1987

13 Speer and the fear of freedom

Frontispiece A. Speer: Entrance to Reichschancellery, Voss Strasse, Berlin
Figure 13.1 Gunnar Asplund and T. Ryberg; Chancellery Project, Stockholm, 1922*
Figure 13.2 Asplund and Ryberg Chancellery Project, Stockholm: ground floor plan*
Figure 13.3 Asplund and Ryberg Chancellery Project, Stockholm: first floor plan
Figure 13.4 Asplund and Ryberg Chancellery Project, Stockholm: cross section and elevations
Figure 13.5 Chancellery Project: elevations
Figure 13.6 Speer: Reichschancellery, Berlin, 1937: plan and elevation
Figure 13.7 Reichschancellery: Entrance from Wilhelm Strasse
Figure 13.8 Reichschancellery: Open courtyard
Figure 13.9 Reichschancellery: Mosaic room
Figure 13.10 Reichschancellery: Round Hall
Figure 13.11 Reichschancellery: Long Gallery
Figure 13.12 Reichschancellery: Entrance to Fuhrer's Reception Room
Figure 13.13 Reichschancellery: Fuhrer's Reception Room
Figure 13.14 Reichschancellery: Facade to Long Gallery
Figure 13.15 Poché of Stockholm Chancellery
Figure 13.16 Poché of Berlin Chancellery
Figure 13.17 Charlie Chaplin in 'The Great Dictator', 1937

14 Sacred games

Frontispiece (upper) Q. Terry: Vent shaft for Underground, Gibson Square, London, 1969 *(lower)* Sir R. Rogers and R. Piano: Centre Pompidou, Paris, 1972–77
Figure 14.1 A. Rossi: Gallaratese Housing Block, Milan, 1969–73
Figure 14.2 A. Rossi: Cemetery at Modena, 1971–84
Figure 14.3 R. Bofil and Taller de Arquitectura: Palace of Abraxas, Marne-la-Vallée, 1978–82
Figure 14.4 J. Simpson: Paternoster Project, London, 1990
Figure 14.5 A. Aalto: sketch of amphitheatre at Delphi
Figure 14.6 M. Duchamp: 'Fontaine' by R. Mutt, 1917 © ADAGP, Paris and DACS, London 1992
Figure 14.7 G. de Chirico: 'The Great Metaphysician', 1918. © DACS 1992
Figure 14.8 A. Rossi: Compositional study, 1978
Figure 14.9 G. de Chirico 'Victory', 1928. © DACS 1992

15 England builds

16 A grand project: a design for the law courts by Alfred Waterhouse

Index